Mixed-Race Identity in the American South

New Studies in Southern History

Series Editor: John David Smith, The University of North Carolina at Charlotte

Race and Masculinity in Southern Memory: History of Richmond, Virginia's Monument Avenue, 1948–1996
By Matthew Mace Barbee

Racial Cleansing in Arkansas, 1883–1924: Politics, Land, Labor, and Criminality
By Guy Lancaster

George Galphin and the Transformation of the George-South Carolina Backcountry
By Michael P. Morris

Race, Gender, and Film Censorship in Virginia, 1922–1965
By Melissa Ooten

Leisure, Plantations, and the Making of a New South: The Sporting Plantations of the South Carolina Lowcountry and Red Hills Region, 1900–1940
Edited by Julia Brock and Daniel Vivian

The Federal Theatre Project in the American South: The Carolina Playmakers and the Quest for American Drama
By Cecelia Moore

The Development of Southern Public Libraries and the African American Quest for Library Access, 1898–1963
By Dallas Hanbury

Backcountry Slave Trader: William James Smith's Enterprise, 1844–54
Edited by Philip Noel Racine and Frances Melton Racine

Setting Slavery's Limits: Physical Confrontations in Antebellum Virginia, 1801–1860
By Christopher H. Bouton

The Development of Southern Public Libraries and the African American Quest for Library Access, 1898–1963
By Dallas Hanbury

Mixed-Race Identity in the American South: Roots, Memory, and Family Secrets
By Julia Sattler

Mixed-Race Identity in the American South

Roots, Memory, and Family Secrets

Julia Sattler

LEXINGTON BOOKS
Lanham • Boulder • New York • London

Published by Lexington Books
An imprint of The Rowman & Littlefield Publishing Group, Inc.
4501 Forbes Boulevard, Suite 200, Lanham, Maryland 20706
www.rowman.com

Copyright © 2021 The Rowman & Littlefield Publishing Group, Inc.

All rights reserved. No part of this book may be reproduced in any form or by any electronic or mechanical means, including information storage and retrieval systems, without written permission from the publisher, except by a reviewer who may quote passages in a review.

British Library Cataloguing in Publication Information Available

Library of Congress Cataloging-in-Publication Data

Library of Congress Control Number: 2021932943

ISBN 978-1-7936-2706-3 (cloth)
ISBN 978-1-7936-2708-7 (pbk)
ISBN 978-1-7936-2707-0 (electronic)

"My story begins before I was born."

—Julie Dash, *Daughters of the Dust* (1991)

Contents

Acknowledgments	ix
Introduction: *Memoir of the Search*: The Emergence of a Mixed-Race Literary Genre	1
1 Writing Mixed Selves at the Turn of the Millennium	11
2 Family Secrets: Uncovering Mixed-Race Heritage	41
3 Media of Memory: Generating the Family	87
4 Narrating the Mixed-Race Nation	119
5 The Past in the Present: Encounters with the South	157
Conclusion: Making History at the Turn of the Millennium	187
References	205
Index	213
About the Author	225

Acknowledgments

This book is based on my doctoral thesis submitted to Fakultät Kulturwissenschaften at TU Dortmund University in 2012 and further research. I would like to take the opportunity to thank my advisors Walter Grünzweig (TU Dortmund University) and Leigh Anne Duck (University of Mississippi) for their input and support, for encouraging and trusting me and providing guidance, space, and freedom to grow. A number of Dortmund researchers, especially Randi Gunzenhäuser, Ellen Risholm, and Ute Gerhard, gave helpful advice regarding my writing and my argument in this book and offered useful feedback regarding my research and teaching at large.

In Dortmund's American Studies program, there is a weekly opportunity for PhD students and junior researchers to present their ongoing work and receive valuable input. This research seminar has been vital to my growth as a researcher, and the feedback I have received over the years has been invaluable for this work, as well as for all my projects beyond. I would like to thank all former and current colleagues, visiting researchers, and others who thereby—directly and indirectly—contributed to this book, and who have warmly supported my work.

My students in my classes on American Literature and Culture have been a constant source of inspiration. Their questions and remarks and our subsequent discussion have led me to reconsider some of my assumptions and have guided my thinking about the importance of the past in the present and what this may mean for the future.

The Ruhr PhD Forum, which assembles all Americanists working at the three universities in the Ruhr region (and often beyond) has been an important resource. I was able to count on everyone's support of my work and have received important feedback from colleagues at Bochum and Duisburg-Essen all the way up to my completion of this book.

Over time, many international visitors to the Dortmund's American Studies program offered their indispensable input and support to me. I would especially like to mention Margaret Cotroneo (University of Pennsylvania) and Erin McGlothlin (Washington University in St. Louis), who have helped shape my ways of thinking about families and their stories to find ways to work through a difficult past. Elizabeth Rosner (Berkeley) and the late Meena Alexander (City University of New York) have encouraged me to think about these questions from the angle of writing and the writing process, which has been crucial to my analysis in this book.

The groundwork for this book was laid long before I started my research on the topic. For precious advice during my studies at Dortmund, I would like to thank Meni Syrou, who, in my first semester as a student, encouraged me to dive into the study of African American literature, and Fulbright-Professor Chip Rhodes (now Western New England University) for his seminar on the Harlem Renaissance taught at Dortmund in 2003, which enabled me to look at American Literature and Art from an entirely new angle. I would like to thank Günter Nold (Dortmund) for offering me space to reflect about how to include African American literature into the German school curriculum. Guest professor Lawrence Meredith (University of the Pacific), and, later on, Jay Williams and Ricardo Samuel at Hamilton College, led me to think about questions of a global humanity, the complexities of human relations, and about issues surrounding reparative justice for the past. Jon Smith (then University of Montevallo, now Simon Fraser University) inspired me to look at the US South and in a global context, especially in relation to its dealing with the aftermath of slavery in the twentieth century. Jeanne Cortiel (then Dortmund, now Bayreuth) and Christine Gerhardt (then Dortmund, now Bamberg) gave me the opportunity to carry these ideas further by helping me build my own projects around such questions. I could not have written this work without all your classes and the discussion spaces you offered to me.

The publication of this book has received enormous support by Blake Bronson-Bartlett, who made important suggestions for final revisions, and Brian Hess, who helped me format and put together the final version of this work.

Turning the idea for a thesis into a larger research project also means much personal growth and a lot of change along the way, and I would like to thank my friends and family who have supported and at times carried me through this time. I will never be able to express in words how much this means to me.

I am dedicating this book to my parents, Gabriele and Günter Sattler, and my sister, Annika.

Julia Sattler
December 2020

Introduction
Memoir of the Search: *The Emergence of a Mixed-Race Literary Genre*

The subject of racial mixing has long been central to the American national and literary imagination. Since colonial times, it has been the subject of political debates and law-making procedures across the country. It has given birth to terms and concepts including "mulatto" and "miscegenation," "passing" and the "one-drop rule." Even in the new millennium, it continues to shape the discussion of topics such as the family and the nation, from the classroom to the courtroom, the church to the kitchen.

Alongside its ongoing impact on debates both private and public, the mixed-race character as a literary figure has left her lasting imprint. Texts such as William Wells Brown's *Clotel, Or: The President's Daughter* (1853), Pauline Hopkins's *Of One Blood: Or, the Hidden Self* (1902), and Octavia E. Butler's *Kindred* (1979), among others, have defined how the public looks at race and specifically at racial mixing both in the past and in the present. These texts each promote strategies of seeing and reading mixed race as undeniably rooted in the social context out of which they emerged. In their complex negotiations of the subject of mixed race, these texts also enable specific ways of addressing the topic with all its implications, including the writing of such narratives, in turn. In their use of a defined set of literary figures and tropes, such narratives play a decisive role in pushing forward, or backward, for that matter, the limits of what can be spoken about.

These texts contribute to the conception of the American family at a specific point in time. This includes questions about who can be a member of the family, and how the mixed-race family can be told and negotiated in public discourse. They also make statements on how the past shapes the present, and how the mixed self positions and sees herself in relation to complex and oftentimes vexed processes of nation-building. If there is one factor that unites very different types of texts relating to the crossing of racial boundaries in the United States, then it is that they participate in the formation of specific discourses addressing identity. At the same time, such texts are shaped by how society reflects upon the subject of mixed race at a given time: they can potentially conform to established patterns, or rewrite them, and hence, the subject itself.

These types of texts, as Ashraf A. H. Rushdy (1999) argues in his seminal study, *Neo-Slave Narratives: Studies in the Social Logic of a Literary Form*, necessarily follow a social logic giving shape to a specific literary form. Specific discourses and social, technological, and other developments make space for different literary forms at different times. Narratives emerging out of particular social contexts make clear how a culture reflects upon itself at a certain moment in history. A literary text can therefore show where the United States stands in terms of race relations, while at the same time pointing to the ways in which people can speak about this topic. Narrative certainly has constitutive power.

In Shirlee Taylor Haizlip's 1994 memoir, *The Sweeter the Juice: A Family Memoir in Black and White*, the narrator makes the following statement about her origins and racial background:

> Genes and chromosomes from Africa, Europe, and a pristine America commingled and created me. I have been called Egyptian, Italian, Jewish, French, Iranian, Armenian, Syrian, Spanish, Portuguese and Greek. I have also been called black and Peola and nigger and high yellow and bright. I am an American anomaly. I am an American ideal. I am the American nightmare. I am the Martin Luther King Dream. I am the new America. (Haizlip 1995, 15)

In this passage, the voice switches from the passive to the active form. In just a few lines, the narrator addresses several different dimensions of her selfhood. The first is biological; it refers to the genetic makeup of a person, and specifically, her persona. The narrator considers herself the result of a process of amalgamation from different "ingredients"—African, European, and Native American genes and chromosomes. The narrator also locates herself in a specific time, namely, when observations relating to genes and chromosomes have become thinkable due to the availability of DNA testing. Such practices give inquiries about a person's heritage a scientific quality and a claim to "truth"—the idea that a person is her genes, and that genes shape identity.

The second dimension of the passage above refers to how the narrator is seen by others: Due to her background, her essential mixedness, her ethnic and racial origins are not easy to determine. Consequently, she has been perceived and identified in many different ways, including ways infused by racism and negative stereotypes. Those who have misrepresented her, and who are not named or described in any detail in the passage, projected their concepts and definitions onto her, making her into somebody she is not.

The third dimension is both spatial and temporal: the narrator locates herself in the context of a specific past, present, and future, and in a specific country, the United States. In this passage, the narrator actively positions herself both at odds and in harmony with established notions of citizenship and belonging. She constructs herself as a representative of her country, as well as an "anomaly" within this context. The narrator makes clear that while she has been "created," and "has been called" several different and at times offensive names, she is now actively taking a stance on who she is: over and over she states "I am, I am, I am." She undergoes a process of making herself, defining herself. Similarly, this very passage complicates notions of selfhood in that the narrator embodies both "the dream" and "the nightmare"—two categories that are usually considered mutually exclusive. The self can be seen, and see herself, from more than just one angle. The verdict here is positive, though: in claiming "I am the new America," the narrator points to her future potential—that she *is* the future; she quite literally embodies it in her racial mixedness and its complex legacy.

This final statement—the recognition and celebration that she is "the new America"—relates to a specific history and to a specific dream evoked in the passage: a dream of freedom and harmony, of equality, a country where people "will not be judged by the color of their skin but by the content of their character" (King 1963, 5). The exclamation that concludes the narrator's meditation of her identity is the result of historical processes following slavery—the Great Migration, the Civil Rights Movement. It is the result of political decisions—the Civil Rights Act of 1964, the Voting Rights Act of 1965. It is a result of specific discourses surrounding ideas of racial mixing in the late twentieth century: the idea of essential genetic mixedness, the idea of a shared humanity of all people, and the idea that "mixed race" represents the future of the United States.

The passage quoted above echoes Walt Whitman's ([1885] 1983) "I can hear America singing" and Langston Hughes's ([1926]) "I, too"—both in the evocation of diversity and in the emphasis on equality as a central principle. The passage implies that the nation has finally progressed to a point where its true potential will be realized and a "new America" will come into being. It also shows that "identity cannot be divorced from history; rather, one's ancestry and origins are crucial to an understanding of the self" (Leverette 2006, 83).

In framing the narrator's identity in these terms, the passage points to several different objectives. Firstly, it confirms identity as a process resulting from how one sees oneself and how one is seen by others. This process is both, active and passive. The passage quoted above also relates well to the postmodern concept of "making the self" and the idea that one's identity is not stable, but in flux, subject to constant creation and re-creation. Secondly, the passage alludes to identity being shaped in the face of experiences, thus being a result of a specific past and present. Thirdly, it locates mixedness—the "commingling" of genes and chromosomes—at the center of the American nation: in the country's past, present, and, most importantly, its future.

The passage analyzed above is somewhat paradigmatic of the negotiation of self-making in the mixed-race memoirs that emerged in abundance starting in the 1990s. Narratives such as Shirlee Taylor Haizlip's *The Sweeter the Juice* (1994) quoted above, or Neil Henry's *Pearl's Secret: A Black Man's Search for His White Family* (2001) all work with similar tropes of creating and defining the mixed self in its complex and oftentimes vexed relationship to American history. In the 1990s, the emergence of these types of narratives occurred alongside the emergence of memoirs addressing similar concerns but from the point of view of those who had contributed—directly and indirectly—to the system that divides people into such categories as "black" and "white": the descendants of slaveholders. In Edward Ball's (1998, 14) memoir, *Slaves in the Family*, the narrator observes that "black" and "white" history usually are thought of as separate, while they are intrinsically linked. In exploring how the plantation past has shaped his family into the present, the narrator in this text tries to provide a more complete and coherent picture of American society, and arrive at a different sense of self.

Both these *types* of texts, texts like Neil Henry's *Pearl's Secret* and texts like Edward Ball's *Slaves in the Family*, rewrite *and* conform to dominant narratives of family-building and nation-making in the US context. While they make clear that different groups in history were affected differently by the past and so have developed different patterns to deal with the present, the memoirs provide insight into how race relations as well as family relations are evaluated at the time of their emergence in the 1990s and into the early 2000s. Both types of texts are not so much texts *about* slavery, but rather are texts about the long-term *consequences* of slavery, segregation, and the color-conscious society that emerged in the United States as a result of these. They are texts reflecting the meaning of the past for the present.

In her study *The Souls of Mixed Folk: Race, Politics and Aesthetics in the New Millennium*, Michelle Elam (2011, 44) argues that mixed-race narratives take on a definable form since approximately the 1990s. She lists features such as their narrative framing via a quest for identity. She also argues that these kinds of texts step back from the tragic mulatto as a central motif used in mixed-race literature at an earlier moment. By contrast, the narrators in those texts look to establish connections and accept themselves. In the same publication, she continues to argue that while these narratives may appear new, they follow rather conventional patterns and use established tropes of identity construction (44). Building on this research, my study suggests the emergence of a new literary genre that uses racial transgression, *passing*, and the trope of mixedness as a starting point of an inquiry about the meaning of the self and the family, the past and the present, race and identity from a variety of perspectives. I will refer to this mixed-race genre as *memoir of the search*. The genre stands in clear relation to earlier texts addressing mixed heritage, but by reinscribing those earlier narratives into the present, it also voices essential concerns of its own time.

To characterize and define this genre, my study will address four different dimensions or layers of the *memoir of the search*. First, I will locate the genre with regard to the specific literary shape it takes—the memoir. Second, I will define the *memoir of the search* by way of its literary tropes and symbols; first and foremost, the family secret that triggers the search for identity and for the self that is described in the text. Third, I will explore the genre in its use of media and genealogy. Fourth, I will focus on how the *memoir of the search* relates to the United States, and specifically to the Southern United States.

In linking the past to the present, the genre centrally reflects US and Southern history from today's perspective and enables a new point of view on the relationship between the nation and the region. These texts do not constitute an alternative literary tradition of "mixed race writing," but rather, they need to be contextualized within an existing canon of texts (45). I will end with a critique of the *memoir of the search* as a genre addressing the meaning of the past for the present. Using the notions of heritage, responsibility, and accountability as my starting points, I will show how this genre that proclaims to be "open" toward alternative readings of history still contributes to the continuous silencing of the past.

My central line of argument is that the *memoir of the search* as a literary genre represents an instance of *passing*, or bending established boundaries of speakability to fit into a canon of more traditional stories we tell about family and about identity. In taking up a very defined set of narrative patterns, literary motifs, and storylines, this genre literally makes itself fit into mainstream ways of discussing mixed heritage and family around the turn of the millennium, while at the same time, at least on the outside, these types of texts are trying to tell a new story. Consequently, the genre texts reflects, and possibly pushes forward, the limits of speakability with regard to mixed-race heritage and its implications at the point of writing. At the same time, it also points to the danger of silencing stories that cannot be made to conform to the established discourses and patterns of crossing supposed racial boundaries.

By tying racial mixedness to immigration from Europe, these texts show that even in the early twenty-first century, inclusion in the national project is dependent on *whiteness*. At the same time, they contribute to the normalization of racial mixing using specific families as examples. They make clear that what is commonly perceived as "normal" or "normality" is a discursive construction and not a neutral fact (Link 1998, 15). In his studies of normalization and normality, the German scholar Jürgen Link has pointed out that normality is specific to its spatiotemporal setting (22ff.). While the concept of protonormalism refers to fixed boundaries of what is perceived as "normal," the contemporary era is characterized by what Link refers to as a flexible-normalistic approach, where the borders of normality constantly change and shift (Link and Hall 2004, 38). Storytelling contributes to such processes of normalization.

The *memoir of the search* is a confessional genre. Confessional literature is strongly connected to tactics of self-normalization. Such publications may change the boundaries of what is considered "normal" by presenting new examples of a life lived and its difficulties confronted (Link 1998, 387). Confessional writing therefore challenges and potentially overcomes the borders of normality. The *memoir of the search* can be read as a narrative of *coming out*; a type of text that, in itself, is a challenge to protonormalist approaches. In the *memoir of the search*, the narrators, and, by implication, their families, come out as mixed race. *Coming out* stories are compelling displays of placing the self alongside or within the mainstream (390)—a tendency that the memoirs discussed here exhibit in powerful ways.

This study makes use of four exemplary texts that can be defined as *memoirs of the search*. Nevertheless, it will be hard to argue that these four are in some ways more representative of the genre than several other such texts that have emerged since the 1990s, such as James McBride's *The Color of Water* (1998), Henry Wiencek's *The Hairstons: An American Family in Black and White* (1999), June Cross's *Secret Daughter: A Mixed-Race Daughter and the Mother Who Gave Her Away* (2007), or the very recent *White Like Her: My Family's Story of Race and Racial Passing* (2017) by Gail Lukasik. Rather, these texts have been chosen for this work because their specific ways of negotiating mixed-race identities enable a dialogic reading throughout this study. They speak from the perspectives of narrators identifying as white and from the perspectives of narrators identifying as black. They vary enough in their approach to filter out what defines the genre, but are similar enough to be characterized as texts of the same kind, for example, due to their use of media, their tropes, and their general storylines.

Shirlee Taylor Haizlip's *The Sweeter the Juice: A Family Memoir in Black and White* (1994) is often considered an early and yet typical representative of biracial biography (e.g., Spickard 2001), but I argue that it is more than that. In this text, the narrator grows up as the daughter of a very well-loved black minister in Connecticut and begins to investigate her family's past as an adult. Finding out about the complex legacies of her family's past—from the Founding Period into the Civil Rights Movement, from Colonial Virginia to contemporary California—allows her to understand better what it means to be black in America.

Edward Ball's *Slaves in the Family* (1998) investigates the narrator's family history as one of the most prominent slaveholding families in Charleston, South Carolina. Ball, being white, wants to find out whether he has relatives on the other side of the color line, and to understand how his family could have become so involved in the slave trade. He voices many ethical questions and concerns, and even attempts to apologize for the sins committed by his ancestors. This approach to his family and to Southern regional history is rather rare and does not go uncontested.

The narrator in Neil Henry's *Pearl's Secret: A Black Man's Search for His White Family* (1999) learns to understand himself better as a black American as he traces his great-great-grandmother's romance with a white plantation overseer. As a young man, he had traveled to Africa only to discover that his true home is in the United States. His search leads him to develop a relationship with some of his white family members, and to the understanding that his family members contributed in significant ways to American history.

In Bliss Broyard's *One Drop: My Father's Hidden Life—A Story of Race and Family Secrets* (2007), the narrator grows up identifying as white, but, as she finds out more about her famous father's black Louisiana Creole background, she begins to challenge the narration of history as well as whiteness as a category. She discovers the secret history of *passing* and its continuing legacy in contemporary America, as well as in her own immediate family.

Even from these very short and introductory descriptions of the four narratives it is clear that they—however different in content, outlook on the future, structure, or degree of relation to the history that they are principally investigating—share more than the superficial fact that a narrator researches his or her family's mixed-race history. All narrators comment on their family's as well as on America's process of becoming; they attempt to provide a more comprehensive picture of their family and of the country as a whole. They do so by including specific media of memory, generating a rather similar *type* of story. By pointing to gaps in the family history, all the narrators evaluate the past's consequences for their family into contemporary times, and interrogate the decisions taken by their ancestors whose former homes they sometimes seek out in order to gain a better idea of these ancestors' lives and the circumstances that may have led them to make certain decisions. All these texts deal, though from different points of view, with *passing* and its implications for the family and the nation. Here, the ongoing legacy of race in the United States is highlighted as "these works foreground the capacity of racial passing to challenge the enduring canards of identity formation itself" (Elam 2007, 750).

In addition, the travel these narrators undertake during their quest for their roots and their family's pasts helps them to evaluate not only their perception of those who came before them, but also their own attitudes toward Africa, toward the American South—the region most prominently associated with slavery and segregation—and toward their current location in the Northern or Western United States. Further, they transcend borders of social class. As much as racial- and class-belonging is constructed spatially in the United States, these narratives can also be read as stories of migration, stories of travel, or as renegotiations of space and memory.

As becomes evident throughout this study, the *memoir of the search* resonates with its social context and takes up concerns of its time: "During those moments when racial tensions and anxieties are most severe, mixed race becomes centralized in public forums" (Leverette 2006, 82). New findings regarding the Jefferson–Hemings controversy sparked such discourse, as did the powerful emergence in recent decades of DNA testing as a tool to learn about one's ancestry. The 1990s also saw, for example, the emergence of a so-called multiracial movement arguing for a "multiracial" option on the census form as a testament to self-identification that goes beyond the established categories.

What might at first sound like a liberal, inclusive idea could in fact have significantly weakened Civil Rights legislation, and was thus met with significant resistance in the African American community (Williams 2006, 111). By 2000, the introduction of the so-called MOOM-option (Mark-One-Or-More) changed the US Census form significantly, "allowing Americans to identify officially with as many racial groups as they saw fit" (2). Here, technically, for the first time in US history it was possible to identify oneself as black and simultaneously as white—to mark two categories that were previously considered mutually exclusive. Since the 1990s, the United States has been confronted with a large-scale debate regarding "the viability of race" (Elam 2007, 750), despite the idea that this is a "post-race" era.

Alongside these debates about the contemporary meanings of "race," a renewed concern about slavery and its long-term consequences developed. This concern led to a discussion about the visual manifestations of the past, such as the meaning of statues and memorial plaques. The concern also referred to the idea of renaming sites, taking down Confederate flags, and tearing down monuments celebrating what was now considered white pride. Ultimately, this debate about the spatial consequences of the past accumulated into a public discussion about whether this would be the time to apologize for slavery and to issue a financial compensation to those who had suffered the losses. The 1990s were in many ways the decade when the open "secret" of slavery and race was lifted: it became a topic to be discussed at the dinner table, in churches and in libraries, as well as in a growing number of university classrooms across the country.

The *memoir of the search* as a genre responds to the idea of uncovering this long-held secret as well as to the popular trend of undertaking genealogical research in the name of coming to terms with not one, but multiple identities. Paul Spickard (2001, 93) argues in his article relating to the steady emergence of such texts, "The Subject Is Mixed Race: The Boom in Biracial Biography," that "these books have an audience, not because there are dramatically more mixed people now, but because Americans of many racial identities have a new sense of the multiplicity around them and an interest in learning about the mixedness that is us all."

This political climate gave rise to the *memoir of the search* and its specific literary devices, which publicly negotiate questions about mixed ethnicities. Significantly, none of the narrators in these texts define themselves as "multiracial": they describe themselves as black, white, or mixed. Nevertheless, these texts comment on questions voiced by the multiracial movement. In its portrayal of so-called generationally mixed people, the *memoir of the search* makes clear that mixedness has always been a central part of America's ethnic makeup. These texts take a stance in locating "mixed race" both temporally and spatially.

While the *memoir of the search* as a genre, and thus all narratives discussed in this study, had emerged before 2008, it can be argued that it contributed to giving rise to the Obama presidency, as well. Not only did Barack Obama himself write and publish a book that is in many ways best described as a *memoir of the search*, *Dreams from My Father: A Story of Race and Inheritance* (1995), but the public debate about his supposed "illegitimacy" as a president, as a citizen, points to many issues already voiced in the *memoir of the search*. The discussions that emerged around his election show that people in the United States have begun a new process of reflection on what it means to be American. In these terms, the potential of such texts as the ones in this study to comment on and intervene in processes of defining both the personal and national family cannot and should not be underestimated and are thus worthy of such detailed analysis as provided here.

Chapter 1

Writing Mixed Selves at the Turn of the Millennium

When Barack Hussein Obama was elected president of the United States on November 4, 2008, many different interest groups across the United States perceived, celebrated, and proclaimed this moment as a turning point in history. Indeed, Obama had seemed an unlikely candidate for the presidency: a young senator with a powerful voice, but not very experienced in the political arena overall; a lawyer with a family and with a background as a community organizer in the notoriously disadvantaged African American neighborhoods of Chicago. A black man running for president—not the first to do so, but the first to win the primary of one of the two major parties—in a nation where, for the longest time, the black population had been struggling for freedom, for political recognition, for the vote, for equal opportunity. Obama became the Democratic Party's presidential candidate and then the forty-fourth president of the United States of America in a tension-filled moment: an age of international terrorist threats, a global financial crisis, and devastating wars in which the United States was a major combatant.

Possibly, he was elected president because dissatisfaction with his predecessor, George W. Bush, had reached new heights in the aftermaths of 9/11, Hurricane Katrina, and the government's failure to successfully install political stability and peace in Afghanistan. Or, it was because Obama was able to mobilize the population, and especially those who traditionally do not vote, by using unconventional and new outreach methods such as social networking websites during his campaign—an innovation at the time. Maybe he was elected president because of his powerful campaign speeches captured audiences nationally and internationally; because the people believed he had a vision, an understanding of their needs and problems; and because he stood for "change"—a change they felt was desperately needed.

Whichever factors worked together to bring about Obama's success in the 2008 election, his victory *was* quickly proclaimed as a true sign of racial progress (Gavrilos 2010, 3), or even as a powerful indication of the end of "race" (e.g., Squires, Harris, and Moffitt 2010, xvii). As Michele Elam states in the previously mentioned study *The Souls of Mixed Folk*, "[t]he election of President Barack Obama is a case study in the cultural invention of mixed race" (Elam 2011, 7). Obama has never referred to himself as "multiracial," but rather described himself as "African American" on the 2010 census (14), and "[i]n the media [. . .] is generally referred to as black or African American, rarely as multiracial or biracial" (Daniel 2009, 52).

Not for the first time in US history, questions about racial mixing and its significance came to occupy the public discourse throughout Obama's election campaign; the question of whether Barack Obama could even be a "real" American citizen was raised, as was his ability to genuinely represent "America." In the immediate aftermath of Obama's election victory, however, the country came together to celebrate its "first black president" (Elam 2011, 7). For a time, so it seemed, the American Dream had finally fulfilled its ultimate legacy—a black man could rise to the status of US president and thus reconcile differences between black and white. The nation could move forward into the new millennium: America's postracial moment—the moment of fulfillment of the American Dream for *everyone*, regardless of racial or ethnic background—had finally arrived, or so it seemed.

Fast forward less than ten years to the summer of 2017, when, following a large number of instances of racially motivated violence including the so-called Charleston Church Shooting of 2015, the Unite the Right rally took place in Charlottesville, Virginia, a historically liberal town and home to the University of Virginia. Unmistakably, this event made clear that despite all talk of unity, reconciliation, and racial integration, the country had no shortage of people identifying with neo-Nazi, anti-Semitic, and other white supremacist ideologies. Protestors were claiming that "diversity is just another word for white genocide," meaning that America's multiculturalism poses a threat to national integrity (Helmore and Beckett 2017).

These groups gathered in Charlottesville in order to unify their movements and form a supremacist alliance. A large crowd of counter-protestors met the rally's participants, and soon the rally escalated into violence. One counter-protestor was killed and many were injured. Certainly, the incidents of Charlottesville caused people to have a hard time "grappling with the blatant display of attitudes that many believed had been buried" (Astor, Caron, and Victor 2017) and that led to the public shaming of several of the white nationalist participants (ibid.). The rally left the national as well as the international public both shocked and puzzled.

If nothing else, the Charlottesville incident makes clear that despite talk of inclusion and diversity, the past matters and representation matters. Even though the American nation had a black president for two terms, it is not clear yet how disputes about the memory of the Confederate past will be resolved across the South or the nation, or how the rise of white supremacist groups may be curtailed. What added fuel to the fire in Charlottesville was that, while Republican as well as Democratic politicians criticized the rally, the Trump administration did not condemn the white supremacists as harshly as would have been expected. Instead President Trump, in the days following the incident, blamed "many sides" for what had occurred, leading to widespread bewilderment and the feeling that Trump did not categorically condemn the alt-right (Helmore and Beckett 2017). A fundamental question the American public is still confronting is whether these protests amount to antidiversity action of a new order, or whether this strain of racism has always been part of the political undercurrent—and has gained new traction since the turn of the millennium and throughout the Obama presidency.

It can be argued that some twenty years earlier the signs of the time were pointing in a different direction. The nation appeared to be moving against the rise of white supremacy and toward the emergence of a more differentiated understanding of the American past. This understanding involved a candid, difficult account of slavery and its multiple meanings leading up to today, which may have helped lead to Obama's election. In the 1990s and into the early 2000s, the United States experienced what Ashraf H. A. Rushdy (2001, 135) has described as a "moment of anti-nostalgic reflection" that led to the possibility to reconsider the past and its meanings.

Public debates addressing the concept of diversity in the face of changing patterns of immigration, as well as a large-scale conversation about the crucial role of slavery for American national development and consciousness, gained a lot of traction. The conversation was led by the country's most prestigious scholars of African American Studies, such as Henry Louis Gates Jr. The United States saw the call for a reevaluation of, for example, the spatial and visual memory of slavery and segregation that also contributed to the escalations of 2017. The attention given to the meaning of the Confederate Flag, the naming of streets or public places after Confederate generals, or the ways the past should be exhibited in museums or monuments was unprecedented.

In the context of these public negotiations, the past and its meaning for the present became the subject of countless publications and media releases. Examples include the TV-miniseries *African American Lives* (PBS, 2006–2008, directed and presented by Henry Louis Gates Jr.), the drama *Sankofa* (1993, dir. Haile Gerima), and the Hollywood blockbuster *Amistad* (1997, dir. Steven Spielberg), but also book collections such as *Slavery and Public*

History: The Tough Stuff of American Memory (2009, ed. James Oliver Horton and Lois E. Horton), and fictional texts like *The Known World* (Edward P. Jones, 2003), a fictional work addressing the issue of black slave ownership in antebellum America. Similarly, the 1990s saw a renewed evaluation of the responsibilities of the then-current generation and their accountability for the ongoing effects of the wrongs committed by their ancestors. For example, Americans debated the question of whether reparations should be made to the descendants of former slaves. As Rushdy (2001, 140) writes, this is certainly a complicated notion because it assumes that people will feel implicated in wrongdoings they have not committed themselves, and that happened before they were born.

The rhetoric of obligation toward those one is not immediately related to, a concept prominent at the time, at first glance suggests a more empathetic approach to the nation as well as to personal freedom and its achievement. But at the same time, these types of discourses of the 1990s and beyond blatantly fueled a more conservative "politics of postethnic ideology [that in the long run] represses the formation of diverse identities and neutralizes resistance to inequality and injustice" (Ahokas 2007, 240). This "not only entails racial and ethnic self-erasure, but, by extension, it also promotes the denial of differences in gender and sexuality" (240). If equality has been reached and we are now living in a "post-racial" era, so such thinking goes, no support system is required anymore. Affirmative action can be done away with.

Considered from this perspective, when seemingly liberal slogans are used to hide a rather conformist and conservative agenda, even the celebration of diversity negates individual difference and forces assimilation. Paying reparations for slavery in the name of diversity and equality may, as a consequence, lead to ignorance instead of liberation—if the money has been paid, then it is time to be "done" once and for all with the past. Such rationale is simplistic in a nation where social opportunity is often still based on race, and strategies to address slavery more openly still have to be developed. For example, it took the United States until 2016 to open its National Museum of African American History and Culture in the nation's capital.

INTRODUCING THE *MEMOIR OF THE SEARCH*

The moments in (more or less) recent American history alluded to above—the election of America's first black president in 2008, the Charlottesville rally of 2017, the opening of a new museum that both commemorates the African American contribution to national culture and addresses the traumas of slavery and racism—point to the fault lines of public discussions about race in the contemporary United States, but also about the legacy of the deeper past. These moments relate to ideas of the self and the *Other*, as well as to larger discussions of American national identity. Who can be and should be a citizen? Who gets a say in how the past is remembered? How should the past be visually and spatially negotiated? Who "owns" which spaces, and which stories? Is there any way to move beyond race and its complicated legacies at all?

This study aims to provide an extensive analysis of a type of literary narrative that arguably contributed and responded to the public sentiments alluded to above. For a period of time, around the turn of the millennium, such narratives promised a more open and inclusive mode of addressing topics such as collective memory and racial mixing, namely via stories of the mixed self and the mixed family coming to terms with the past and its long-term legacy. These texts, in their strategy of placing mixed-race heritage at the center of the American experience, engage in a double movement of opening up new discussions about the topic, while at the same time silencing stories that cannot be told in terms of the American tenets of individualism and success. In this way, they situate themselves in the direct context of debates at the time of their emergence. The texts also speak back to earlier moments in literary and cultural history in which questions of race and national identity, the family, and personal freedom were at the center of such discussions.

Working with texts pointing to the rhetorical construction of mixed-race identity at the turn of the millennium, my analysis shows how addressing and narrating hybridity situates mixed-race individuals "as racialized subjects in history" (Elam 2011, 50). This first chapter contextualizes millennial mixed-race family narratives in their cultural and literary frameworks to show that they pick up on and feed back into extra-textual discourses of their time. In order to place themselves at the center of the national discussion, these memoirs speak back to other texts about race and specifically mixed race that came before them. While I cannot provide a detailed intertextual reading, as this would make for a different study, I still hope to be able to point out that such an approach is productive and that mixed-race family narratives from the turn of the millennium lend themselves to dialogues with a variety of narratives from both the black and white traditions: ethnic and immigrant autobiography, slave- and neo-slave narratives, as well as their ultimate predecessor, Alex Haley's (1976) *Roots: The Saga of an American Family*, are only some points of reference encouraging such an intertextual reading.

Centrally, in the American context, fictional as well as nonfictional negotiations about race, identity, and the self have manifested themselves in melodramatic forms, appealing to the audience's emotions and calling for personal involvement and investment. In her comprehensive study of what she terms race melodrama, *Playing the Race Card: Melodramas of Black and White from Uncle Tom to O.J. Simpson* (2001), Linda Williams discusses a variety of texts and their public reverberations through the past two centuries, claiming that "melodrama has been, for the better or the worse, the primary way in which mainstream American culture has dealt with the moral dilemma of having first enslaved and then withheld equal rights to generations of African Americans" (Williams 2002, 44). Williams argues that this conflict has been central to US national identity into the present, specifically with regard "to the question of who we mean when we say 'we' are a nation" (44). She explains how the "race card" has been played repeatedly and extensively in black/white relations in the United States, both by blacks and by whites, in a quasi-back-and-forth pattern between the two communities in which one card is always potentially trumping another, keeping racial melodrama at the center of public attention (5).

Melodrama has been described by Linda Williams as a "leaping fish," jumping from one genre to another and thereby always transforming itself and in turn transforming its genre of choice. Since the post-Civil Rights era, Williams argues, race melodrama has mostly taken place in "reality-based forms" (220). This means that the media is used to attest to a particular "truthfulness" of the story told. In addition, as becomes evident in the iconic example of *Roots* by Alex Haley, a text "telling the story of slavery from an African-American, post-civil rights perspective" (221), following the Civil Rights era African Americans increasingly became part of the mainstream and could no longer be excluded from the public discourse. Finally, they could also tell their family story in terms of a "saga" and contextualize themselves in American history—a sign of arrival at the center of society (221). This development is also significant for the texts discussed in this study, directly speaking back to *Roots*.

The genre henceforth referred to as *memoir of the search* follows Neil Henry's description of his autobiographical narrative *Pearl's Secret* as "a memoir of his search" (Henry 2001, 14) that led him to a more detailed understanding of his and his fellow African Americans' identity in the United States. Around the turn of the millennium, this genre appealed to the emotions of readers, all the while complicating established notions of victim and perpetrator central to the melodramatic mode by leveling the central questions of whiteness, blackness, and the issue of race (Haizlip 1995, 34) at the most idealized of American institutions: the heteronormative family. This focus is rather unsurprising given the time of emergence of these texts: "Late modernity has spotlit intimate relations. Families, feelings and love lives have been opened to public politics through diverse pressures" (Jolly 2011, v). In the *memoir of the search*, the reader encounters families who are both living as black and living as white, and who, after years without contact between each other, often even without any knowledge of each other's existence, unite in the present moment in order to reflect on what connects them and to "share [their] recollections, feelings, and dreams, and make the story whole" (Ball 1999, 14).

The narrators, some of whom identify as white and some as black, point out how the same questions about the family can be voiced from multiple standpoints. In turn, these questions can also be responded to in several ways: the answers actually depend upon an individual's perspective and on social positioning, lived experience, and frame of reference. The answers, too, are intensely shaped by patterns of relating. The underlying theme here is how a family, and by implication, a nation, can unify after such a long period of time apart and in a framework characterized by disunity.

Much in tune with these themes, the narrators' personal reflections, as well as their inquiries into American history through the process of piecing together their family history, make the memoirs prime examples of life writing around the turn of the millennium. These reflections and inquiries add to placing these texts in a complex relationship with race melodrama, not least because their appeal to social uplift and individualism speaks from a standpoint of social privilege. "Melodrama," as Lauren Berlant argues, first and foremost "is bourgeois tragedy" (Berlant and Prosser 2001, 185).

By the 1990s many narratives of the mixed self—its discovery and negotiation—had taken on a definable form as well as a definable and closely circumscribed content. These narratives had established a normative kind of profile of people of mixed-race descent (Elam 2011, 10): the *memoir of the search*. A dual outlook defines the genre. These texts understand the past through stories, but at the same time recognize that any story, and, by implication, all past, is constructed. The format of the memoir about the resolution of a family secret with larger social implications is much in tune with trends in the book market at the time. More generally speaking, the 1980s and 1990s were characterized by a move toward underlining the role of personal histories in their larger contexts. Sharon O'Brien (1996, 1) claims that this period was a time of "breaking silences" in writing. She explains that "[w]riters [were] challenging the boundaries supposedly distinguishing fiction from nonfiction, memoir from biography, essay from poetry, autobiography from criticism" (1). Nikola Herweg has argued that the biographies available then make a statement about the relationship between the community and its collective memory: they relate to what the community of readers finds worth remembering. These texts thus do not only make a statement about the personal choices of authors, readers, or the personnel of publishing houses, but also about the current state of national memory and the available means for such processes of remembering (Herweg 2005, 206).

The 1990s and the years following saw the large-scale emergence of texts that have been characterized as "life writing" in its diverse manifestations, from journal to confessional to ethnography to memoir, to mention just a few of the possible shapes in which personal narratives emerged as the indicative way of speaking and writing in "our confessional times" (Zinsser 1998, 3). As William Zinsser argues, "Never have personal narratives gushed so profusely from the American soil as in the closing decade of the twentieth century. Everyone has a story to tell, and everyone is telling it" (1). The period was characterized by an increased blurring between the boundaries of public and private; everything became scrutinized, and intimacies were revealed in front of a mass audience.

Efforts were being made in this context to resolve the cultural family secret of slavery, and to find new ways of talking about "the color line"—a term popularized by W. E. B. Du Bois in *The Souls of Black Folk* (1903)— and mixed race in the United States. A cultural secret is one that people are aware of, but that has become unspeakable or unimaginable, it is something that "seems continually to elude our understanding" (Rushdy 2001, 2). The *memoir of the search* therefore operates under the assumption that there is a part of American history that has not yet been revealed, but that concerns the nation as well as the individual family. The narrators of such memoirs need to break this cultural secret to their textual family members, and, by implication, the reading public, in order to establish that secret at the center of what it means to be American. This attests to an altered sense of the past and to new approaches of dealing with it, or not: It means that individuals as well as communities have to invest time into thinking about the meaning of the past in the contemporary moment and potentially have to reconsider their role in relation to how the present power constellation came to be, especially if it is the result of exploitation, war, or another atrocity (3).

The agenda of the *memoir of the search* is to develop and move forward an existing narrative about the supposedly monoracial American family and, by implication, about the American nation, in order to create a "usable past" (Zamora 2008) that will help determine the future.

The texts work on building a more comprehensive past and writing a narrative of familial and national reconciliation from there. Extensive periods of research using a variety of media, including microfilm, newspaper articles, archival material from architectural sketches, and obituaries, in reality-based fashion (to use Linda Williams's terms), lead the narrator of this type of text to travel cross-country and then to engage in a process of negotiating their family's past in depth (Henry 2001, 3). Still, the *memoir of the search* remains firmly situated in the present. There is no time travel or physical encounter with the supposed ghosts of the past. Rather, the genre speaks from a "realist" stance; the narrator addresses the subject of reconciliation as a contemporary American to other contemporary Americans—the reading public.

This stance forces the narrators to position themselves vis-à-vis their lived and experienced social privilege, but also in relation to the long-term political consequences of integrating mixed-race individuals into both their present family and the larger national family up to the point of their investigation. Within the narrative of the stories in question, the family has up to this point perceived itself as either black or white, and the members have not been part of a kinship system across perceived racial and social boundaries. The national family was predominantly coded as white.

In these terms, the texts discussed throughout this study bear striking resemblance to the *Bildungsroman* since it asks questions about the relationship between the individual and society, and how the individual becomes part of society (Elam 2011, 125). These narratives address an educational process of reconciling the self with a complex world. In different ways, and to varying detail, the *memoir of the search* tells the story of how the narrator and the narrator's family have become "mixed," how the character moves beyond the mutual exclusiveness of "blackness" and "whiteness," and how the resulting "mixedness" finally becomes merged with "Americanness" at large. By implication, these texts take a dual stance looking from the present into the past, as well as toward the evidently postracial future; they propose that inclusion of mixed race into the nation will lead to the resolution of central national conflicts and a brighter outlook. Still, they address some of the difficulties and challenges relating to such an inclusion.

The inquiry into the past requires the narrator to reverse previous assumptions about the (individual and national) family and how it came to be, as well as about the meaning of being American in the twentieth or early twenty-first century. These reversals of assumptions are central to the quest undertaken in the narratives. In essence, the genre engages with the question of what racial mixedness and diversity signify at the time of the texts' genesis. It also questions how the postmodern self can fulfill all of the different dimensions and social roles and responsibilities an individual may have to bear in the face of racial mixedness and its multiple legacies. Finally, the genre asks questions about how the narrators and, by extension, all members of the present generation are implicated in their ancestors' decisions.

Ashraf H. A. Rushdy (2001, 135) links such ideas to a philosophical model that he calls *narrative model*. This model speaks to the responsibility of corporate bodies for events that have happened at an earlier moment in time. It builds on the assumption that a person cannot choose whether or not they would like to be responsible or morally connected to an earlier event or crime they have not committed or participated in in any way. Rather, it suggests continuity between the past and the present by assuming that the present is the way it is because it is constituted by a specific past in which specific actors took defined actions. According to this model, there is an obligation toward the community, and also, in the national sense, a need to be able to take up responsibility for past mistakes, for example, in the context of colonialism (138).

At the same time, perceiving oneself as part of a larger group and its identity is a matter of choice. For collective responsibility to emerge, there needs to be a sense of collective identity first (Rushdy 2001, 140). This understanding suggests that contemporary Americans will only assume responsibility for slavery and its long-term legacy if it is part of their national story, or the story they consider their own. In addition to examining the wrongs their ancestors committed, the narrators in the *memoirs of the search* try to achieve such placement of the past in the mainstream. By taking up a defined set of narrative elements and by speaking back to other texts set in a similar mode of conflict, these texts represent a form of transferring this particular storyline into the mainstream narratives of the United States of America itself.

The identifying author of the text—the "I" speaking to its reading audience—constructs her identity through a specific narrative arc: beginning with the moment she begins to seek out, in one way or another, the family history she had been denied as a child growing up and ending in the moment where she comes clean with the past. Between these two states is a search for answers and a gathering with those the narrator encounters along the way and identifies as family. While the voice speaking in these texts identifies as the author—the "real" person who has written the text—this study refers to the main persona in the *memoir of the search* as its narrator or narrative voice, as this work is limited to analyzing and understanding the *memoir of the search* as a literary genre.

According to Lauren Berlant (2008, xii), "[t]he autobiographical is not the personal": "In the contemporary consumer public, and in the long durée [. . .] all sorts of narratives are read as autobiographies of collective experience. The personal is the general." This study does not seek to comment on any aspect relating to an author's life or lived experience; the goal of the analysis provided here is not to refer to any extra-textual events that may have conspired in an author's life and led this "real" person to take certain decisions regarding the text. Rather, the goal of this study is to understand the narrative conventions of writing the mixed self around the turn of the millennium. One of these conventions is the autobiographical outlook.

This particular outlook is useful in telling stories that are not (yet) "closed," stories that ask questions: "Autobiography produces so many questions within or without texts because questions are ultimately what the texts express" (Perreault 1990, 130). Questions—in contrast to statements—can neither be true nor false; they do not describe anything, but rather, they open up possibilities, expressing a desire, or even a need, to know (131) that has so far not been satisfied. This quality interlinks the *memoir of the search* with other forms of autobiographical writing, which "appears to share with questions a distinctive brand of truth, open-endedness, self-referentiality, the speaker/writer's drive for coherence and an affirmation of his will to know more" (131). Donna Perreault (1990) argues that autobiography is "a meaningful response to questions which cannot, and usually claim not, to answer." Autobiographical writing lends itself to introspection and is, in those terms, a quest in and of itself (132).

The need for intense introspection is clearly evident in the memoirs under consideration. In Neil Henry's *Pearl's Secret*, the narrator grows up thinking—and feels confirmed in this line of thinking by his parents—that racial injustices and inequalities are integral to the black experience in the United States (Henry 2001, 45). This view enables him to move on despite the backlash he also experiences (45). But during his process of investigating his family history, he cannot isolate his existence from these events anymore: While he had previously "stow[ed] them [racial prejudices] away in a little box inside [his] soul somewhere," during the process of uncovering the past, they hit him with full force once he starts his investigation (45). He goes on to explain that this is a challenge to him, as keepsakes from the past trigger memories and can become "a kind of key to a locked portal to [his] psyche, releasing all sorts of long pent-up personal memories about race" (45–46).

It is particularly interesting how the persona makes use of metaphors in these passages. The narrator uses ideas such as the "lock" and the "key" to talk about his subconsciousness. These ideas allude to strategies of avoidance and sublimation—whether conscious or unconscious—that the narrator has to overcome in order to be able to confront the past. Thus, in the process of "unlocking" the secret door to the past, the narrator is also led to reevaluate his life and previous experiences, meaning he has to contemplate what his findings mean for him and for his life.

In effect, the matters taken up in these narratives can only take the form of the quest, or the memoir-as-question, as the long-term meaning of mixed heritage is yet to be resolved. In the past, the subject could not be openly addressed due to the supposed mutual exclusiveness of black and white in American culture. Now, it can only be formulated in inquiries and be approached in the shape of research undertaken in the text, as a redefinition of identity is necessary. The meaning of mixedness had come under scrutiny around the turn of the millennium in the context of the so-called multiracial movement, which at the time rose up to create a new "multiracial" history and a distinct census category for a mixed-race population, thereby threatening established Civil Rights era legislation, for example, Affirmative Action, which used census records to attest to the harsher conditions for African Americans (Williams 2006, 3).

The multiracial movement by and large pushed forward the argument that, in the years and decades following the Civil Rights Movement, a new population had emerged that was in need of support and that supposedly had not been properly taken care of before. But this argument has an ahistorical premise. Racial mixedness is not a new phenomenon, especially not in the African American community: "Because of their history of the past four hundred years, Afro-Americans are one of the most (if not the most) genetically mixed populations in the United States" (Spencer 2006, 4). Nevertheless, as Rainier Spencer has explained, the idea of a newly emerging multiracialism might just be another strategy of keeping the African American population outside of the mainstream and thus to deny historical injustice (4). In this context it becomes particularly interesting that the *memoir of the search* works on the basis of intergenerational mixedness, meaning that all families encountered by a reader have been mixed for a long period of time. They are not a new population.

The reader is familiarized with the narrator by closely following the investigation of the character's singular but representative family history. This includes learning about the frustrations within the process of searching and the ambivalence of the narrator toward what is found. The narrative's autobiographical perspective cultivates the reader's empathy. At the same time, the narrator maintains a distance to the reader: Apart from the narrator's research, the reader does not learn much about the central character. If a relationship or marriage is mentioned, for example, it is usually not expanded on in much detail, unless it is a vital part of the research process. In *One Drop*, we learn that the narrator's boyfriend accompanies her on a trip to New Orleans, during which he—as a person unrelated to her family history—has a much easier time dealing with the poverty they discover upon visiting the family's former street (Broyard 2007, 94).

Even *The Sweeter the Juice*, which of all the texts discussed here offers the most extensive information about the narrator's personal circumstances—information about her husband and daughters, as well as the different stops along her professional career—only provides such information when there is a direct link to the process of the search itself, or to the motivations driving the search: the narrator says of her childhood that she thought everyone was living like her family, but she comes to understand how exceptional her family and the opportunities she was provided with truly were (Haizlip 1995, 124). The unusual nature of her upbringing is evident in the daily experiences she recounts, including encounters with well-known members of the African American community (150) and being well respected in their religious institution (151). The narrator's upbringing in a relatively privileged setting means that she did not have a detailed understanding of the complex dynamics of race in America when growing up (145). The opportunity to get a good education and connect with important people in the African American community all contribute to her later interest in investigating family history. A reader recognizes this narrator—like most narrators in the genre—as unusually socially advantaged.

It might seem that there is a contradiction between the narrators' relative silence on personal matters and the revealing of information about their family history. This seeming contradiction is a feature of the genre that enables its rather academic perspective. Adding too much information about personal matters would distract the reader from following the central character's process of investigation. Moreover, the meaning of privacy—if not its importance—shifts over time. It is easier to expose those dimensions of the family life and the family secret that are rooted in the (relatively) distant past.

The narratives include an ethical dimension in that they ask complex questions regarding the past's impact on the present. They point to the fact that the matter of who belongs to a family at any given point in time is shaped by decisions made in the past that are hard to comprehend and the effects of which are difficult to overcome in the present. Even more importantly, the narrators in this genre question the decisions taken by their ancestors and wonder whether they themselves would have reacted in the same way if given the choice. Would they have, for example, left behind a family member due to their skin color? Would they have *passed* if given the opportunity and risked losing those whose skin was not light enough to *pass*?

The past and the decisions taken in it linger over all relationships established throughout the texts. The past overshadows meetings with new family members as well as others, for example, the descendants of the slaves the family once owned. The narrator's position in society changes because of their investigation. It becomes clear that the present generation in these texts feels accountable for and implied in past actions. Feeling an overwhelming sense of kinship for his white relative Rita, the narrator in *Pearl's Secret*, Neil, observes that her story is rather sad (Henry 2001, 241). The narrator also learns that some of his relatives did not and still do not share Rita's open-minded attitude and refuse to acknowledge their black kin (248). Even Pearl's father, the narrator concludes, was unfair and a fraud since he had conceived a child with a black woman but still did not change his mind about the inferiority of African Americans (254). No matter how this man, A. J. Beaumont, might have felt inside, on the outside, Pearl's father acted in a racist manner. While this event happened before the narrator's lifetime, it still pains him and is incomprehensible to him.

Along similar lines, the narrator in Edward Ball's *Slaves in the Family* is confronted with the past and the complexities of addressing it from a present perspective. As a white man looking for the descendants of those his ancestors enslaved, the narrator must accept that the very people he seeks to understand and possibly befriend might not be interested in getting to know him and hearing what he has to say. After a meeting with one of these descendants of slaves, Katie Heyward, he comes to understand that the undercurrent of the conversation is distrust, and that this distrust is due to his family's legacy with this woman's family, whose members were enslaved by the Balls. He is a member of the family who kept them enslaved, and there is nothing he can do to change that (Ball 1999, 66). He understands that it takes more than one conversation to resolve the past's complex legacy and that he may not be able to convey his message. Historically, after all, the narrator's family has broken the Heyward family's trust, and the distrust between the families continues to the present.

Despite the fact that the reader learns only relatively marginal information about the narrator's personal life, the latter still becomes a "real" character in the *memoir of the search*, a character with enough depth to be believable and who is considered serious in her intentions. The construction of the narrator as both a family-oriented person, probably not totally unlike the imagined reader, and as a serious researcher and investigator of family history, creates a sense of connection between reader and narrator. Her struggles through the story, her hurt feelings and ambivalences, further humanize her.

The reader is taken along on the quest, encountering a research process that appears reasonable: It begins by examining under close scrutiny items that have always been part of the family heritage and then extends outward into books and archival material. The narrator in *Pearl's Secret* gives a rather extensive description of this process. He starts from three leads: a photograph, a newspaper obituary, and an old letter written by Pearl's father to his daughter (Henry 2001, 20). He explains how, fueled by an obsessive energy, he begins to investigate every so little trace about the white Beaumont family that he can get a hold of, including census materials and data stored on microfilm (20). He even establishes contacts to Great Britain, receiving support from institutions that keep archives relating to the time and geographical locations he is interested in (20).

His description makes clear how extensive the research process is, and how much energy, time, and also money are needed to undertake such a quest. Beyond access to the materials, it takes specific knowledge to commit to this type of scholarship. Still, despite this research orientation, the narrator's relationship to the work is neither passive nor clinical. The narrators in all texts experience setbacks and difficulties; they follow paths that do not lead anywhere in the process, and there is disappointment until a new clue is revealed.

The pattern of secrecy and revelation makes for an entertaining read. The creation of a bond between the narrator and her reader, to whom these intimate family secrets are shared, renders the cultural secret of the "color line" less and less abstract: it becomes, for the reader, a matter of personal concerns.

The narrators in the texts chosen for this study all describe and construct themselves as professional writers of one type or another—as journalists, as professors or instructors, as graduates of writing programs. While this may be a coincidence that ultimately has more to do with the selection of texts for this particular study rather than with the nature of the *memoir of the search* as a genre, it does confirm that these texts are speaking from the specific social location of the educated middle class. As members of such a group, the narrators are aware of the predecessors of their own texts, the common tropes associated with writing about mixed-race backgrounds, and the power of autobiographical writing. It appears that their education ultimately stimulates an interest in undertaking this type of research.

The connection between education and finding access to one's family history is most explicitly present in Bliss Broyard's *One Drop*, in which the narrator commits to some preliminary research about her family, but neglects it until she starts her graduate education in Fiction Writing at the University of Virginia. Surrounded by her academic environment, she becomes more open-minded with regard to investing time in studying her family history. She acknowledges that while she had only read about race before then, when enrolled at the University of Virginia she started having conversations about race and identity. In a process of "outing" herself as mixed race first to another member of the university community and then multiple others on campus, as a graduate student she learns that while she had up to then considered her father's story rather unique, *passing* and leaving one's family members behind was not a rare thing to happen (Broyard 2007, 97). Knowing that she is not alone in this makes it easier for her to develop strategies to deal with and address her family history. She finds a community.

By describing the process of disclosing her racial background to other people at the University of Virginia as a process of "outing," the narrator links herself to those who, in "coming out," disclose themselves to others as outside of heteronormative conceptions of sexuality and, by implication, family. It appears that mixed heritage and a family legacy of *passing*—in the case of this narrator a factor that is, by and large, "invisible" to others— is connected to the same kind of shame that homosexuality (or bi-, or transsexuality) potentially (still) evokes in public discussion, even though sexual orientation is, like mixed heritage, something an individual cannot impact or "change" in any way. Much like "coming out" as "non-straight," it is a difficult process for the narrator to "come out" as "non-white" to those around her, for fear that these people might change their ways of seeing her after the fact. She might lose her white privilege, much like someone outing themselves as "non-straight" loses their straight privilege. The narrator is now outside the supposed mainstream, giving her ambivalent feelings that she reflects on at length throughout the memoir.

An instance of "outing" herself at a party, or rather calling herself "'[b]iracial'" (Broyard 2007, 294) to Deforest, a black-identifying fellow dancer, leads to their falling out. Reflecting on the occasion, the narrator states that even years later, this memory is uncomfortable to her as it reminds her of her insecurities associated with having to place herself in relation to race (295). Her internal battle depicted in the narrative alludes to questions of authenticity, as well as to the idea of what it means to use particular labels to describe oneself. The narrator is not sure that she is "black enough," having been socialized in an exclusively white environment despite her mixed background.

Following a partial resolution of the family secret—by understanding that her father has *passed* as white—the narrator feels the urge to try her new identity out, yet also knows that this is essentially not possible in contemporary society without causing alarm, bewilderment, misunderstanding, and disregard. She feels caught between "worlds" of racial identities, and, with her previous conception of herself now under contestation, she no longer knows who she is. Her circumstances at times resemble common notions of the tragic mulatta: the narrator feels neither black nor white enough. At the same time, for her, identification is a matter of choice. She can return to white privilege after amusing herself in her biracial role. That her apparent ability to select her racial identity is not received positively in the African American community is something she has to understand first.

As a second consequence of speaking more openly to each other about the past and the family, the father–daughter relationship becomes a matter the narrator of *One Drop* explores extensively in her writing during graduate school. There, she begins to think about publishing her father's story in book-length format, but only after she has earned some merits as a writer of fiction (104). At the same time, she becomes very much aware of her own racist attitudes, which shock her to some degree (99). Since she is ultimately aware of patterns of white supremacy engrained in her own behavior, she attempts to change such thoughts even though this proves to be hard in many instances (100). Still, in the context of the narrative at large, this admission is another moment where a narrator becomes fairly open and honest with the reader, and in a rather exceptional way: by admitting a weakness and difficulty, by sharing a narrative of personal struggle. Having mixed heritage, she makes clear, does not automatically make you less racist.

While the connection of the *memoir of the search* to coming out stories is definitely feasible, Michelle Elam has argued these texts are a function of ethnic narrative (Elam 2011, 50). This necessitates commentary on their approach, as according to Elam, exploration from this angle would enable the placement of such texts in the context of existing ethnic literary traditions (50). This would make for a productive reading including the recognition of patterns of writing and telling hybridity at the time of their emergence. Ethnic narratives and the autobiographical form have always been interlinked in American culture and beyond; they are a strategy of and commentary on the necessary process of "Americanization." Autobiographical texts in the present "represent a far more multicultural past than had previously been told" (Bergland 1994, 68). As Betty Ann Bergland has argued, "issues surrounding representations in ethnic autobiographies in the United States can be meaningfully situated within the central cultural debates over multiculturalism" (68).

William Boelhower has studied ethnic autobiographies and their narrative structures and elements in his *Immigrant Autobiography in the United States* (1982), as well as in his subsequent work. He has found that autobiographies by European immigrants to the United States use specific narrative devices to inscribe themselves into American history. These narratives are cultural constructions, in addition to being personal stories. In the *memoir of the search*, a similar tendency can be observed with regard to the narrators and their families: For example, these narratives use the paradigmatic American immigrant story to refer to their own story of becoming American (see chapter 4).

Also, and in different ways from European immigrant literature, African American writing has often made use of autobiographical forms, frequently in the attempt to construct a narrative and identity recognizable to the mainstream (i.e., dominating) society (Drake 1997, 91). As an oppressed population, African Americans needed to find ways to tell their stories, to attest to their humanity, to speak up against the erasure of the past, to bear witness in the present. This is a crucial matter:

> Hostilities and crises among people emerge not only over land and resources but also over the systematic denial of history and memory; thus, the muted pasts of oppressed people remain at the centre of these debates, representing the silenced histories and memories that often challenge prevailing ideologies and commonsensical traditions (Bergland 1994, 69).

Taking this into account, the *memoir of the search* with its inherently autobiographical outlook is not only aware of these earlier narratives, traditions, and functions, but also uses them productively and creatively. It comments on them from a late twentieth-century perspective and adds to the telling of a new story.

These texts use the narrative strategies of autobiographical writing to attest to this story's "truth," and do so in a legible way. To participate in both these traditions—immigrant and African American—and to comment on the postmodern construction of the self, no other form but the personal could have been used. This is the pattern available to communicate stories of this kind. There is a close connection between autobiographical storytelling and the creation of a national community. Via such narratives, it is communicated who and what is "American" at a particular point in time (Smith and Watson 1996, 4).

Certainly, genre, including the autobiographical genre, always has "taming" and normalizing functions; sticking to genre conventions helps make a specific story available in a readable form at a specific time. By implication, the use of the memoir, and not another form, to comment on mixed race and its historical legacies may not actually tell us so much about the perceived reality of mixed race in terms of numbers in the late 1990s, but rather point to how the topic could be addressed. This is because everyday practice has "establish[ed] cultural conditions determining who can speak, what can be spoken, what narrative forms can be understood, and to whom personal narrative can be addressed" (12).

The *memoir of the search* emerged out of a specific sociocultural setting and political context in which certain contested topics could only be addressed in this predefined way. The genre emerged in the 1990s because at this time its concerns could be voiced. Additionally, the genre focuses on a specific agenda and speaks from an established mainstream standpoint. The development and high visibility of these texts is then not necessarily the result of more people suddenly becoming mixed, or suddenly realizing they are mixed, and thus needing to solve a long-kept family secret. Rather, it makes clear that at the time of these texts' publication, the question of how to address mixed-race heritage was a subject of widespread public debate—even obsession—and that this debate had entered the mainstream, the circle of the American middle-class family, which needed to address it in the form of a question. The widespread public interest in mixed-race backgrounds has consequences for both the narrative mode in these texts, as well as the potentials and limits of the genre at large. This concerns questions of authorship and authority just as much as to agency and a perceived "authentic" quality of the *memoir of the search*.

By telling the discovery of the narrator's mixed self from a first-person perspective, the story becomes both a personal narrative and a report about an experience an individual went through at a specific point in time. And still, the personal is always political. This factor, while opening multiple opportunities of telling a story of the search for and the becoming of the self, also makes these texts interpretations—rather than neutral, detached and scholarly descriptions—of a process of the discovery of a family history shaped by secrets.

While the *memoir of the search* by and large, and as one of its specific features, uses scholarly methods of inquiry that are at times described to the reader in much detail so as to attend to the "truthfulness" of the experience, the narrative itself is the narrator's personal analysis of the investigative acts undertaken. In some ways, these texts can be read as personalized responses to the multiplicity of self-help guides to genealogy that have emerged in the United States over the past decades. These self-help guides have made genealogy more open to groups who were at first excluded from such research, and in part came out, like the memoirs, in response to *Roots*.

The genre comments on the role of race and related concepts—such as blackness and whiteness—in the United States around the turn of the millennium. Characteristically, the *memoir of the search* addresses the long-term consequences of Jim Crow and the "color line" in the present. Slavery and its aftermath are important subtexts in these narratives. The reader does not encounter the voices of slaves, nor is there much of a direct engagement with slavery in terms of its emotional or physical cruelty. Ball's (1998) *Slaves in the Family* is the text addressing maltreatments and the horrors of slavery most explicitly. But even then, there are no flashbacks or instances of time travel.

The storyline negotiated in the *memoir of the search* does not enter the plantations, but sticks to the present, arguing that the horrors of slavery still linger in the American consciousness and exert a continuous influence on American society. The central interface and site for this encounter remains the family. The *memoir of the search* is not a fictional plantation saga like *Gone with the Wind* (1936), but rather a meditation on slavery at a time when slaves and their children are no longer alive to tell their stories. It is the narrative of mixed-race America from different perspectives, black and white. It develops its own voice, while listening to multiple others, and while making yet unheard ones heard, it also silences others. By and large, the genre makes a move toward a more democratic approach to history, albeit still within strict limits.

OF ROOTS AND ROUTES

Michelle Elam poses an important question regarding the negotiation of mixed race around the turn of the millennium that is significant with regard to the memoirs analyzed in this study and the traditions in which these texts can be located: "Does the mixed race category productively complicate all racial boundaries or does it risk instituting and reifying yet another kind of racial categorization—in effect, does the designation of 'mixed race' dissemble or merely replicate models of race?" (Elam 2011, 51). She points out the specific problems and dangers resulting from the widespread attempt to rewrite the African American literary and political tradition from the stance of the emerging mixed-race identities. According to Elam, practices of reading such texts independently from their specific traditions, freeing them from associations with blackness by placing them in a new, multiracial line of thought and tradition (43), are dangerous, and potentially lead to disunity rather than a more refined understanding of mixed-race identities and their respective literary discourses fueled by a diversity of traditions and narratives.

It would be limiting to place these texts solely in the American literary tradition or solely in the context of what is usually referred to as African American literature—a term that has more recently also come under scrutiny: In his work *What Was African American literature?* (2011), Kenneth W. Warren (2012, 1) claims that "African American literature was a postemancipation phenomenon" that, following the Civil Rights Movement, has come to its logical end since it "gained its coherence as an undertaking in the social world defined by the system of Jim Crow segregation, which ensued after the nation's retreat from Reconstruction." As Jim Crow segregation has come to an end, the coherence of this category of writing has recently "eroded" (3): the social context and the conditions of these texts' emergence no longer exist.

This does not mean that contemporary black literature does not relate to (past) African American literature, but that the perception and interpretation of such texts has to be extended, especially since concerns of unity and identity have become central to literature since the 1980s, making it possible to read texts by such different authors as Toni Morrison and the Native American Leslie Marmon Silko in a productive dialogue: "Once it no longer became necessary for black writers to consider contesting Jim Crow as the point of their efforts, they were freed to become exclusively involved with the problem of identity" (107).

The question of identity is central to the *memoir of the search*, as is the question of belonging both in relation to the family and the nation. Matters of race and past racial mixing further fuel these essential questions of belonging. The mixed-race focus of these texts encourages the reading-in-dialogue provided here. While certainly the narrators in these texts do not "know" each other, they tell a similar story from different points of view, be it from the position of the descendant of a slaveholding dynasty, or the position of a person whose family has been torn apart by racial discrimination.

A dialogic analysis is not only productive in terms of gaining a better idea of where America stood in terms of race relations at the turn to the twenty-first century, but also in terms of the memoir's dealing with the long-term effects of slavery and racial segregation from opposing—or maybe rather not-so-opposing—points of view. All narrators, independent of their skin color, struggle with the absence of certain other family members from their family tree and family history; all of them bring up complex questions about family and national identity, voice ethical concerns, and wonder how they may contribute to resolving the situation. The fact that many of the issues brought up in the narratives are similar may point to the importance of not only knowing one's individual (symbolic) "roots" and one's family history, but also to questioning dominant narratives about the making of the nation and the roles that were played by different groups in society.

This approach places mixed-race memoirs emerging since the 1990s in the context of a variety of existing traditions, and specifically in relation to other texts addressing the meaning of mixed heritage, slavery, and the role of the past. Over the past two centuries, such texts shaped the national and political discourses about racial mixing and race relations. The best-known example of this phenomenon is likely Harriet Beecher Stowe's *Uncle Tom's Cabin* (1852), but it is also true for texts such as Margaret Mitchell's previously mentioned saga, *Gone with the Wind*, or Alex Haley's *Roots* (1976), all of which have been studied by Linda Williams in the context of race melodrama. Just as these earlier texts fueled specific developments—from activism against slavery, to a widespread romanticization of the "Old South" and slavery, to the popularization of genealogy in the African American community—the *memoir of the search*, too, potentially brings forward new discourses and constructions of America's mixed-race heritage by speaking back to earlier texts and responding to them creatively.

The idea of *passing* is central to these memoirs. Werner Sollors (1999, 247) locates *passing* narratives in the nineteenth and in the first half of the twentieth century, meaning that these newer texts on the topic speak back to an earlier tradition of talking about the process of challenging perceived racial and other boundaries. It is worth considering why this type of text—albeit in a different shape—has returned. As a theme, *passing* "links literary texts with sociology and investigative journalism" (255), which may make those texts specifically appealing to late twentieth-/early twenty-first-century audiences interested in attesting to hidden "truths" in a world that is getting steadily more complex.

Sollors (1999, 35) claims that "[t]here may be something about representations of interracial couples and their descendants that provokes audiences to read them as myths of origins, foundational stories rather than stories about just any couple." Along with the attractiveness of genealogical projects and the large-scale availability of DNA testing in the late twentieth century, this mythological appeal may have contributed to the emergence of the *memoir of the search* with its renewed emphasis on *passing*. Moreover, the postmodern conception of identity is firmly based on the assumption that anyone can be anything. The memoirs contest this idea to some degree, as they allude to the necessity of knowing one's background, one's history, and one's intergenerational connections in order to feel "complete." They play with the concept of a fragmented self that is lost without knowing its origins.

The texts studied here are aware of slavery's persisting impact on life in the United States. This understanding places them in line with slave narratives. According to Kimberly Drake (1997, 91), "[s]laves' (or more accurately, ex-slaves') autobiographies record the process in which the ex-slave writes his or herself into an existence recognized by dominant American society." Consequently, and as analyzed in detail by James Olney, the slave narrative takes up a definable form, which, despite its variety of features—from drawings or photographs to newspaper clippings to the precise descriptions of human encounters—follows a similar pattern in each case, placing it in a complex relationship with autobiography. If autobiographical writing is the recollection of one's life from a teleological standpoint, how can these texts still follow such specific conventions (Olney 1984, 149ff.)?

Olney describes slave narratives not so much as literature, but rather as "a non-memorial description fitted to a pre-formed mold, a mold with regular depressions here and equally regular prominences there—virtually obligatory figures, scenes, turns of phrase, observances, and authentications" (151). Because of this "mold," the critic is able to perceive these texts as a more or less coherent and recognizable "group" of texts. To expose slavery "like it really was," and to negate it as a practice, slave narratives as a genre have to be readable as the calls for freedom and humanity they are at their center; and they have to address mainstream culture, thus speaking to "America." Despite such mainstream norms being at odds with the narrators' ways of experiencing the world, then, slave narratives—both in content and in form— pay a tribute to true American selfhood (Drake 1997, 92).

Along similar lines, the *memoir of the search* follows the goal of exposing America's family secret of racial transgressions of various sorts, and including involuntary acts such as rape, and at different times in history. In a concerted effort, the narrators write their mixed selves into dominant narratives of American national identity (see chapter 4). The texts discussed here within the *memoir of the search* genre all share similar contents—a particular narrative mode, descriptions of work with sources, false traces, encounters with family, the use of family trees and family photographs—and strategies of speaking to the American mainstream. These contents also link them to slave narratives in various ways. The *memoirs of the search* are predictable—another feature they share with each other, but also with slave narratives—but in their emphasis on the commonality of racial mixing they shape a discourse for interpreting America's cultural secret that is contemporary. The discourse will also open new paths of perceiving racial mixing for its essential "American-ness." The supposed conventionality of the story being told in these publications makes it mainstream—if the same story circulates over and over again, it becomes normal. This is what this type of text does in order to break a taboo and reevaluate American history as well as the various ways of narrating the American national story. In these terms, it also contributes to reversing the argument about the noncentrality of slavery for the present and by contrast makes it and its aftermath defining to the meaning of being American in the twentieth century.

The *memoir of the search* is not the first twentieth-century genre to talk back to slave narratives. Rather, its talking back to slavery is a feature it shares with those texts commonly defined as neo-slave narratives—a term coined by Ishmael Reed and referring to fictional texts set during slavery or in its aftermath and telling the experience of the transformation from slavery to freedom from a first-person perspective. Like slave narratives, neo-slave narratives make use of the narrative features and conventions of the antebellum slave narrative (Rushdy 1999, 3), even though they are twentieth-century texts firmly embedded in the social logic of the 1970s. In this way, they comment both on the continuing legacy of slave narratives, and, by implication, slavery. Neo-slave narratives also make a statement about the ongoing repression of slavery's legacy in the present, for example, in terms of the by-and-large absence of it from public places and museums, and the way history was (and often is) taught in schools.

These practices of repression had come under scrutiny alongside the emergence of the New Left and the Black Power Movement in the 1960s, and therefore neo-slave narratives constitute their specific logic from these discussions (4ff.). Examples of this type of text range from Gayl Jones's *Corregidora* (1975), to Octavia E. Butler's *Kindred* (1979), to David Bradley's *The Chaneysville Incident* (1981), to Toni Morrison's *Beloved* (1987). Neo-slave narratives push for the recognition that slavery still matters in the American public and needs to be incorporated into the mainstream. They also make a critical statement about agency and authority, reflecting at length on who should be telling the story, how it can be spoken, and how exactly it should be preserved and memorialized.

The *memoir of the search* shares with the neo-slave narrative a preoccupation with the role of memory in the present. In both types of text, slavery and systematic oppression constitute this present. That past must not be forgotten, because it is still there, however invisibly. While the neo-slave narrative often also makes use of a first-person narrator to allude to the original slave narratives, it is clearly located in the fictional realm. At times, the reader travels back in time, encounters elements of magical realism, or finds herself in a setting that is clearly not "authentic." This stands in stark contrast to the *memoir of the search*, which, more like the original slave narratives, continuously attests to the veracity of the story being told through the inclusion of documentation and references to archival material. These latter texts seem to operate under the assumption that in order for America's mixed-race heritage to be recognized and included, its "truth" needs to be attested to over and over again.

The *memoir of the search* can furthermore be productively linked to texts that George Handley has qualified as postslavery narratives, meaning texts ranging from Alejo Carpentier's *Explosion in a Cathedral* (1962), to Jean Rhys's *Wide Sargasso Sea* (1966), to Rosario Ferré's *Sweet Diamond Dust* (1988), and other texts emerging in the United States and across the former plantation belt. Postslavery narratives, as Handley (2000, 3) claims, are texts written following the end of slavery but that engage with slavery's consequences into the time of their writing. These texts mainly focus on the social relations between slaves and masters before and after abolition. They do not make the same moralizing and humanizing move as slave narratives, focusing on the struggle for individuality. Instead, they operate in terms of centralizing family history to "revise the metaphorical meanings of genealogy that have been assumed by the plantocraty and by emergent nationalists and that have contributed to a consolidation of their landowning social power" (3).

These texts invite a transnational reading that listens to the calls for a broader conception of the plantation, one that goes beyond the United States and takes into account that while the South may have an exceptional history within its national context, there is an entire "belt" of countries that also had a system of chattel slavery, where social relations to this day are ordered based on this historical legacy. Several Latin American writers speak back to American authors such as William Faulkner when addressing the past's role for the present. These writers also encourage a reading that traverses national boundaries. In its use of genealogy, its complex narration of family history as intertwined in a system of oppression, and its statements on the continuous presence of the past in the narrated time, the *memoir of the search* makes for productive reading-in-dialogue with these Latin American texts. Nevertheless, its nonfictional stance differentiates the stories from what Handley subsumes under the header of the postslavery narrative.

Another possibility is to place the *memoir of the search* in a dialogue with an entirely different set of texts from an entirely different context, namely, post-Holocaust fiction and nonfiction. This connection may at first seem absurd, considering that the *memoir of the search* is firmly based in the United States and that it constantly alludes to the specific role of race in its national context. Post-Holocaust writing, on the other hand, is not as firmly nationally based, and, due to the long-term impact of the diaspora due to the Holocaust, can originate across the world. While post-Holocaust literature is diverse as a genre, it bears acknowledging that there is a branch of post-Holocaust literature that does not only address its ongoing legacy among the descendants of victims, but that also engages with the descendants of Nazis.

Erin McGlothlin has studied such texts in her work *Second-Generation Holocaust Literature: Legacies of Survival and Perpetration* (2006). The *memoir of the search* shares with at least some post-Holocaust literature an intense focus on the family, as well as a preoccupation with secrecy and the resolution of secrets. Both types of texts have an intergenerational dimension: they ask complex questions about how the past and present are intertwined, how guilt is transmitted and negotiated, and how past suffering impinges on the present.

Addressing the texts subsumed here under the heading of the *memoir of the search* in dialogue with other texts begs the more general question of "where intertextual dialogue ends and dependency begins" (Ryan 2008, 186). To what extent do these texts rely on their readerships' knowledge of a different kind of text that came before, and that may be regarded as their "Ur-text" (186)? To what extent do these texts require their readers to know at all what came before them? A very detailed intertextual reading would make for a very different kind of study and will not be provided here. Still, it is important to be aware of these texts' more general positioning among other earlier texts.

To recognize intertextuality as the only quality of the *memoir of the search* would be to deny the otherwise innovative nature of the texts studied here. Studying only their linkages to other texts would consider them solely as perpetuations of already existing texts. Nevertheless, it cannot be denied— both with regard to content as well as form—that these narratives use earlier texts as their points of departure, such as, quite obviously, Haley's *Roots*. This legacy is also acknowledged in the texts, such as when the narrator in *Pearl's Secret* explains in the prelude that he had thought of turning the story of *Roots* around and engaging with finding his ancestors (Henry 2001, 13). *Pearl's Secret* also lists Ball's *Slaves in the Family* and another text that can easily be classified as a *memoir of the search*, but which is not part of this study, Henry Wiencek's *The Hairstons: An American Family in Black and White* (1999), as an inspiration. The narrator states that these works all engage with black/white relations and with families from a scholarly angle (4). This situates the texts firmly in a more or less academic context and also shows that they are aware of each other and talking to each other: intertextuality is a dimension of the genre that can hardly be ignored.

To go beyond common-scale definitions of intertextuality, Ashraf A. H. Rushdy (1999, 14) suggests ways of reading that may lead to a redefinition of intertextuality and enable researchers to recognize not only where texts may be related to each other, but to understand "the way texts mediate the social conditions of their formal production." This approach considers processes of canonization—famously described by Toni Morrison (1988, 132) as processes of "empire building."

The tendency of scholars "to construct a coherent black literary tradition concerned with slavery that stands in stark opposition to a white canon of works on the subject" (Ryan 2008, 188) is limiting in the context of narratives such as *Pearl's Secret*, because these texts point to the interdependencies of both black and white American traditions and their interrelatedness—their similar origins. Instead of thinking of literary traditions as stable, one might begin to analyze the necessity of the emergence of such traditions at large (Rushdy 1999, 10), in order to arrive at a more detailed analysis of this type of text in relation to "American" stories at large. The *memoir of the search* encourages a look beyond the obvious: these texts require their readers to understand black and white cultures and traditions in dialogue, as this study demonstrates through four exemplary texts of this decidedly mixed-race genre.

WRITING MIXED SELVES—INTO THE MAINSTREAM

At the time of its emergence in the mid-1990s and beyond, the *memoir of the search* became one of the possible performances of mixed-race identity, which is now accepted as such. The sheer number of narratives of this type being written and published around this time makes the point. In the introduction to their volume, *Getting a Life: Everyday Uses of Autobiography* (1996), Sidonie Smith and Julia Watson argue that "everyday occasions, and the practices attached to them, function as one form of 'discipline' in the Foucauldian sense" (Smith and Watson 1996, 12). Narratives, such as those discussed throughout this study, in their circulation and public discussion, contribute to the normalization of mixed-race heritage as a legitimate way of addressing American identity in the present time. If something is perceived as "normal" by the mainstream, it becomes socially acceptable and doable (Link 1998, 21). The question of who can be an American citizen and a member of the mainstream is a specifically precarious one that is strongly linked to ideas of normality. Due to the increased publication of stories of mixed race, the phenomenon of racial mixing itself becomes increasingly normalized. The *memoir of the search* represents a successful case study in "being mixed," thus supporting the topic's entry into the mainstream.

This points to the liberating potential of the genre: It makes for a more open negotiation of the past in terms of individual families' strategies for finding and connecting to each other and to the past, all the while pointing to potential difficulties, such as when communication about this past is anything but easy. At the same time, the established pattern of how this identity can become voiced—using a specific type of narrator and a rather predictable storyline to negotiate this content, for example—potentially silences other stories which do not conform or cannot be told as conforming to the narrative patterns and angles of the *memoir of the search*. This concerns stories that cannot be told in terms of the American narratives of immigration and success, for example. This is also true for mixed identities that cannot be located on the spectrum of black/white mixing.

In some cases, the narrators the reader encounters in the genre seem mindful of this limitation and point to it in their own negotiations of their identities. In *The Sweeter the Juice*, the narrator lists the different parts of her heritage, but without explicating them or what they mean to her. Certainly, one reason for this "silencing" of identities other than black/white is the predominant focus on this very topic within American culture at large. The narrator is also aware that she is, as many others are, usually identified as "ambivalent" by the public due to her black/white heritage, and not due to any other of the lines of descent contributing to her makeup.

Hence, it is possible to argue that the black/white identity is so strong in these texts, not because the narrators do not know or deny that mixedness can go beyond this very paradigm, but because this paradigm is the most "obvious" one. It is the one that figures most prominently in the public imagination due to the supposed mutual exclusiveness of these two categories, "black" and "white," across American history. It is this formation that has led to regulations such as the "One-Drop Rule," and not any other. It is this type of mixed heritage that could decide over matters of life and death, freedom or slavery. Hence, these narratives try to address strategies of change by turning to this crucial matter in their own family's context. By ending the mutual exclusiveness of "blackness" and "whiteness" and addressing it in its historical legacy and in its impact on the family, they point to the possibility of moving beyond "race." This change concerns the understanding of the past, but more than that, it addresses strategies of identity negotiation in the present and future.

In its strategies of accessing the past and provoking change in the present, the *memoir of the search* can be read with texts that emerged before it. *Roots: The Saga of an American Family* tells the story of an African American family—from Africa to America—as a "representative experience" (Ryan 2008, 221), making it possible for black and white audiences to be captured by the saga. The texts here subsumed under the heading of the *memoir of the search* pick up on this very title, but, by and large, they tell the story of an *American* family that is not only defined by its Americanness, but also by its mixedness: It is, quite literally, the saga of an *American* family in black and white. If nothing else, this shows that the topic of mixed-race identity and its history can be placed in front of a mass audience by the 1990s, albeit in a rather defined and predictable form.

This reliance on mainstream narrative conventions, as Tim Ryan (2008, 116) argues, is also problematic with regard to *Roots*. It remains firmly linked to Africa and looks back to the past in a "home 'space of innocence,'" albeit in an attempt to discover "an American home that is not burdened with the fatherless, mother-centered heritage of slavery" (L. Williams 2002, 234). At the same time, its major accomplishment "is to have exalted the impossibly singular root of the past African heritage over the multiple roots of American hybridity, even as it accommodates to a future hybridity and assimilation" (234). The observations made with reference to *Roots* point to the larger issue of moving within or even just relating to an established framework or set of literary conventions.

Tim Ryan suggests that in order to be different, or revolutionary, a narrative necessarily has to move beyond such established forms. At the same time, in order to remain accessible and in order to be heard, the "readability" of a text also depends on its picking up or relating to an existing discourse. There is constant tension between innovation and stagnation, hinting at the complexities behind narratives such as Ball's *Slaves in the Family* or Broyard's *One Drop*. To move beyond known formats, a break with conventions would be necessary, while to remain accessible to a large audience a narrative has to stay in tune with performative and reading practices that can be understood by this very audience. A similar tension can, for example, be detected with the poetry of the Harlem Renaissance, which was mostly conventional in its literary forms, but at the same time voiced revolutionary concerns in its content. Arguably, the *memoir of the search* engages in a similar type of movement: The genre uses established practices of narrating racial mixing and identity conflict, but voices them from a nonfictional stance, and places them in the narrator's own family. The genre turns the narrator into a central agent of progress and democracy by opening up the past—rendering it legible—for the current, and possibly future, generations.

Despite this rather original move of placing mixed-race heritage and its complications into a middle-class context, and following its complex legacies from the present into the past, the *memoir of the search* with its specific features and narrative patterns has started to become a stable discourse of its own. Thus, these texts participate in determining which versions of mixed-race identity can be negotiated in public, and how so. Certainly, the narratives represent an instance where something that was heretofore unspeakable is placed in front of a mass audience, and they do so in a readable way. It is therefore possible to understand the *memoir of the search* as a new type of *passing* narrative, for example, albeit without the tragic mulatto at its center. But rather than addressing the tragic failures of identity creation, the narrators in these texts from the 1990s and beyond commit to analyzing their feelings of inadequacy and incompleteness at the start of their stories, but then go on to discover a new and supposedly more complete sense of self via scientific investigation, family exploration, and finally, national inclusion, hinting at the idea that mixed-race identity and its exploration are inherently progressive, and that mixed-race identity is indeed representative "of the [American] melting pot" (Elam 2011, 55).

Undeniably, addressing these questions provides an opportunity to change the rather fixed existing discourse on race through a more participatory and inclusive practice. But the danger is that the mixed-race narrative genre does not offer new opportunities for dealing with these urgent matters. By establishing one possible, acceptable, or "authorized" pattern of how the story of mixed-race identity in America can be told, the genre codifies a new type of nonspeakability that may potentially prevent—rather than reinvent—national dialogue on the problematic legacies of a past that continues to divide living Americans along the "color line."

Altogether, the fact that the texts remain very much caught within the confines of the master narrative derives from their emergence out of a specific political and social situation. But it is also due to the texts' strategies of responding to very specific existing traditions and narrative patterns, which they attempt to challenge, if not rewrite, through a scheme of taking up a known pattern and then challenging or changing it by making evident the limits of this very pattern or device.

Chapter 2

Family Secrets
Uncovering Mixed-Race Heritage

This chapter addresses the main theme negotiated in the *memoir of the search* as a literary genre, namely, the family secret and the process of investigating it. This process leads the narrator to revise prevalent ideas about the family and, by implication, the American nation. The chapter aims to analyze how the family secret gives shape to the story told in the text, how the secret literally moves the text forward on the narrative and content levels, and how its investigation requires specific techniques that significantly shape the genre. The pattern of secret–investigation–revelation, which Rushdy (2001, 147) refers to as a paradigmatic feature of the storytelling practices of slaveholding families, becomes transferable to texts in which the narrator is the descendant of slaves. The family secret and the search for truth are defining markers of the genre of the *memoir of the search*. Thus, while the previous chapter has addressed the *memoir*-related aspects that shape the *memoir of the search*, the emphasis here will be on *the search* as the second decisive marker of the genre. This chapter, as the chapter on narrating the nation, will be centered around extensive literary analysis of the texts selected for this study in order to provide a detailed reading of the genre at large.

THE FAMILY AND THE FAMILY SECRET

The family is the most important social unit portrayed in the *memoir of the search*. The story is always about family, or, by implication, about the family that is not there. The genre deals with family ties as well as with their disruption, and with the invention and reinvention of the family through the reestablishment of contact. It is a *memoir of the search* for family and its meaning at the nexus between two categories that significantly shape the American experience: nation and race. In these memoirs, the narrators describe their lives as embedded into specific family structures and stories defined and at times limited by skin color. The narration focuses on how the narrators' families' self-perception changes through the process of investigating and (re-)writing its story.

The narrators show how the family came into being under very specific historical and social circumstances, and how it subsequently reinvented itself through practices of investigation, strategies of revising the existing family narratives, and confronting US history. The underlying assumption here is that by way of approaching the center of the "family secret," the narrators get to know their family better, but they also experience themselves from a different angle; they go through a process of reevaluation of the self and of the family on the whole. In these terms, the *memoir of the search* buys into late twentieth-century concepts of alienation and disintegration of the self that can be resolved through listening to one's true calling, getting to know oneself, and, in this case, investigating the family secret. The narrator cannot feel complete until the quest has been completed. Like many *coming out* stories, the *memoir of the search* is also a narrative of personal growth.

The central significance of the family for the storyline as well as for the genre of the *memoir of the search* already is evident in the titles chosen for these texts: *The Sweeter the Juice: A Family Memoir in Black and White*; *Pearl's Secret: A Black Man's Search for His White Family*; *Slaves in the Family*; or *One Drop: My Father's Hidden Life–A Story of Race and Family Secrets*. While these titles point to the preferences of the book market around their time of publication, they also refer to the main topics addressed in the texts: the family, the role of skin color at a time when black and white are no longer mutually exclusive, the history of such exclusiveness, the decisive role of the past for the present, the search process, and the central motif of secrecy with regard to the family. Taken together, these titles indicate that an investigation of some sort is to be undertaken in the text.

Among the themes mentioned above, the family secret is the most significant and especially the most decisive for the storyline developed in the genre. The family secret is both situated at the heart of the text, and present as a stylistic device in the *memoir of the search*. The family secret—about race and *passing*, albeit in different constellations and in different historical and spatial settings—is not only central to the development of the events told in the text. There would not be a plot at all if the family secret was not there as a starting point for the narrators' investigations. This is not to say that there are no other subplots in these texts, but that any other plot ultimately revolves around or relates back to the family secret.

More than that, the presence of the secret structures the narratives and moves them forward. The secret therefore works like a riddle connecting the text's layers to each other; it is the thread interweaving the past and the present. Through the family secret, its investigation, and finally its revelation, in effect, the text comes full circle. The conclusion, even if it does not offer a "happy ending," provides closure for the text as well as the narrators, but it also and undeniably leads to more questions and more secrets to be explored.

Due to its strong presence across multiple layers of the narrative, the secret complicates the meaning of family in the *memoir of the search*. Ultimately, the secret governs the relationships between the characters in the text. It shapes where characters can go in their daily lives and which obstacles they have to overcome. Typically, they can or cannot interact with each other because of the secret. They know or do not know about each other's lives both in the tightly knit circle of the family as well as outside of it. Oftentimes, the characters are unable to address the secret without knowing why. They can or cannot voice certain facts or concerns as a result of the secret, meaning the secret impacts every conversation in the text. By the same token, the secret helps establish and sustain connections and cooperations as well as support structures between certain characters and not others. In effect, the characters, specifically the narrators, at least on the surface level, are empowered once they know what has been hidden from them for most of their lives.

The reader accompanies the narrators during their quest to find answers and reveal the family secret—even though the story is told retrospectively, from a position where the narrator has already learned their true family history. The texts look back at the investigation and revelation, instead of describing the process in the present tense. One question to contemplate is why this type of story, told at the end of the twentieth and in the early twenty-first century, can still create suspense. It is possible to argue that the narrators are on a quest for their own identity and speak to the idea that it is both possible and desirable to know everything about the self; that this knowledge will in the long run enable a better life. The narrators acquire a detective-like role, and in this context the family secret, as a storytelling device, produces this suspense in the narrative. The *memoir of the search* shares this characteristic with crime and detective novels, in which the storyline typically moves forward as the central character follows a riddle—and where at times it is clear to the reader from the start what the resolution of the case will be.

Ashraf H. A. Rushdy (2001, 21), in his comprehensive work on texts he refers to as *palimpsest narratives*, *Remembering Generations: Race and Family in Contemporary African American Fiction*, has argued that the family secret is a generative force in these texts from the 1970s and 1980s. Due to the secret's central role in the texts discussed in this study, this notion can be extended to the *memoir of the search*. To both—the *palimpsest narrative* and the *memoir of the search*—it is crucial that the "family secrets [. . .] are transgenerational, [. . .]" (21), and connect previous trauma from the past to the present generation. The "haunting" quality of the family secret further complicates the notion of the secret itself and emphasizes that even though it may not always be "visible" or perceived at the outset, the secret is still there.

Using the family secret as a central motif to uncover a story of supposedly hidden racial legacies allows for a type of storytelling that does not place the blame on any of the involved parties. Since the secret demanded silence, nobody—among the family members of either the present or of earlier generations—could address it openly. In that sense, there is no character or generation centrally at fault. If anything, it is the secrecy itself and the different characters who remained complicit with this silence that are at fault.

The intergenerational quality of the family secret—a secret from an earlier generation that shapes the contemporary narrator and her peers—determines some of its functions in the genre. It serves as a point of connection or disconnection, respectively, between the different generations of the family portrayed. This is true for children and their parents, but also for the parents' parents and generations further back in time. The family secret determines who belongs to the family at the moment the story begins, and who does not belong. The revelation of the family secret leads to a redefinition of who is, or who can potentially be, family. The resolution of the secret thus signifies a reevaluation of seemingly fixed boundaries.

In the *memoir of the search*, the intergenerational secret is always investigated from the point of view of the present. The narrator is firmly located in the present. The *memoir of the search* works the other way around. Here, the narrator is investigating the past and relates the findings back to the present situation, and the revelation of the family secret does not change the past, but it does change the present. These texts also comment on contemporary practices of archiving and representing the past. The *memoir of the search* as a genre is acutely aware of the fact that slavery has given rise to "whiteness," and the privileges associated with this ascribed—not achieved—identity (24–25). Instead of reaching a point of clarity, texts within the genre make clear that no investigation of the past alone—but rather, concrete acts in the present—will contribute to a change in race relations in the United States.

As the mixedness in the text is intergenerational, it cannot in any way be attributed, for example, to the achievements made during the Civil Rights Movement, or due to changed legislation making it more likely for mixed-race couples to pursue a relationship, get married, and have children—the *Loving vs. Virginia* decision of 1967. The narrators' mixedness precedes all of these developments and is located at the nexus between slavery and freedom. With regard to their family and how it came to be, the narrators in the texts are reflecting and commenting on a racial mixing that occurred long before their own lifetime. Still, this factor shapes their own identity and practices of relating to family and the world in general around the late 1990s or early 2000s. The texts thus point to the long-term psychological and physical legacies of the nineteenth century. This idea runs against the so-called "Loving Legend" at times brought up by supporters of the multiracial movement (Spencer 2006).

According to the "Loving Legend," the number of Americans of mixed-race descent rose exponentially following the legalization of interracial unions, a claim that makes a distinction between Americans of mixed descent before the 1960s and supposedly "multiracial" Americans born after *Loving vs. Virginia* (Spencer 2006, 63ff.). This idea and its possible long-term consequences for Civil Rights legislation potentially impacts and alters the discussion about mixed race as it was led in the 1990s and into the 2000s. The *memoir of the search* genre shows that the rules of speaking and the power of narrative agency determine the meaning of mixed race and that it is possible to intervene in an ongoing discourse by questioning racial categories as well as by looking backward to the past. Even on the verge of the twenty-first century, race still matters in terms of how an individual family, as well as the nation at large, define and constitute themselves.

Circumscribing the complex legacy of racial mixing in American culture with the help of a "family secret" that can finally be revealed at the end of the twentieth century offers a critical statement about the status of such revelations at this time. While of course it was always well known that racial mixing existed before the Civil War, it was treated as a nonissue for the purposes of advancing certain legal, financial, educational, and other interests over others. The keeping of this well-guarded "secret" has contributed to the development of very specific, supposedly separate, identities and ways of dealing with race that are discussed in these texts. One of these ways is the attempt of silencing the fact of racial mixing in the first place. It has contributed to the color-coding of American society, and to the imposition of invisible borders separating a so-called white and a so-called black community from each other. In the *memoir of the search*, two parts of the same family are divided by the "family secret" and by implication, by race. In the storyline, they are united through the disclosure of a supposedly shared past.

The *memoir of the search* plays with the idea that the resolution of the "family secret" will lead to a moment of familial and national revelation and absolution. If mixed race really is, as was sometimes claimed in the 1990s, a *frontier* (as claimed by Maria P. P. Root in her 1995 publication *The Multiracial Experience: Racial Borders as the New Frontier*), then an exploration and quest narrative will likely be needed in order to push this *frontier* forward (Leverette 2006, 79). In the *memoir of the search*, the narrator becomes both a detective piecing together her family history as well as a curious explorer along this last *frontier*. Both of these metaphoric roles are worth considering further.

A detective is in charge of solving a crime and has specific agency and responsibility to explore a case in detail. The narrators in the *memoir of the search* do not undertake their work for professional reasons, of course. Rather they investigate their own family story and its silences. They pose their own questions and follow a riddle linking the present to the past. If one were to consider this genre in the context of detective fiction, the "detectives" represented in it would come close to the private detectives typical in the Hardboiled tradition, who develop a personal curiosity in a subject (here: race relations) and make sure that justice (of some sort) is served.

The concept of the narrator as an explorer of the *frontier* is equally interesting and can be related to the specific way of seeing that is established in the texts. The person exploring a *frontier* is endowed with certain economic and cultural privileges; they are an established member of their society, and have the means to undertake an at times risky process of investigation. In these terms, the depiction of the narrators in the *memoir of the search* as explorers of sorts points to their middle-class status, their educational and economic privilege, and their fundamental curiosity in what history suppresses.

This chapter now closely examines how the family secret functions in the *memoir of the search*: How is the secret characterized and by whom, what is at its center, and how is it employed as a narrative tool within the texts? Theoretically, there is a multiplicity of ways in which a family secret could be negotiated in such texts, but upon close study, the *memoir of the search* uses strikingly similar plots in order to establish the secret and to carry it through the text. Indirectly, the narratives ask where race and family are connected to each other, and in which instances and constellations race was a decisive factor in who could be considered a member of the family.

Rather unsurprisingly, the secret investigated relates to skin color and to how skin color shapes a family at a given point in time. More precisely, the secret always deals with matters of *passing* and familial abandonment, which relate back to skin color. In his comprehensive study *Neither Black Nor White Yet Both: Thematic Explorations of Interracial Literature* (1997), Werner Sollors defines the term *passing* as "the crossing of any line that divides social groups" (Sollors 1999, 247). However, the term is most frequently used in the US context when addressing instances of crossing the "color line" from black to white, that is, when a person or a character in a text *passes* for white, often with complex implications for their identity.

In this genre, the narrator examines the phenomenon of black/white *passing* and explores how the relation of *passing* to skin color played out within their family. Part of why skin color and its negotiation play such a big role in these narratives is related to the time and the settings in these texts: Most narrators locate the origin of the secret of *passing* in the nineteenth and earlier part of the twentieth century before desegregation. At that time skin color could be a matter of life and death, meaning there was greater urgency to maintain the secret among earlier generations of the family.

Another reason why *passing* is at the center of the genre is likely that it deals with the concealment of identity. Despite the taboos associated with it, the American public is rather familiar—and rather obsessed—with *passing* stories, and with what *passing* for someone else means for a society (Elam 2007, 751). It is a well-known trope in American culture, and one that has been prominent in American literature over time (e.g., Sollors 1999).

This being said, secrets about *passing* are specifically interesting with regard to their implications that lead beyond race or skin color alone. They are also secrets about access, about social and familial privilege, and about class stratification in the country of the "self-made man" and of the "American Dream," where supposedly everyone can be successful via hard work, regardless of their background. As is well known, people who choose to *pass* for something or someone else do so in order to achieve a better socio-economic situation for themselves, and possibly for their family members and further relatives. By implication, *passing* is oftentimes associated with freedom. If one is able to *pass* for someone or something else, this will help to gain previously denied access to places—physically and socially. This is why family members may not necessarily look down on a person taking this step: it is a way to self-actualization that would otherwise be limited by race.

Simultaneously, however, *passing* is a limitation and potentially poses restrictions on access and on behavior. *Passing* essentially equals a situation where a person is *closeted* with regard to their identity. It establishes a very fragile sense of security. There is always the fear of one's cover being discovered, with disastrous, possibly fatal, consequences. If one *passes*, the threat of discovery potentially looms large over every step one takes—a person could be recognized and *outed* to the public. Still, often there is pressure to *pass* in order to rise socially and/or economically. Taking this into account, not-*passing* does not seem to be an option because it would ruin the family's attempts to preserve its sense of security.

However, in the *memoir of the search*, *passing* always brings about negative consequences that manifest themselves at the time of narration: It leads to the isolation of characters and their feelings of incompleteness; it has broken apart families. These effects are long-lasting and become the central subject of these texts.

ESTABLISHING THE FAMILY SECRET

In the *memoir of the search*, narrators typically introduce the family secret early in the text, using specific narrative strategies leading to encourage the reader's empathy and to introduce tension or suspense. Usually, the family secret stems from something that is missing or that has been silenced and cannot be talked about. The narrator is presented as a character with a very specific understanding of what is happening around them, almost amounting to a sixth sense. Even though they do not know what the secret is about, a clear perception of something being different or "off" is voiced in the texts. This also ensures that, from early on, the reader recognizes that the narrator is the moral authority and guide to follow throughout the narrative.

In *One Drop*, the narrator only learns about the presence of a secret as an adult, but in the opening paragraph describes how she had perceived an absence regarding her identity, and the identity of her family (Broyard 2007, 3), which leads her to extensively search her parent's home when she is still a child. Even then, the narrator acts like a quasi-detective trying to find missing information. She is aware of an absence without her parents ever mentioning a lack of any sort. Evidently, she is not the only family member who feels that something she should know is absent from her knowledge, and has been kept from her. Later in the text, the reader comes to know that the narrator's brother also searched through his father's belongings (31). The subconscious awareness of the secret is a shared trait between the siblings, an invisible bond. At the same time, brother and sister keep this awareness a secret from each other into their adult years.

Still, in *One Drop*, the secret defines the narrator's identity and sense of self from early on; her entire life centers on the presence of the secret. This also concerns her brother. The secret in its entirety shapes the small family that the reader encounters in the text. Significantly, the family is characterized by absence. The story centers on these four characters of father, mother, son, and daughter; their social situation is marked by their isolation from the larger family context and lack of contact with the extended family, the narrator explains (30). Apparently, the common obligations of, for example, attending family functions or celebrations do not apply to this family. The children are not introduced to these practices. The secret, or rather its keeping, necessitates the isolation of the narrator's immediate family from the other family members. Here, it becomes very clear that the secret poses, above all, a limitation on the family—it restricts the possibility of their communicating with each other openly and also hinders encounters with members of the extended family.

Several times in the story, the narrator struggles with the feeling that she is not true to herself, or that she does not know who she is and where she belongs. She recounts a story from before she was aware of her father's heritage and had to take a personality test in order to get hired for a job. With every promotion, she has had to retake this test. While these test results are usually not given to the employees, she is confronted with her result by the human resources administrator. This is because it places her in line with an impostor, thus someone who is untrue to their real self (63). In this way, while she is not consciously aware that there really is a hidden dimension to her family life, the secret still impacts all aspects of her life, including her job opportunities. Here, quite obviously, the text argues that the secret has shaped her psyche in such a way that a test would recognize it.

A similar awareness of an absence from early on, and of this very lack determining her life, is described by the narrator in *The Sweeter the Juice*, who addresses her perception that "big chunks of [her] life were missing" (Haizlip 1995, 31). The feeling of something lacking originates in her childhood and also manifests itself in the absence of an extended family the narrator is firmly aware of (31–32). Both texts, *One Drop* and *The Sweeter the Juice*, build on the idea that the narrator's childhood was already impacted by an absence and a feeling of incompleteness or fragmentation. From early on, the narrator has a special role in the family—not only is she the later investigator of the past, but more than that, hers is a role that has long been in the making, that has been a part of her life since childhood.

It is defining for the genre of the *memoir of the search* that the narrator's childhood was spent in subtle awareness of a secret and that this early awareness triggers the research process when the narrator is an adult with the resources and abilities necessary to undertake such an investigation. The same plot development is true for *Pearl's Secret*, where the narrator's white forebear fascinates him as a child. The mysterious man, whose photograph is kept by the family, is sometimes brought up in conversation, but then it is only in hushed whispers between the adults (Henry 2001, 10). Of course, this type of secretive behavior leads to the narrator's special fascination with the secret and the man behind it, the man whose name must not be mentioned. The way the text introduces the ancestor, Beaumont, suggests to the reader that this person will be of special importance for the later events, thus enticing the reader's desire to read on.

Open communication about ancestors is not possible for the families portrayed because the secret influences, even determines, what can be said, when it can be said, and by whom it can be said (Imber-Black 1993, 13). This idea is also central to Ball's *Slaves in the Family*, which begins with the narrator's childhood memory of a conversation between his father and mother, and relating to topics that cannot be addressed in their family: "'Religion, sex, death, money and the Negroes'" (Ball 1999, 7). The silence about the past, and especially about the slaveholding past of the family, has effects on the narrator even when he is a child. He recalls that he perceived himself as different because of the privileges his family had enjoyed in the past: "'Our people' had once controlled a slave dynasty" (9). The narrator does not qualify this short statement any further, but the statement does achieve two objectives.

On the one hand, it introduces the reader to the Southern setting of this text—this is the background story and the narrator's socialization process. In this family, there are specific rules governing family communication in relation to Southern regional identity: Custom suggests that there are taboos on communication, that there are matters that should be kept private. On the other hand the passage raises questions about how the family's slaveholding past may have impacted the narrator's childhood: whether it may have instigated pride or rather shame in the young boy who did not know very much about what his ancestors did, how they got to be where they were as he was growing up, and how they had treated their human property. Much like in *Pearl's Secret*, the past is also present in the family home in the shape of a photograph. This time, it is not a photograph of a person, though, but of the family's former plantation home (11).

The former family home fits well all the parameters generally associated with Southern plantation life, which is still present in the photograph as a material object. While in the present the mansion is no longer owned by the family and has fallen into disrepair, it is still important to the family's identity. As an indicator of social and economic privilege, it is a quasi-heirloom that shows how the contemporary family regards its historical social standing. It also attests to what accounts for the family's privileged past: property and the presence of the plantation.

In whichever ways all of these factors may have influenced his upbringing, the narrator's feeling of difference allows him to follow through with his ambitious project of learning about the past in order to write up the story of the Ball family, their slaves, and what became of them (11). The search process is significantly more difficult due to the fact that the Ball slaves mostly did not take the last name Ball after emancipation, and there are no clear written records about where they went after freedom came (352). The only documentation available to the narrator upon starting his investigation is the records of the white family, suggesting that holding records is first and foremost a matter of privilege, economic and otherwise.

When the narrator of *Slaves in the Family* is about eleven years old, his father passes a written family history of the Ball clan on to him and his brother. This is the book which later serves as the starting point in the investigations. It contains a collection of material related to the family that was published in 1909 entitled *Recollections of the Ball Family of South Carolina and the Comingtee Plantation*. The records are given to the boys with the remark that they will want to find out about their family history at one point, something that makes the family patriarch rather nervous. Since the father passes away about a year after giving the book to his sons, the narrator cannot interview his father about his perceptions of the family past, and can only guess that despite all the family pride he sensed in his father, the older man is also aware that there are parts of the past that need to be disclosed (7–8). He perceives this aspect of his family's past as "unfinished business" (9). The narrator attributes special importance to the passing on of the family history book and considers it an incentive to break the silence and find out about the past, despite the taboo he grew up with. The passage also foreshadows what happens later in the text: the narrator indeed follows the task given to him by his father, as he tries to "finish" the business of the plantation by telling the story of his discovery and resolution of the family secret.

While the earlier passage addressing the taboo—the list of matters not to be addressed—at first sounds like an insider joke or just a casual family saying, it also points to the shame that is connected to the secret. Just like when the adults lower their voices in *Pearl's Secret* when talking about the white ancestor, the "Negroes" in Ball's story are essentially an unspeakable subject. It is significant that the "Negroes" are named together with "religion, sex, death, money"—topics that are culturally contested and strongly related to matters of privacy.

Since they govern everything that can be said in the textual family, the secrets are given a lot of power within these conversations: They potentially impact, and limit, every interaction. Clearly, once the matter has become a taboo, there is no adequate way of addressing it anymore—the sole idea of discussing what happened to the slaves after emancipation has become unspeakable in the Ball family. This is an unwritten rule that is observed by everyone in the family, even during their frequent extensive family gatherings. These gatherings assure the family members of their identity across the generations and enable them to hold onto their identity, including the secret. The family meetings remind the Balls of their family privilege as well as the rules and limits of speakability. Still, the narrator decides to investigate the matter, breaking with the unspoken rules that have upheld family stability from generation to generation and challenging its identity.

The family secret in the *memoir of the search* lays the groundwork for the following general storyline: Based on the narrator's childhood, the secret determines the relationships between the parents and the children as presented in the text. It also, by implication, governs how different generations of the family relate to each other. The elder generations have established the rules of speakability and taboo and pass these unwritten laws on to the younger family members. The secret and the unwritten rules relating to it create a bond between the family members; these factors determine familial relations at the time of investigation. The secret and the rules of speakability govern who is considered a family member and who is excluded from the family.

At first, the secret appears to be kept from the children in the family, suggesting they must be protected from the shame it could bring. Such a secret is what the psychotherapist Karpel (1980, 259) would likely characterize as an *internal family secret*, meaning a secret the content of which is at least in some capacity known to some family members, but not to others. At the same time, the child is made aware or becomes aware that there *is* a secret in the first place.

In these texts, the narrator-as-child is always left out of the secret, which stirs curiosity in this character and in the reader and thus helps move forward the story and foreshadow the later plot: Both the narrator and the reader are eager to investigate what the secret could be. But even as the narrators in these texts grow up, the content of the secret is not released to them—in some cases, as it turns out, because even the parental and/or grandparental generation is no longer clear about the content of the secret themselves. This collective ignorance suggests that the secret, or rather the silence or unspeakability, has been passed on without the reason for the silence being known, usually out of loyalty to an even earlier generation, such as the parents' parents or grandparents. It is only through their respective processes of investigation that the narrators and their families learn about *what exactly* has been unspeakable.

In *Pearl's Secret*, for example, Beaumont and his fate are mysterious, as well (Henry 2001, 20). This part of the family history is moreover described as located far in the past (20). The events relating to Beaumont did not happen especially long ago, but the reference to a different, faraway time helps establish detachment between Beaumont's life and the lives of the Henry family. Now firmly members of the educated middle class, the Henrys certainly find themselves far away from their Southern origins. Through the character of the narrator, the text suggests it is easier to investigate a painful story from a temporal and geographical distance.

The investigation undertaken in the *memoir of the search* at times comes under scrutiny as the narrator is accused of violating their ancestors. In the Ball family, it is generally the men who worry about uncovering the family past (Ball 1999, 61)—men determine what can be said, and what remains silent. It is the privilege of white men to dictate power relations in this family, and men serve as the main bearers of tradition. One Ball cousin, Bennett, clearly states he does not want to be involved in the narrator's investigative project for fear that it may stir trouble in the family. He bursts out rather violently that slavery is a long way in the past, and the investigation means that the narrator is "'going to dig up my grandfather and hang him!'" (63). This statement certainly alludes to the process of lynching, though certainly it was much less often white men who got lynched.

Stating that the research project will harm family members posthumously—by changing the image of the family—Bennett appeals to the narrator's loyalty toward the ancestors. He is supposed to value his ancestors, to whom he owes the family history and family privilege. This reaction also places responsibility upon the narrator and adorns him with a powerful role. His investigation can potentially disrupt the heretofore known family story and challenge it for the future. This is an ethical challenge as well—he may cause significant harm to the present family and their reputation, even though these people cannot really be blamed for a past that happened decidedly before their time. But they may be blamed for the privilege they retained from this time.

Notably, the family members, even the narrators, portrayed in these texts at first participate in the secrecy and are complicit in the silence even though they have no idea of what exactly it is they are hiding. They do not speak up. They contribute to the secret by not asking questions about whether anything might be missing, or by accepting the existence of a secret or taboo as a given. Of the texts studied here, the two narrators who recognize their complicity in secret keeping most clearly are the ones in *Slaves in the Family* and *One Drop*. Their recognitions may very well have to do with the fact that in both cases it is the narrator's family members who have gained economically and culturally from the secret, while in Haizlip's and Henry's texts the narrators come from families who have been abandoned by family members and thus, by and large, have suffered more negative consequences associated with *passing* and the silencing of the past.

Certainly the families who have committed the wrongs have a different power position than those who have been denied or abandoned, even if this occurred in the past; this is not only true for the characters in the nuclear families portrayed in the texts, but also for the society we encounter through the *memoir of the search*. In the case of family members who have contributed to the wrongs being done, the secret keeping is not punished; rather, it becomes necessary so as not to be found out and to potentially lose one's privilege. In *One Drop*, the narrator understands that even though she and her brother Todd did not know about the content of the family secret while they were growing up, they both contributed to keeping it intact and only confront it after their father's passing (Broyard 2007, 31). Investigating the secret does not seem feasible: The secret belongs to the family and quite literally defines it. It is part of its inherent makeup. The secret lends the family structure stability and holds the members together. Addressing the secret could lead to disruption and injury.

By implication, becoming involved in the process of solving the secret can be painful as this entails the potential for changes and revisions in the family, in terms both of the power structure and its constitutive storytelling. The truth can hurt, but so can the very act of challenging parents and grandparents on why they maintained the secret in first place. Investigating the secret will trigger further complicated questions either way. When the family in *One Drop* needs to go through the father's belongings following his death, this entails the literal closet, and thus, there is no way the taboo of his heritage can remain unbroken. The identity of the father is however not the only thing that had so far remained in their closet: it stays there "along with the ashes of [the narrator's] grandparents" (31)—the father, Anatole, has kept them there, giving them space in the family home, without talking about them. His death represents a turning point (31). The idea of the secret staying "in the closet" (31) suggests that while the secret is hidden and stored away, it is still in the room. Nobody can see it, but everyone in the room also knows it is there. The expression of keeping something "in the closet" is often used in narratives of *coming out*—the question in the narratives discussed here is who or what will come out once the closet is opened.

While the secret at the center of all these texts prevents open conversations from taking place, especially between parents and children, the texts make clear that it simultaneously serves to bring the family members closer together. Bound to each other by the secret, the family members in *One Drop* stay among themselves, as a "tribe of four" (24). Here, the family is circumscribed using "tribal" and "colonial" terminology. The members apparently share something with each other that nobody else has access to or insight into. The family has developed its own inherent communicative practices, rules, and strategies to deal with each of the members. As this makes the family seem "special and forsaken" (24) there may not always be pressure to explore the secret: it is not comfortable to question one's own family, especially the parents that have sustained the family.

At the same time, the ideal family is breakable (24), meaning that the slightest disruption can potentially lead to its breakdown. Thus, the secret must remain "closeted." The family portrayed in *One Drop* therefore is rather isolated: The narrator recalls frequent moves and also that her parents were rather lonely, with the exception of times when they invited friends from New York City or traveled to Martha's Vineyard for longer periods of time (55). The locations specified also make evident that there is much to lose: this is a socially and economically privileged family.

Typically, in many *memoirs of the search*, a well-defined nuclear family is at the center of the story. This raises the underlying question of whether children have a right to encounter their extended family if the members of this family are still alive. In these texts, the existence of the extended family represents a threat to the nuclear family's integrity and identity, as well as its positioning in relation to the "color line." Despite the air of privileged exclusiveness about these families, growing up in such a limited familial circle can lead to isolation and to the need to search for those lost along the way: The lack of an extended family is typically experienced as a problem by the narrators—not only in their childhood memories, but also during their youth and adulthood. This feeling of deficiency oftentimes leads to specific behaviors, such as the speaker in *The Sweeter the Juice* observing other people in public locations in order to see whether there are enough visual similarities to suggest relatedness by blood (Haizlip 1995, 13). Regarding this particular habit, the narrator voices that she has had it since before her teenage years. The unusual absence of an extended family ultimately leads the narrator to question their family history. The "difference" narrators perceive in their families is not solely one of storytelling and addressing the past, but is also one that becomes very evident in their small families that have been diminished by isolation.

Even in *Slaves in the Family*, where an extensive family circle *is* very present and regularly gathers in order to pass on the "plantation story" to the younger generation as part of their tradition, the narrator senses from early on that part of the story is missing as it is characterized by division between black and white people, despite them living in close proximity with each other (Ball 1999, 13). Supposedly, one half of the story can be told by itself; according to the family legacy, these two halves of the story can be entirely separated from each other, and they should be separated. Apparently, only one side of the story counts—the other remains hidden from view, discredited as "unimportant" and not passed on to the next generation. This absence creates a feeling of lack in the narrator in *Slaves in the Family*, who is somewhat aware of the long-term social consequences of chattel slavery.

This narrator, as the descendant of a slaveholding dynasty, inherits a different legacy of slavery from other narrators in this study. Still, he voices similar concerns to those narrators who identify as "black": "The plantation heritage was not 'ours,' like a piece of family property, and not 'theirs,' belonging to black families, but a shared history" (14). The narrator expresses that the fates of both groups are interlinked, and that there are blood relationships between them, though this will not be acknowledged by everyone in the family. His statements allude to the exertion of power wielded by the slave owners and point to the fact that this part of American history plays a role 150 years after the end of slavery, that its legacy will reverberate into the future as well. For the Ball family in particular, these statements suggest a more intimate entanglement between the "white" and the "black" family members than is usually communicated at the Ball family gatherings—it refers to relationships that are not openly discussed by the white family.

According to the narrator, there is however only one story of his family, and it is a story he shares not only with his "white" relatives, but also with the descendants of the slaves the family once kept. Understanding his role as a storyteller finally triggers the narrator's desire to complete the story (14), to actively participate in the creation of a more comprehensive narrative, and to become an agent in his family history. By and large, these texts—at least on the superficial level—aim to produce family histories that are more "complete," in that they no longer consider "white" and "black" as mutually exclusive but as inherently intertwined through multiple generations.

In the *memoir of the search*, the emphasis on the family secret that can and should become known is strongly linked to the idea that the past is essential "family business." But the secret also connects to ideas of individuality and selfhood central to American national identity. In these texts, the narrator needs to resolve the secret in order to know herself and fill an apparent hole in her life—there is an absence that hurts and ultimately requires a resolution. The narrator needs to intervene actively in the ongoing discourse about racial mixedness.

The quest for the secret is as much a quest for relatives as it is a quest for the self, for an identity that is "true" or "real" (Haizlip 1995, 14–15). Hence, the narrator has to redefine the meanings of whiteness and blackness in her own life (34). The narrator thus fills a gap in the family story that has for decades been an accepted part of the family story. Her intervention places her in a position of power relative to the other family members, but also helps her feel completion.

DIMENSIONS OF THE FAMILY SECRET

Generally speaking, in the *memoir of the search* the family secret prevents the family from discussing its origins. In each text, however, the actual content and construction of the secret is different. While the central motif and its presentation remain more or less the same throughout the genre, the storyline itself varies to some degree. Nevertheless, what is common among the family secrets is that they relate to race, to abandonment, and to power. These issues are approached in several ways and from several different points of view.

In Shirlee Taylor Haizlip's *The Sweeter the Juice*, the unspeakable topic is familial abandonment and the disruption of family ties due to difference—mainly difference in skin color, but also sexual orientation. Familial abandonment due to difference is a pattern that repeats itself variously throughout the family's history for several generations. Neither the mixed heritage in the narrator's family nor the act of *passing* constitutes a secret in the text; rather, the consequences of both have become unspeakable. The very extreme breach of family ties due to skin color and the exact circumstances of this disruption counteract all attempts at parental love and family solidarity, and hinder contact between family members.

The family described in *The Sweeter the Juice* has been confronted with the "color line" and social limitations due to skin color in so many ways across the generations that a steady pattern of abandonment has been established. This pattern repeats itself over and over again. The narrator's mother had been left behind by the father because of her inability to *pass* as white. Her own mother, the narrator's grandmother, had also already been painfully separated from her family, albeit in the other direction, having been left behind by her white family members because of her relationship with a black man. As a consequence of both the system of supposed racial inferiority, and the possibility of *passing*, the extended family in the text is in effect nullified. Even if family members would recognize each other on the street, it is impossible for them to talk to each other (72)—both out of shame and in order to protect those who have actually *passed*.

The narrator's mother suffers from her abandonment all her life and is unable to talk about her younger years (78). Her past is best not addressed with her; a coping strategy that would likely be considered problematic by a therapist, but also by her daughter in the text. In addition to not being able to speak about her past, she is surrounded by an aura of pain even as an adult (33), indicating a lack of imagination that has emerged in the aftermath of the trauma she experienced. During her childhood and younger adult years, basically until she meets the man who later becomes her husband, the mother's life was an unhappy one characterized by loss and lack of family connections. When the children learn that their mother was abandoned due to her dark skin color, they are left bewildered, as to them, the mother is light skinned (32). This puzzlement, however, is a matter of perception, as to her family, her looks would offer clues to the family's nonwhite ancestry (77). What to the narrator is a gradual difference of skin color at the most has had terrible consequences for her mother's life.

This type of secret associated with *passing* does not only affect the mother, and by implication, the family she founded after the fact. Her preference for a darker-skinned man results from it, as does her difficulty of dealing with her lighter-skinned son. Her secret also impacts those who have left in the first place, those who have to constantly keep up the façade, and who have to be careful not to be revealed or to reveal themselves by accident—the family members, who need to remain "closeted." Her knowledge about her extended family members' complicated strategies of *passing* puts the narrator in a position of power.

If she were to find her mother's lost relatives, she could potentially destroy these people's lives by exposing their secret. This knowledge, while empowering, also places the narrator in a moral dilemma and leads her to think that some of her younger family members living as white have no idea about what happened in the past (33). She wonders to what degree these young people are still implicated in their parents' deeds, and whether they should be concerned with what has happened a long time ago. The narrator herself has suffered, having, as she claims, "absorbed" her mother's pain into her own life (33).

Since racial difference has led to various forms of abandonment in the family before, openly addressing any differences, even within the trusted circle of the nuclear family, has become impossible. As the text progresses, the reader learns about three more secret, hidden, or unspeakable topics that hinder open conversation in the family. One relates to the narrator's father, with whom the narrator has a difficult relationship because he has a distant personality, as she describes (132). In these terms, the father remains a "secret," even though he is a popular and well-loved man with a huge social circle. As is stated by the narrator, the father also had some problems in the past. These are not addressed in detail but remain vague and mostly unknown to the reader (133). The only fact the reader later learns is that the father was married once before and divorced his wife when he was still a young man. It is significant that in a text dealing with the resolution of secrets, there are secrets that are not revealed. With regard to the father's past, resolution is found in the fact that he had changed his life following his marriage to the narrator's mother (133), making clear that the revelation of this particular secret is no longer needed and closure has been reached.

In this text, both the mother and the father share a "dark past" and through their marriage absolve one another. Marriage enables the father to break with his painful life before, and in turn it enables the mother to free herself from her traumatic childhood and youth, at least to some extent. The fact that the father's past is not entirely revealed also shows that for the reader just as for the family members themselves it is not necessary to be aware of every private aspect of life. In this story, there is a notable difference between secrecy and privacy, and since the father's past does not shape the family in the same way that the mother's past does, there is a sense in which it no longer matters. The family can move on from there.

Another family secret the reader encounters in *The Sweeter the Juice* is that the narrator's brother, a very light-skinned man, has not been able to develop an integral sense of self. This, the narrator supposes, might be related to the fact that he was too light skinned to be accepted as a "true" member of the family. He struggles with his identity and also commits smaller crimes that send him to prison (Haizlip 1995, 161). He gets married five times and attempts to kill himself (159–61). The brother's life is not a topic of conversation in the family as a whole, but rather, only the women would sometimes bring it up to each other (163). Thus, as an internal family secret, this one creates a bond between the women in the text and possibly distances the "unknowable" father even further from the narrator.

This secret surrounding the brother is also one of skin color and abandonment, as the brother was rejected because his skin tone made him unrecognizable as a family member in the black family. The mother is unable to build a healthy relationship to her son; as the text makes clear, she has difficulties getting along with men other than the narrator's father. Her son, due to his light skin, stirs up negative memories in her, and this negatively impacts not only her motherly feelings, but also, in turn, her child's ability to fully grow into himself. The son's feelings of incompleteness and loss are shared by the narrator. Nevertheless, the son is very intelligent and attends therapy in order to cope with his problems, even as a boy. This family member is referred to as "brother" throughout the text and remains rather unknown to the reader— he is also called "brother" by his parents. The absence of his first name in the text demonstrates how this character has no opportunity to develop his own, nonfamilial identity: He remains unknowable both to the narrator and the reader. Through him, the family's unconscious rejection of those who are able to *pass* becomes evident.

The final secret is that the narrator's uncle, Percy, is gay. While this secret does not appear to be related to skin color and *passing*, upon closer observation it becomes clear that Percy has been *passing* as straight and has even participated in cultural rituals coded as "straight" by getting married to a woman, however briefly (240). The narrator only learns about Percy's sexual orientation as an adult, when she is already married herself, and, upon discussing the matter with her mother finds out that it was not supposed to be a topic of conversation as it is not relevant to the mother or the father (241). Percy was rejected for his homosexuality by his other family members and so moved from his childhood home to New York, and from then on presented a cleansed life to his family members, as well as establishing himself under a different name among his gay friends (241).

Like in a play or a dance performance, Percy's life is carefully scripted and his freedom of movement is severely restricted, not by the mere fact of his homosexuality, but rather by having to keep his sexual orientation a secret. Percy entertains a rather close relationship with the narrator's mother—likely resulting from their shared experience within the family of being unable to *pass* as someone they are not: the mother cannot change her skin color, while Percy is unable to live the life of a heterosexual man.

In *The Sweeter the Juice* one family secret undeniably triggers the next. The family portrayed in the text is caught up in a complex web of secrets, mysteries, and unspeakable things. The past cannot be talked about, and the present cannot be addressed either, at least not every dimension of it, because that would lead to bringing up the past in turn. Each decision made in the family is impacted by the secret, which haunts the family (138). To improve the situation, the daughter must seek out the family that once abandoned her mother. In effect, the family members' pledge not to break the covenant needs to be broken, so that the family can overcome the past, heal, and grow.

The secret explored in Bliss Broyard's (2007) *One Drop* also relates to matters of *passing* and abandonment, but is one where the narrator is a woman who grows up identifying as white. In that sense, *One Drop* presents the flipside to *The Sweeter the Juice*. As she is growing up, the narrator is not aware that her father was the descendant of black Louisiana Creoles, that he had been *passing* for white for a very long time, and that he had abandoned his original family in the course of his *passing*. Since this narrator is the daughter of someone who has abandoned his family—rather than someone who has *been abandoned* by his relatives—her point of view differs from the narrator's view in *The Sweeter the Juice*. Significantly, however, in both cases the past instance of *passing* continues to impact the present family.

In *One Drop*, it is only when the narrator's highly educated father, a writer and literary critic, is on his deathbed that the children learn there is something that needs to come out into the open, finally confirming their vague notion that something had been kept from them for a long time (Broyard 2007, 9). At this admission, both children conclude that the secret must be related to sex or death, with the narrator recalling her relief that her suspicion has been correct all this time (13). She considers the breaking of the secret her last chance at true intimacy with her father, who has little time left to live (13). Knowing that there is a secret gives the narrator a feeling of control over her father.

Even years later, the narrator remembers her feelings during the conversation as she participated in pushing her father to tell the truth about himself (12). In *One Drop*, the power dynamics between the parents and the children shift as the parents admit that they have been keeping something from the children. When the father becomes too ill to tell the children himself, it is the mother who exposes the secret of the father being of mixed descent (16). This is not an uncomfortable situation for the characters, but rather just a strange one. In the context of the text as a whole, it represents a break from the established family script, and a moment of honesty that the members have not prepared for. While their communication patterns are usually carefully scripted and rehearsed, this intervention comes without any possibility to react according to a prescribed pattern. Hence, the narrator reacts with laughter and her brother asks whether this is it (16), essentially breaking the tension that has emerged from the situation.

In what follows it becomes clear that both children do not feel shocked at all, but simply curious, as they begin to ask their mother some questions regarding their father's family history. The mother explains that coming from New Orleans, a multicultural city, the father's heritage is Creole (16). This suggests that their family's fate is not rare. She adds that the parents—the narrator's grandparents—*passed* for white when they got to New York in order to get a job, leading for Anatole, the father, who was light skinned to begin with, to act in a similar way. In turn, she goes on to state that the father's sisters lived as black, which kept the family apart (17).

The father has no agency at all in the telling of this story to his children. Apparently, he also did not have any agency in his own *passing*, as it was the result of "confusion" (17), as the mother explains. The mother's story determines the children's perception of the secret at this point. It emphasizes his supposed "lightness," which can be paraphrased as "whiteness." She also normalizes the story by emphasizing that in New Orleans at the time, *passing* and racial mixing were not rare (16). As the story moves on, Sandy, the mother, speaks about the father's history in terms of what can almost be called the essence of the well-circulated *tragic mulatto* story: The father never belonged, he was not black enough and not white enough, and did not want his children to suffer like him (17). The mother's way of telling is supposed to turn a story of pain into a positive narrative.

Unlike in *The Sweeter the Juice*, where there is considerable sadness and shame involved in the confrontation with the mother's history of neglect, both children in *One Drop* feel empowered instead of ashamed because of their family history. Nevertheless, their mother issues a warning for them to keep their new knowledge to themselves, and she also reminds them that this does not change anything for them as they are white (17). The mother, who has apparently urged her husband to come clean about his past for many years (74), thus attempts to extricate the children from their father's history by telling them, in effect, that they have nothing to do with it. They have been socialized as white, and thus should not be making any claims toward other parts of their identity.

The mother is putting herself in a strong position of power by determining what the children can know and how they should best deal with this information, namely, that they should ignore it. It is most painful to the children in this context that, while they are not supposed to talk about their newly discovered heritage, their mother has been quite freely spreading the story. Whenever the narrator tells other people about her father's background—in effect, breaking the rule her mother had given her—she learns from these other people that they already knew. Everyone but Bliss and Todd—the children—seems to have been aware of the father's racial background and family story. This is problematic, of course, because other people have known more about the siblings' heritage than they had known themselves, even though the two always sensed something was "off."

While *One Drop* and *The Sweeter the Juice* are both about the *passing* of family members into white society, the consequences of revealing the secret are radically different. The blurred line between blackness and whiteness is as important in *The Sweeter the Juice* as in *One Drop*, but it plays out in opposite direction. Since the narrator in *The Sweeter the Juice* describes herself as very light skinned, she explains that she herself and her family members identify as black not because of anything in their appearance, but because of the way they have lived their lives, moving in African American social circles (Haizlip 1995, 13). By contrast, the narrator in *One Drop* is firmly rooted in white society and is very unsure at first what her newly revealed family heritage might mean for her. In her family, race was never a topic of conversation (Broyard 2007, 41). This admission is unexpected, because, although the father's heritage was kept a secret from the narrator and her brother, the subject of race could have been discussed separately from the family's history. There could have been conversations about political issues in the household, especially in an educated household like this, or in a school-related context. That these issues were not mentioned at all demonstrates how the father tried to isolate himself from his heritage and from blackness altogether. He lives in a place that is characterized by whiteness.

Consequently, the narrator now feels very insecure talking about blackness, black history, and race more generally. She does not have an automatic ability to serve as a bridge between the races, an ability that is oftentimes attributed to people of mixed heritage; she has no familiarity with these supposedly color-coded subjects and feels overwhelmed discussing race with members of her father's family. There does not seem to be an "automatic" connection between her and relatives on her father's side. Instead, she finds it exceptionally difficult to find the words to talk with them about these matters.

She learns more about the topic of race when she enters graduate school at the University of Virginia and *passing* is discussed in class (96ff.). The understanding she gains enables her to lead conversations about race and finally be able to tell her story. In the process, she begins to critically examine her own thoughts regarding African Americans, her own stereotypes, and to trace racially coded messages in the public sphere (98). This process of "learning by doing" does not come naturally. There are several instances in the text where the narrator struggles to come to terms with what her blackness means to her.

Overall, blackness and whiteness in these texts are not so much matters of one's actual skin color or tone, but are matters of socialization and of knowing which side one belongs to or feels most affiliated with. They inform the questions one asks and what conversations are conducted in the family home, but also outside of it. The knowledge about which side of racial identity to choose is sharply informed by the process of *passing* that is central to the secret and the secret keeping in the texts.

In *One Drop*, the narrator—despite her excitement about her newly found identity—does not discuss the topic of *passing* or racial identity with her dying father. Essentially, the secret persists between the father and the daughter. Even though both know about it, and even about its details, they do not talk about it. The narrator consciously chooses not to address the secret (19). In that sense, she determines for herself that the subject is unspeakable. She sticks to their familiar scripts instead of adding something new to the ongoing father/daughter conversation.

At the same time, the topic *is* addressed in the hospital room where her father is resting. When friends come in and out to say goodbye, the family talks about the secret history of skin color in the presence of these friends—with the friends often sharing a family secret of their own in return. Even though the family mainly defined itself through shared activities, rather than extended dialogue between family members, the narrator feels that she knows more about her father than most daughters: He had at one point revealed to her that he had been married and got two other women pregnant before meeting and marrying her mother. She had therefore assumed his secrets were mostly about his qualities as a seducer of women (75). Now, however, she feels that this is no longer the case.

It is notable that in this family, sex is less of a taboo than race. In retrospective, the narrator recalls that her father had once openly lied to her when she questioned him about his ancestry, which he claimed was French and maybe a little Portuguese. The worst part about this lie is that she feels betrayed because other people knew about it (75). To the narrator, he has treated them, his own children, much more unfairly than anyone else he surrounded himself with, driving a wedge between father and children even posthumously.

In the circle of the immediate family, the father kept much of his past a secret (23). He did not refer to any ancestors in the presence of his children and considered authors such as Franz Kafka and Charles Baudelaire his "family"—until he married their mother and had his own children who became his family, without him needing anyone else (23). To him, family is a matter of choice, selection, and decision. Much like the problems for the characters in *The Sweeter the Juice* relating to speaking about difference, there are strong conventions in the Broyard family governing what can and cannot be said. Feelings between family members also appear to be more or less secret; without the grounding of a stable familial connection, they are rebuilding their connections through everyday interactions. Family members choose to hide their feelings, and making it so means that, essentially, open communication is hindered because it could lead to one or more family members making different choices.

While *The Sweeter the Juice* and *One Drop* deal with *passing* and family abandonment from more or less opposite directions, they function similarly, both in how the family secret is introduced to the reader and how the presence of the secret has brought about feelings of inadequateness, insecurity, and doubt in the characters. In *The Sweeter the Juice*, the narrator claims that she has "absorbed" her mother's pain by "osmosis" (Haizlip 1995, 33). Osmosis is a natural process that cannot be stopped or stymied. While the narrator in this text is rather ambivalent toward her own "whiteness" (14), the narrator in *One Drop* is at first curious and positively excited about her supposed "mixedness" (Broyard 2007, 17).

She even wants to try on her newly found blackness, an effort that is received with skepticism in the black community (294). Her concerns are not unfounded. While she becomes very unsure when "trying to locate herself on this racial landscape or even recogniz[ing] its terrain" (295), she also learns that "identity [is] a performance of sorts" and that becoming oneself is a process (296). That this narrator will "play" with her "blackness" while the narrator in *The Sweeter the Juice* is skeptical about her "whiteness" makes clear that these two speak from very different positions of power.

Only when the narrator in *One Drop* learns more about her father's past does she become more doubtful of her motivation to identify as mixed race. Getting to know her father's family is a rocky road instead of a fun-filled joyride. Through her research, she learns about the history of race and inequality in the United States, and the devastating poverty suffered by black Americans. This knowledge turns her into a person who is unsure about the meaning of blackness and the importance of race and white privilege in American society.

The narrator comes to recognize that the privilege she has taken for granted throughout her life is a result of access and therefore skin color. This same privilege has made it difficult for her to relate to the experiences of her father's family. This is especially true at the beginning of her quest. When she first travels to New Orleans to visit her father's birth place, she is shocked by the poverty she encounters in the community and abandons her search; she feels shame as he had been unaware of her family's poverty and social standing, and she feels affected by this more than she had previously thought (94). She does not further her inquiry but tries to store it away—in fact, placing it "in the closet" so to say (94). Years later, it is her studies in graduate school stimulate her interest again in researching her family history.

The narrator in *Slaves in the Family*, as the descendant of a slaveholding dynasty, speaks from a rather different vantage point to begin with. Still, what might be the most obvious subject that would lend itself to a textual family secret is not very contested: He knows that his family once owned slaves. The secret is not the mere fact of slave ownership, which the narrator is aware of, and in detail (Ball 1999, 7). Rather, the secret stems from what happened to these people during slavery.

The narrator is interested in how the slaves were treated by his forebears and in what became of them after the end of slavery. Across many generations, there has been no contact between his family and the slaves and their descendants that he knows of. He is ignorant of these peoples' lives, wondering who they were and what they may have experienced and whether there were any living descendants in the present (7). His questions about the slaves and their descendants are ultimately triggered by his ownership of the book containing the "white" side of the family history. The supposedly "other" side he does not know. It is quite significant that even this narrator, who has been raised in a very sheltered home and has experienced regular family gatherings, feels an absence in his life—that something is supposedly "missing." The "color line" has created the division.

The narrator has the perception that the treatment of the slaves and where they went after emancipation is an "unfinished business" in his family (9). This means it concerns the family members whether they want it or not. The narrator makes it his "business" to resolve the secret. He grew up with stories about his family, but these focused on the rice planters instead of the people who sustained the plantations by way of their labor. It becomes very clear in the text that this family has for the past centuries constructed their identity around their past as slaveholders, as an empire, as a powerful dynasty. The Civil War, the end of slavery, even the Civil Rights Movement have seemingly not changed this self-perception of the family.

Everything the narrator learns from his family members about the slaves the family once owned stands in stark contrast to what he, as a college-educated journalist, knows about slavery. He seems altogether well educated about the history of slavery, though this does not mean that he is informed about all its dimensions and long-term consequences. The stories he is being told by family members upon embarking on his quest for truth go against the family records that take stock of beatings that slaves have received. But still, and even though the narrator confronts family members about these findings, the family likes to remember the ancestors as benevolent slaveholders who never hesitated to support their slaves. As the Ball family historian tells him, the white Balls did not only treat their slaves very well, but that white people suffered greatly from the conditions on the plantations, in contrast to the slaves who apparently lived rather good lives. The family historian relates that the lives of the white ancestors on the plantations were shaped by boredom and isolation through long parts of the day (48).

In contrast, the slaves could rely on each other (49). This understanding trivializes the situation the slaves experienced on the plantations and adds to the perceived contrast the narrator detects between his knowledge about the subject and the stories he encounters in his family. Despite these remarks by the family historian, as well as similar stories about how the Balls considered their slaves family, how they never beat them, and did not tear families apart (56), the narrator is also repeatedly warned that he might hear the wrong kinds of stories from other people (60). This ultimately disqualifies all stories the narrator might hear from the descendants of the slaves.

It appears that the story depends on who is asked about the slaves, and other versions of the story cannot be trusted. The narrator is put into a complicated situation, because asking those "other people" would mean breaking with family loyalties and family tradition. At the same time, he feels that his family, in their glorification of the past and their role in it, may have reduced the events to legend. His unease inspires him to continue inquiring into the matter, whatever he may find out.

In addition to the slaves' treatment and their lives after slavery, the narrator in *Slaves in the Family* is especially interested in another societal taboo, namely, in whether there were any sexual relations between the Balls and their slaves. He assumes that this was the case (49). Here, too, though, the narrator's family members also cannot or do not want to answer his questions: They either claim not to know of such relations, or deem such stories "folklore" (49). "Folklore" of course suggests that these relations are legends—this idea fits with the overall secrecy in the family relating to these matters.

Another relative he interviews suggests that relationships between the Balls and their slaves are not worth investigating. This relative, an elderly woman named Dorothy, claims such contacts only happened in other parts of the region, naming Louisiana as an example of a state where sexual contacts across the "color line" took place (57). By locating the actual event far away from the Ball plantations, to a different state, she places it outside of her own family, and outside of her line of heritage. Her later allusion to "Virginia" (57) can be understood as a direct reference to the relationship between Thomas Jefferson and Sally Hemings, which had been confirmed and was the subject of much research around the time of the publication of *Slaves in the Family*.

According to Dorothy, this elderly relative, African Americans in Virginia did not follow the same moral principles as those in South Carolina, who would apparently never do such a thing as bed a white person—omitting that they may not have had a choice in this matter at all. This relative also dismisses the subject of interracial relationships or rape from her family history by linking it to her national heritage and claiming that in contrast to the English, the French settlers were the ones to cross over boundaries of skin color (58). She, in tune with her ancestors' values, is still against integration and believes that it would be best if schools and the entire social sphere were segregated in order to prevent intermarriages in the long run (58).

Dorothy insists that she had never heard about an intimate sexual relationship between a Ball slave and their master, and does not think that this has previously been a subject of discussion in the family. Her attitude convinces the narrator that there is not much reason to believe that his white relatives will, in fact, openly acknowledge sexual relations between their ancestors and the slaves they held, no matter whether this actually happened or not (58).

The subject has been moved to the area of taboo: it is not supposed to be mentioned, and family will dodge it when it *is* mentioned.

As before, the answer will depend on who is being asked in the first place. While this relative does not oppose the narrator's quest, about which he clearly informs her, she also warns him that he might get the wrong information from the people he may encounter along the way. She admits an uneasiness about meeting African Americans which she claims she has not had before (60). Her remarks make clear that she has no contact with the African American community herself.

The main question that amounts to a family secret in the text concerns the life of a perceived *Other*, who is intimately related to the family and at the same time isolated from it and its stories. In *Slaves in the Family*, the assumption that slavery still matters today leads the narrator to investigate a deeper "truth" regarding his family's past that will supposedly also make him discover a "truth" about himself, as he sees himself implicated in his ancestors' deeds. He knows next to nothing about the slaves' lives, which, considering how closely intertwined the lives of the Balls and their slaves once were, amounts to a kind of abandonment of his family's history and himself.

For some time, the narrator seems able to repress his wish to get more information about the past, but as the narrative progresses, the unanswered questions that have been with him since childhood come back to trouble him: He describes how his perception of the place where he grew up has transformed, and how he "sometimes shovel[s] the graves [the mass graves where those who had not survived the quarantine were buried, and sometimes also washed ashore in Charleston] in my sleep" (90). Here, he feels guilty for sins he has not committed, but that his blood relatives have committed. As their descendant, he is a part of this history and feels implicated in their sins. Along similar lines, the narrator feels haunted by the unknown past and apparently has no other choice than to seek the revelation of the family secret, despite all the risks associated with it. More than once in the text the narrator describes how he encounters serious opposition from his family members with regard to his project of finding the descendants of the Ball slaves.

He goes on to state that "death is a master from England" (90), clearly alluding to Paul Celan's poem "Todesfuge" (written 1944/45), about the killing of Jews across Europe by the National Socialist regime. The narrator's statement, with its allusion to National Socialist Germany and to England, where the Ball family originated, significantly complicates the passage. On the one hand, it states that the English—and by implication, the narrator's ancestors—committed the harms of slavery on American soil, as slave masters. Europe is implicated in the sins of slavery because Europeans acted as slave masters following their immigration to colonial America, but also, because they operated the Transatlantic Slave Trade: a fact that English cities such as Liverpool have only slowly been coming to terms with since the 1990s. On the other hand, the passage establishes a link between slavery and the Holocaust. This link is problematic, but in the context of *Slaves in the Family* helps convey several messages. It alludes to the idea that slavery, like the Holocaust, has lasting consequences, yet lacks the same type of memorialization that is known with regard to the Holocaust. The link also points out that many slaves lost their lives, not only following their arrival in the United States, but also before that, during their passage across the Atlantic.

Last, but not least, the narrator is aware of the fact that his family is on the side of those who committed the horror, that he is a descendant of the "master from England." He does not refute that his ancestors have participated in the exploitation of those who worked for them and thus contributed to their social status and ability to build a dynasty: His family heritage and heirloom is built on the backs of others. His legacy is the legacy of a perpetrator rather than a victim. This acknowledgment causes intense feelings of guilt and regret in the narrator. At the same time, he also seems to think at times that he, through his actions, can undo the past or make up for some of the injustices committed. This belief puts him into a vexed situation for which he has no words.

If *Slaves in the Family* explores the fate of a black family from the perspective of a white journalist, *Pearl's Secret* undertakes just the opposite quest. At the center, there is a black journalist trying to find the white family he is connected to by blood. This story is only indirectly about a secret related to mixed race, as the narrator, at least from the age of twelve (Henry 2001, 43), and his parents and grandparents, are very well aware that they have a white ancestor named Henry Beaumont and are of mixed descent. Several documents relating to the man are passed on in the family from one generation to the next. There is a letter Beaumont sent to the narrator's great-grandmother Pearl in 1901 acknowledging her as his daughter, a photograph he also sent her, and Beaumont's short obituary (7).

These documents are not kept secret, just the opposite. They are treated "almost as if they were relics" (9), the choice of the word "relic" hinting at their sanctified, almost "untouchable" status. What is not clear, though, is whether Beaumont, after conceiving his daughter Pearl with a former slave named Laura, did indeed start a second family, a white family (29). *Pearl's Secret* investigates this question. Since it transpires that there is such a second family, this "white" family, the text deals with the narrator exposing the secret of the "black" family's existence to these relatives. Up to this point in time, the Beaumont descendants had thought that Pearl, the narrator's great-grandmother, was of Native American ancestry. While the relationship between Beaumont and Laura Brumley was not discussed openly, the family remembers that the mother was in touch with the grandfather's child and had cared about this person. But the family members had thought this woman to be of Indian (Native American) descent (121). This shows that the black/white race mixing is a taboo subject in the white family. This is not very surprising, as it later turns out that the white family in part supported the Confederacy and the Ku Klux Klan.

The narrator attributes the keeping of the secret about Beaumont in his own family to their attitudes toward African Americans (20). Thus, the keeping of the secret is related to shame, but also to the fact that there are many black people in the family history whom the family can be proud of (20), leading to a situation where this middle-class family has developed its stable identity based on the black family members alone. His family is one of lawyers and doctors, well respected and solidly located in the middle class across several generations.

Because of his own family's successes, the narrator feels guilty about his desire to explore the white family's history and links it to the idea of "peeling back the pulpy layers of some forbidden fruit" (49), unaware of the troubling truths he might find. The "forbidden fruit" metaphor used here evokes Billie Holiday's "Strange Fruit," as well as the complications of mixed-race family histories in the American South.

The image suggests that it is in part the forbidden aspect of his undertaking that attracts the narrator to it. He is an active agent in this process; he is doing the "peeling." The layered quality of the fruit suggests that it is not an easy undertaking to get to the core of the secret and that the process will be messy. The "forbidden fruit" also recalls the story of Eden: The narrator might learn things he does not want to know. He might see the world in a light he had so far been sheltered from. New knowledge might provide relief, but can also be the source of painful recognitions. Time has shaped the family the narrator is seeking, and in the first place, they might not be willing to associate with him. Still, the image of the fruit builds on the assumption that there is a "truth" at the core worth exploring and that in fact lends itself to such inquiry.

The narrator in *Pearl's Secret*, as becomes evident in this passage, is likely the most reluctant among the narrators studied here. He is constantly wondering whether he is making a mistake by investing so much money and time into his quest, rather than into the people who already support him—his black family members (32). He feels it might be an act of disloyalty, which potentially hurts his family, especially since he does not know whether Beaumont's white descendants will care for him and his family or not. Since many of his family members, including his parents and siblings, have experienced great achievements and have profited from being part of the later Great Migration to the Western United States in the second half of the twentieth century, his investment into a family he knows nothing about seems irrational.

At the same time, the narrator appears to need this type of investigation to confront his ongoing feelings of alienation from himself. He feels conflicted spending time looking for a distant white forebear who apparently did not fulfill his family obligations to the narrator's ancestors. The underlying question here may very well be what it means to be a family, both in the past and in the present time. How much should one invest in this question, in the search for unknown relatives?

In contrast to the black family in *Pearl's Secret*, whose members talk quite openly about mixed ancestry, the "white" Beaumont family evidently did not know about Pearl's ancestry. It had to be kept silent because of social pressures—a convenient excuse. As one of Beaumont's great-granddaughters explains that to her father, Indian heritage would have been advantageous over African American roots, a statement which confuses and pains the narrator (223). He feels hurt and rejected. There are many similar family legends in the South about families with Indian blood in their family tree instead of black/white relationships, a phenomenon sometimes referred to as "Indian Princess Grandmother Myth." Apparently, when it comes to hiding mixed heritage, there was a significant layer of invention in many Southern families of this time, as also becomes clear in relation to this "myth."

In *Pearl's Secret*, a second secret that affects the narrator's family is revealed. This secret is seemingly unrelated to the mixed-race heritage of the family, but is connected to the questions of power and shame voiced earlier and is spatially located in the American South. The family had ended up on the West Coast due to a painful incident, namely, the rape of the narrator's mother one night while her husband, a doctor, was out at work. Because of the specific conditions of their life in the South and the limitations imposed upon them due to their skin color the family moves to a middle-class neighborhood in Seattle, where the narrator's father becomes one of the first black general surgeons (176–81).

His mother's rape is kept from the narrator and his siblings (181). The children are told that at one point someone tried to break into their Southern home, but they do not know the importance and meaning of this incident for the parents (182), or how it triggered the subsequent move to the West Coast. The parents do not share their vulnerability with the children. Even though the narrator describes his mother as an open person (183), he only learns about the rape when he is thirty-one years old.

When he learns about it, he realizes that "[t]he rape was the biggest secret of her life" (183). At this point, the mother has come to realize that in order to heal, she will have to tell her children about this central incident. Her realization may not be conscious, because the narrator is stunned when his mother brings it up (183). This appears to be the first time she presents her son with such a difficult and painful story from her past. Sharing it is also a tribute to the trust between mother and son.

He describes what it is like to have no words, feeling stunned into silence (183–84), before asking his mother a series of questions about what really happened that night in Tennessee. His questions also concern the issue of why the rape was kept secret within the family, and how the mother recovered from this experience. She says that she probably has not completely recovered from it even after all these years and that she has only recently started to feel safe again. Nevertheless, contemplating the event so many years later, she can even find some irony in it, and especially in her own reaction to the rapist's demand for money—she had asked him whether she could write him a check (185–86).

Both these secrets are not "unknown" in terms of people not being aware of the fact that something specific—an instance of race mixing and parental and familial neglect; an event triggering the family's relocation from Tennessee to Washington State—took place. They are "secrets" because it is impossible to talk about the events even within the tightly knit circle of the family: There are no words to do so. It appears that the family members do not want to confront each other with potentially problematic parts of the family story. This is especially true for the parents, who keep secrets even from their adult children.

In telling Pearl's story, and approaching its legacy for two families, one white, one black, *Pearl's Secret* exposes the same story from two more or less opposite points of view. This dual history creates tension in the text and shows that communication across established borders is a difficult and painful undertaking. Once again, the narrator does not automatically have the ability to act as a "bridge" between the different groups. The two families can both claim to have been affected by Pearl's life and her treatment, though ultimately they were affected in very different ways.

For the Henry family, the story's legacy is much more painful and ultimately had to be addressed. In this way, the text offers a statement on white privilege, however indirectly and without summoning the term. Throughout the narrator's conversations with his white family members, it becomes ultimately evident that while their ancestors have contributed to the same historical events, today it is still important which side of the story a person is placed on; and this remains a matter of skin color and the privilege associated with it. The white family has been able to push much of the story aside and keep their convictions intact. This was not possible for the narrator, who felt haunted by the past and needed to get closure. The difficulty of being unable to ignore the past is a consequence of the narrator and his parents not having white privilege.

The "secrets" exposed in the *memoirs of the search* impose problems upon the intergenerational relationships portrayed in the genre. The past betrayals of trust, the long-term consequences of familial abandonment, the legacy of racial *passing*, and the secret keeping itself all pose problems in the present. The current generation has inherited the unsolved problems from their parental generation and beyond. The *memoir of the search* argues that trauma will be transmitted unless it is resolved. In each case, the neglected trauma in the text centers on race and the long-term economic and ethical consequences of the racial divide that still characterizes American society even in the supposedly "post-racial" age. In essence, the genre argues that in order to find new modes of living together in the present, past trauma must be acknowledged and worked through.

Of course, the recognition that the past plays into the present is not new. What is new is that these texts commenting on the long-term effects of the past—and the secrets the reader encounters in them—are in a dialogue with each other. They reflect the same kinds of "secrets," but from supposedly radically different points of view. The narrators all comment on the pains race and the "color line" have caused in their families and on how their family is supposedly "incomplete" because of what transpired in the past. In these terms, the boundaries between victim and perpetrator are blurred—the texts point to the sufferings of both black and white families, due to matters of skin color.

This is certainly a complicated assumption, as the consequences of racial oppression on people identifying as white are completely different from the realities of black life in the United States. Still, by commenting on these issues, the *memoir of the search* breaks boundaries: It is okay to lead a dialogue about these matters, and also about the difference skin color makes in the present. However, at the same time these texts strictly focus on the middle class and on the singular families portrayed. Thus, the genre looks back from the present to the past, but not necessarily from the single family to the entirety of black and white communities.

The clues to unlocking the secret in these texts are found in the present, but the process of investigating the secrets centers on the past. The genre uses a different set of devices in order to explicate the connection between the past and the present—first and foremost a specific methodology based on genealogical practice. Thus, in these texts, while is up to the current generation to gather the courage and the responsibility to find out what has become of those left out of the *family stories* so far, this situation is not the result of an outside force urging the narrators to act. There is no intrusion into their families from the outside, no threat, no pressure from others. Rather, the narrator presents herself as a curious, and also specifically educated and qualified, individual, who wishes to investigate the past because of feelings she has entertained from childhood on and because she is aware that her family has been shaped in a specific way by past events. These aspects all play into 1990s/2000s tenets of self-actualization and well-being.

By implication, the narrators all engage in *writing a new family story*, one that ostensibly provides them with the sense of *completion* they all seem to be lacking as they start out on their investigations—a real saga. At the center of this new family story is the changed role of responsibility and loyalty. At least on the surface, the *memoir of the search* builds on the idea of a shared past that should pave the way into a shared present in which boundaries of race can be overcome. Rewriting the family story in these texts means reknitting long-lost ties and addressing complex questions regarding the meaning of the past for the present situation in the families portrayed.

INVESTIGATING THE SECRET

The family secret and the narrator's decision to resolve it sets in motion a process of investigation and revelation that is described in different degrees of detail within the genre. *Pearl's Secret* capitalizes on this process of research, effectively creating a detective story in which the narrator inspects the past using specific genealogical and research-oriented tools.

By providing a detailed overview of the research process, the narrators demonstrate the lengths they will go to solve their family secrets. The efforts become an all-consuming activity that eventually leads them to their "lost" relatives. It is sometimes an international undertaking and goes beyond boundaries between family and state, church and political institutions, as, for example, Henry describes (Henry 2001, 21).

*Pearl's Secre*t is not the only text with a strong focus on the research undertaken by the narrator. In *Slaves in the Family*, the narrator consistently talks about visiting archives and even relocates from New York City to Charleston in order to be closer to both the story and the sources needed for the study. In *The Sweeter the Juice*, some of the investigative work is done not by the narrator, but by a professional detective agency hired by her. Still, this narrator describes how she becomes obsessed with finding more clues (Haizlip 1995, 43).

In the *memoir of the search*, the process of researching and piecing the family history together is often described metaphorically. The idea of the riddle that one can follow to get to the core is central to *The Sweeter the Juice*, as is the idea of a quilt which links different layers of history and different skin colors and can be stored away once it has been completed (14). This idea makes clear that the narrator is looking to be relieved at the end of her search. Once she has pieced the different parts of the quilt together, creating both something new and something quintessentially American, she can put it in the closet and make her peace with it. Until this process is completed, she will have to keep looking for and obsessing over the missing pieces.

At the same time, the quote also points to the difficulty of this very situation (14), meaning it is very well possible that the desired completion will not be reached. Along similar lines, the expression "wearing it smooth" (14) suggests that the quilt may at first not be a comforting item to cover oneself with because it has a new feeling, not yet softened by use—it requires a revision of the family narrative. Still, the composition of the quilt, a central image in African American literature and culture in and of itself, provides a sense of closure that is present throughout the entire narrative by Haizlip, but also in the genre of the *memoir of the search* in general.

A similar image is used in *Slaves in the Family*. The narrator describes what he is doing in terms of a puzzle (Ball 1999, 21). The emphasis here is on the creation of something—something that has a defined shape—out of the singular items and stories that emerge throughout the research process. The idea that the pieces will necessarily fit together is interesting in this context, as it suggests a type of linearity and completeness of the pieces that may not in fact be achievable due to the long-term legacy of slavery and its aftermath. "Piec[ing] together" (21) a story from the single fragments available sounds almost too simple an activity—a puzzle that can be made to fit if only one spent enough time contemplating and putting together the individual parts.

The idea of the puzzle goes along with another metaphor used in this text, namely, the self-portrait of the family that is addressed in *Slaves in the Family* (62). Here, the narrator describes his role in more extensive terms, as he adds to this portrait in the course of his investigation, and certainly also transforms it. He becomes a creative agent, an artist, who is potentially revising the story that has been told by his family members before. The question is whether it is even desirable to create an image without any gaps; to just "paint over" the past, albeit in producing an image that is supposedly more "true."

Piecing together a puzzle—"the murky details about [his] family's racial past in the United States"—is also central to *Pearl's Secret* (Henry 2001, 13). *One Drop* uses yet another image, but one that fits very well with the ideas voiced above: She thinks of identity in relation to a board game (Broyard 2007, 11). Here, the search is tightly linked to the idea of progress: In order to be able to move on to the next level, a set of tasks needs to be completed. The assumption, again, is that there is a correct way to complete the tasks.

The sense of closure aimed at by these texts becomes especially evident in *Pearl's Secret* where the narrator, upon ending his research process, describes how his family connections come together "like dabs of oil paint completing a long unfinished landscape" (Henry 2001, 250). Still, a painting is a human creation, one that may have flaws and be imbued with irregularity—it is an imaginative, creative work. Broyard's (2007, 141) narrator points to this process of construction by likening her work piecing together her family history to the building of the city of New Orleans, where her family's origins are. Surrounded by swampland, the city of New Orleans has unique physical characteristics: the ever-present levees, drastically mixed elevations. It is a place that grew according to the availability of land, the place's identity being always provisional and subject to change. New Orleans reflects the fact that the process of piecing together the family history is irregular, that it can be delayed, and that it is literally a work-in-progress.

The research practices described within the genre vary from archival investigation to studying family documents to DNA testing to the creation of family trees. Of the texts discussed here, *Pearl's Secret* is the only one in which the narrator's research plan is so detailed as to include a set of specific questions relating to his family members on the other side of the "color line" (Henry 2001, 11). Finding their names in the census records, in the archives, is very important to the narrators because it assures them of their place in history and shows that they have contributed to it in whatever small but significant ways.

In the *memoir of the search*, the investigation is complicated by matters of race as well as by silence (Haizlip 1995, 53), as traces have often been obscured by slavery and its aftermath. In *One Drop*, the narrator addresses hearing stories of whites searching in archives who stopped their research once they found a connection to the black community (Broyard 2007, 233), or who would stop following their family history in the archive due to the understanding that their family was "white"; hence, finding records of "black" family members must be proof that something has been missed and that they have been following the wrong traces, pointing to the idea of the mutual exclusiveness of a light skin tone and African American heritage, as well as blackness and whiteness.

The presence of the family secret adds to these difficulties as it governs the processes of storytelling in the family that are vital to knowing what the family members did in the past. Her basis to start from is much smaller compared to others. She just has a "ball of thread" to start from (89). The images used in this passage, including the idea of an "unraveling [. . .] ball of thread" and a "dusty tangled thing" that has to be unknotted, are rather telling. Both images point to what is at stake here. The narrator quite literally has to take her family history apart without knowing what she is going to find. That it has been neglected, "been kicked under the bed years before," complicates the narrator's task and shows that this effort may not be appreciated by all family members—something that has been kicked under the bed is finally out of sight. The "ball of thread" likely has many knots, small and larger ones, and it is not possible to just make a clean "cut" as that would ultimately destroy the thread. Nevertheless, the unresolved family story has been in the room all of this time, and in the bedroom at that. It is a most private issue, and one that does not disappear just because it was hidden from sight. This image links to something being hidden "in the closet"—it may be closeted, but it is still there and it will not disappear.

In effect, the *memoir of the search* represents the result of this metaphorical process of "unknotting" undertaken by the narrator. The text, both in materiality and in narrative scope, creates a different and new family history that was previously not there, but that can be discovered with the help of official records. The genre then finally establishes a record of the narrator's process of investigating this history and intertwines a personal, family-related story with a larger, historical narrative about the American nation and its becoming. The genre also presents a regional narrative centered on the American South, its practices of slavery and segregation, and the legacy of this past on the present.

For the narrators, it is important to have such a document as they believe it will ground them in history and pass on their family story to the next generation. They oftentimes state that they are undertaking their extensive investigations so that their children will know about their family history from early on (Henry 2001, 13). This narrator in *Pearl's Secret*, as well as the other narrators in these texts, untangles a complex web as part of a creative process, of producing something. Race and prejudice are interwoven with the American experience like the different parts of a quilt; cutting them out of the fabric would ultimately lead to destruction of the material. This is essential for the narrator to understand and to pass on to his daughter. The quote also locates the Henry family firmly in an African American context, since a white father would not have to educate his children about racial matters and the precariousness of black life in the United States from early on.

In addition to helping the next generation understand where they come from, it also becomes clear in the texts that the search is conducted for parents and grandparents whose lives were also impacted by the family secret. In this way, the *memoir of the search* is a rather optimistic genre. The memoirs demonstrate that by unraveling the family history and understanding why certain family members had to make particular decisions with particular consequences, the past can be known and change can come by way of knowing, understanding, and thereby gaining power over the past.

In *The Sweeter the Juice*, the narrator conducts the search so her mother can meet her sister in old age (33). At this time, the narrator consciously wants to give her mother back what was taken from her. She is aware that time might be running out for her mother, and that if she still wants to reacquaint her mother with her "lost" family, this has to happen now. That the daughter would undertake this large-scale quest for her mother's benefit demonstrates their strong relationship. It also shows how parents and children depend on, and are obligated to care for, one another. The mother has nurtured her daughter through childhood and youth; now the grown daughter must return the same caring and effort.

Despite the narrators' ambitions and careful tactics of confronting the past, they already experience feelings of ambivalence and anger during the investigation process described in these texts. In *The Sweeter the Juice*, the narrator is very aware of these feelings that also lead to thoughts of revenge (100). She is envisioning a kind of hell for those people who abandoned her mother and she voices her desire to expose and judge them (100). Thus, she is in a situation where she thinks of avenging the wrongs committed against her mother and, by way of her mother, herself.

These thoughts are not acted upon in the text, but their contemplation alone makes clear how the narrator suffers from the wounds of the past—her mother's past is also her past, her mother's rejection is also hers. She has to assume that the people who abandoned her mother also do not want to meet her, or would reject her on the basis of skin color. Nevertheless, and despite their conflicted thoughts in relation to both *passing* and familial abandonment, the narrators all devote extensive time and money to the process of getting to the heart of the family secret. Their investigations lead them to travel across the United States and beyond in order to meet with relatives and address the past and its legacies. They are willing to face the pain.

INITIATING DIALOGUES

Throughout the process of investigation, the narrators encounter family members with very different backgrounds as compared to their own. These differences do not only concern their racial identification, but also their social class and occupation. These factors play a role in the conversations they have across the supposed "color line" that both divides and unites their families. The "color line" in these texts is also a class line in many instances, though it is not always the black family that has been or is doing worse economically—unlike what the popular stereotype might suggest.

The difficulty of starting a conversation, especially one that goes beyond small talk, between family members rooted in different stories and on different sides of the so-called color line, proves to be another convention of the genre. While the idea of the family secret initially suggests that once the secret is solved—via the process of investigation explained above—there could be a "happy ending," quite the opposite is true. The texts end with more questions than answers, and the dialogue established does not create one unified family among the members who encounter each other, as though by some quasi-automatic process. Rather, the predominant feelings are ambivalence and doubt. As a genre, the *memoir of the search* does not offer the kind of happy ending one might anticipate. It does provide a resolution, but it is bleaker than a reader might expect.

In the process of investigating their tangled family histories, the narrators must begin a conversation about a particular past as well as its potential impact on the present. So much is at stake, and all involved are aware that they are treading on contested terrain in their investigation of where family and race have met in their own family trees.

In his mind, the narrator in *Pearl's Secret* makes up a catalog of questions that he intends to ask his family members. This catalog points directly to what is at stake and to what has remained unsaid in families torn apart by skin color. It addresses the question in how far the family has ever talked about past, and how so, what they remember about the ancestors, but also about the family's identity as Americans (Henry 2001, 60).

While part of this imaginary interview looks to the reader like a collection of conventional questions inquiring about a person's background, the narrator also includes questions relating to hopes and dreams. In addition to seemingly standard questions, this catalog also shares qualities with police (or other types of) interrogations, especially the very first question asking about the family's knowledge about the past, and specifically about Pearl. This question almost seems to imply another that is not voiced directly, namely: "And if you knew about this, what did you do or think about it?" What is even more remarkable, though, is that the narrator does not seem to have a word for what has happened between the common ancestors. Rather, he refers to the events leading to Pearl's conception as "this" and as "it."

The shame is so deep that the narrator cannot even formulate a question regarding the relationship between A. J. Beaumont and his ex-slave great-grandmother in his own mind. Even the imagined replies that he makes up before he encounters his white relatives seem to fill him with a feeling of unease (60), possibly because the answer could lead to follow-up questions that he considers even more important. These questions deal with the family's involvement in the struggles relating to civil rights, the family's opinions on African American history, civil rights leaders, court cases relating to equality, and the more general stance of white Americans regarding these topics, and whether there has been progress in relation to their ideas about race over time (61). Thus, these questions are not so much about personal background or interest, but intimately relate to family loyalties, and to the ways the white family is or is not sympathetic to the concerns of African Americans more generally, beyond their own family members whom they may or may not have known about. The narrator would also like to know whether their attitudes may have changed since the nineteenth century—the living family members may have different ideas than their ancestors. Still, accusations hang in the air.

The list points to the ethical dimension of mixed-race heritage: Ideally, family members should be invested in each other's legal, financial—human—concerns. Such concerns have been absent so far and caused the black-identifying and the white-identifying families to become and remain divided. Interestingly, in *Pearl's Secret* there are no imaginary replies to these questions. Possibly, the narrator does not want to imagine the replies; out of fear of renewed rejection, or he aims to get the reader to answer for herself: what would the reader do when faced with these circumstances, when confronted with those kinds of questions about their family, or about themselves?

The actual conversations taking place between the family members in *Pearl's Secret* are mostly of a nonaccusatory nature, although there is at times a negative tone. Certainly, there are instances in the texts where it becomes very apparent that a conversation is not easy, at times stagnating, and full of hesitancy. This is especially true when the narrator is discussing matters of racism with his white relative, Rita, who tells him that her sister had family connections to the Ku Klux Klan via her marriage (263).

The narrator realizes at this point in the encounter that even though on the outside he gets along with his newly found family members, there is a significant division between them that is not only generational, but that also relates to the mindset and social setting in which they grew up. Later in the conversation, more and more details of the white family's rejection of black people are brought to light, and while the narrator does not engage with this new knowledge in terms of picking a fight or even just openly rejecting the new family members, he understands that the unification of the families will be a struggle and retreats from the conversation. It appears that the white family members do not understand what is at stake in this situation—another mark of white privilege and its consequences.

Something similar becomes evident in *The Sweeter the Juice*. When the family also gathers, the members ask each other a variety of questions. These are questions that family members usually tend not to ask each other during family meetings because they are already familiar with these facts: where someone went to school, where they work, when they got married. Since the communication has been lacking for such a long time, even this kind of information is not available in the family. And even though these questions may appear rather casual, the conversation has to be undertaken with much sensitivity.

More importantly, though, the family members reacquaint themselves with the basic facts of each other's lives. Still, the impossibility to address some topics remains; and rather than bringing up these difficult issues such as the reason for leaving Grace behind, the participants in the meeting carefully navigate around them, as becomes evident in, for example, how similar the sisters look (Haizlip 1995, 265). The sisters, in turn, remain silent witnesses for the most part (265).

As indicated by her rather passive behavior, Grace, the mother's sister, has never learned to speak about her mixed-race background. While her family is aware of it at the time the conversation takes place, she has not been able to develop strategies to talk about what happened in the past. Possibly she is also afraid of being blamed for what has been done to Margaret, the narrator's mother, for the lack of family life before the sisters' reunion, for never admitting her African American heritage and denying her immediate family members this knowledge, and for never trying to get in touch with her sister.

Despite such difficulties, all of the narrators in the texts discussed here try to be open-minded and nonjudgmental about what they learn from their family members. This is so even if the knowledge they acquire is painful, and they are confronted with inconvenient or uncomfortable facts about their family's past, including decisions made by their ancestors. In each case, the narrators reach out to their extended families. The situations brought about by the narrators give rise to complex questions of accountability and of how to approach a person with similar origins, and yet a very different social and racial background (Henry 2001, 263). Identity takes shape in many different ways, and these differences may mean that trust and unity are not easy to build up or even achieve. At the same time, it is possible for individual family members to share details about each other's lives in conversation, to meet and to come to some understanding of what the other family's life is like, and how it has reached this point in the present.

At least according to this genre's agenda, separation cannot be easily overcome, but would require the same careful exploration that the narrators undertake in these texts, but in the form of a larger process. It would mean contemplating each step along the way, finding ways of relating to the past without hurting those one needs to be loyal to, and attempting to acknowledge the wrongs that have been committed.

There are passages in all of the texts where feelings of anger, regret, and/or sadness play an important role. The situations in which these feelings come up by and large relate to missed opportunities of the past, but also at times occur alongside the relief felt when the search—or a part of it—is successful, and a meeting with a family member works out. There is an uneasy tension in passages where the narrators attempt to discuss the ambivalence associated with the investigation with a significant person in their lives such as a spouse or child. The uneasiness is due to the fact that the narrators feel they are in a sense betraying those family members that have been loyal to them: their parents, their spouses.

In *Pearl's Secret*, the narrator directly confronts this concern when stating that he feels conflicted about his investment in the project (32). Other narrators do not voice these concerns, or only bring them up in retrospect. Possibly, they do not want to burden their family members, or perhaps they first need to contemplate and decide for themselves what exactly their newly acquired knowledge means before communicating it to those they are close to. In some cases, the narrators shy away from talking to their immediate family members too early for fear their search might fail and their relations on the other side of the "color line" might refuse to talk to them, or might not be open toward the investigation. This is especially true for the Ball family. In this text, the narrator experiences much resistance from his family members even after his research has been completed and the truth can no longer be denied.

In all the texts, and despite the personal contacts established in the narratives, the conclusion the narrators reach at the end of their search is rather bleak. Even when the secret is resolved and the narrators' family histories are revealed, there is no sense of unity between the families who have previously been divided by the "color line." Rather, the narrators conclude that despite having met their relatives, despite their feelings of success and fulfillment in finding and communicating with these people, they do not really build a common life together, but each party continues on their regular and established path (287). Haizlip (1995, 264) states that the story can now be told in its entirety, but due to their very different circumstances that does not mean the different branches of the family get reunited immediately or easily. Or, as Broyard (2007, 456) explains, she has to come to terms with the fact that her father's family might actually reject her.

Edward Ball's narrative ends with him asking forgiveness of the descendants of his family's slaves. Yet even his memoir has an ambivalent ending. While still in the United States, narrator had been confronted with the fact that forgiveness possibly comes too late because those who could have accepted his apologies are no longer alive (Ball 1999, 416). In the scene that stimulates this line of thought, Emily Frayer, an aged descendant of the Ball slaves, makes clear to him that while the present generation may ask forgiveness or contribute to reconciliation—or at least something akin to it—this comes too late for those generations who have suffered because those have passed away. From this perspective, it is impossible to forgive or make up for the past, as the opportunity has indeed passed. At the same time, there may be an opportunity to reconcile the present generations, who can still have an impact on the future. This is the perspective the narrator carries with him to Africa.

The instances of regret or ongoing disunity about whether reconciliation is possible at all add a complex layer to Ball's narrative, but by implication also to the other texts discussed under the header of the *memoir of the search*, namely, the ethical question of whose role and obligation it is to address the past and to potentially forgive. This ethical imperative resonates well with ongoing discussions about the meaning of the past in the 1990s and early 2000s. It is not clear whether, beyond telling the story, there is anything at all that the contemporary generation can do in order to make up for the past.

In *Slaves in the Family* this question is of particular importance, as the narrator travels to Africa in order to perform a forgiveness ceremony that unites him with the (African) descendants of the slave catchers and sellers, who also participated in slavery. In these families, participation in the slave trade has contributed to their high social status and, as the reader learns, also significant pride (437). When asked about whether the contemporary family would have the same status today without its earlier participation in the slave trade, the answer is seemingly easy: "'No,'" the narrator is told by Chief Modu, whose family was involved with slavery into the twentieth century, until the British forbade it (437). This detail again points to the transnationality of slavery. The African family must have risen to quite some status, with Chief Modu and his wife having traveled to the coronation of Queen Elizabeth II in 1953 (438). At the same time, the contemporary family members recognize that this was a business conducted by their ancestors out of greed, for improving their social standing and to demonstrate power: the ownership of people relates to status, the narrator is told in Africa (440–41). During this same conversation, they recognize that slavery is violent and wrong and that that it has caused much sorrow (441–42).

The narrator also enters into a conversation about forgiveness with the people he encounters during his trip to Sierra Leone. The contemporary descendants of the African slave traders recognize the shared heritage of slavery—a heritage their family shares with the Ball family, but also one that the African West Coast shares with the United States—and they ask the narrator what could possibly be done so many years after the end of slavery, such a long time after the evil was committed (442–43). The narrator offers an act of reconciliation, but also makes the Africans involved in the conversation aware that he does not represent the United States, but is coming as an individual, and out of his own personal interest (443).

This passage is inherently complicated as slavery has had very different effects in Africa as compared to the United States. The narrator does not necessarily include the discussion of power and white privilege that needs to be recognized when debating and understanding slavery from a transatlantic point of view. While pointing out that he is not a government representative, he does appear to believe that his individual act, his participation in the process of commemoration on the African coast, will contribute to a larger-scale change or healing. The ceremony takes place between a white descendant of slaveholders and the descendants of African slave catchers, asking forgiveness from a third party who is not represented in it at all. From a relational perspective, the ceremony may not be useful. It may lead the descendants of the guilty parties to feel better about themselves, as they absolve themselves from guilt they feel for the present situation.

There is no party from whom they can ask forgiveness: Those to whom injustice was done have passed away, and there are no descendants who represent this group on location in Sierra Leone. There is no strategy of absolution for the past, and knowing how the system worked does not change anything either—though it may mean that the secret behind the Ball family's success is evident now. Still, this part of the memoir is moving for the reader because it shows that ultimately both American and African parties—despite their very different backgrounds, cultures, and traditions—accept a shared responsibility for the past. At the same time, the lack of participation of those who were actually harmed, if this is even a possibility, is painful and rather remarkable in a text that focuses so much on finding the descendants of the Ball family's slaves.

The further the original separation is from the time of the narration, the harder it is for the narrators in these texts to actually reach the center of the betrayal because the patterns of neglect have built up over many generations. As the statement by Emily Frayer (417) mentioned above implies, those who should have been asked for their forgiveness are no longer there to give their approval. Nevertheless, the fact that an open conversation is conducted between those living now opens the way to dealing with the past and to overcoming some of the burdens associated with the silences.

The divide is deeper than across one or two generations—the *memoir of the search* points to the fact that it will likely take a long time to make up for what was lost if that is possible at all, and making up will be hard to accomplish if there is no real reason to build trust toward those who have originally betrayed those one feels close to as neglect and betrayal continue into the present. This imbalance, which is hard to reconcile, also becomes evident in the silent hopes of some of the narrators that those who once neglected their ancestors would be doing worse economically than the narrator's own family (Henry 2001, 280), or that those who neglected others were faced with their own demons they had created in their betrayal (Haizlip 1995, 266–67). The narrators thus in one sense voice a question of what could be called "fairness"—would it not be fair if those whose ancestors committed the sins were to fail, while those not guilty could recover from the past?

At the same time, the narrators have to understand that the contemporary generation, while able to talk about the past and lead complex dialogues about what their ancestors may have done and why, has not committed the crime. Thus, while these people can be held responsible for their present actions and their particular ways of approaching family members, and potentially also for their refusal to admit that their ancestors have committed wrongs, they cannot undo the past. Closure can only happen in the present, and even then, it cannot change the past. Closure also cannot make up for the past, or make good out of evil. Rather, it can only establish a different strategy of relating in the present.

While the narrators all report that they understand themselves and the past much better at the end of their search, their reaction toward their new family members introduced in the text is decidedly ambivalent, and understandably more so among those narrators who identify as black. This is something these narrators also struggle with as they know, consciously or unconsciously, that they should not be so ambivalent toward their own kin, but rather take a stance in leading more open conversations about the past, and with their newfound family members. One such way they take a stance is by telling the story itself and in their words: instead of continuing to silence the past, the narrators give it a voice and seek to find ways of understanding it, contextualizing it, and placing it into a framework that may not make it relatable but at least graspable.

In these terms, the disclosure of the family secret has implications for the white as well as for the black family in the story. Both sides are newly able to confront a taboo in their family history, but in that very same moment essentially contribute to the taming and silencing the gist of the story by reducing it to a narrative that can be broken down by way of one particular and closely circumscribable narrative: a genre of its own, even. These texts make a statement about family, about race, about the United States and its dealing with the past in a particular moment. But they also establish a rather conformist way of making this statement that will be rather difficult to transcend in order to make other statements, to tell stories that do not come with a family secret or a family that can be met on the supposedly other side of the "color line."

PASSING AS THEME, *PASSING* AS STRATEGY

As this chapter has shown, the *memoir of the search* in its investigation of the family secret follows a specific and definable set of literary conventions, including a predefined narrative pattern. This predefined characteristic of the genre makes the storylines of these texts appear rather predictable and in those terms normative after one has read a few of these texts. To simplify, there is a family secret about *passing* from black to white and abandonment that challenges the narrator's perception of herself and her family that can be and needs to be investigated to supposedly find closure. The process of investigation is guided by more or less genealogical methods and leads to the establishment of a variety of difficult conversations across the "color line."

While the final aim—solving the secret and being absolved of one's past—is not reached, the narrators arrive at both a more complete picture of their family's past and a more secure sense of self. Here, the genre points to notions of self-care and the multicultural ideals of the time in which the novels were published. These texts are very much in tune with narratives of self-discovery: The idea that you can get to the center of your truest inner self by careful inquiry. It is characteristic of these texts that the self is not found in isolation or meditation, but rather through communication with others and through strategies of relating. The texts play with the idea that everything should be subject to open negotiation, that it is necessary to disclose one's family's past in order to feel complete, and that it is indeed possible (and desirable) to do such a thing.

They also suggest that if one searches long enough, a truth about one's family's past can be found even if this past has heretofore been silenced due to slavery and its multiple legacies, including long-term division. While these texts attempt to provide a family history for those who have not had such a coherent narrative of their family, this apparent disclosure of a family secret largely remains subject to very specific narrative confines and conventions. There is, in essence, not a new story in each of the texts discussed here, but rather the same story in several variations. It is the story being told by the genre—story and genre depend on each other in these terms.

The *memoir of the search* contributes to establishing a rather normative profile for black/white mixed-race family histories that conforms to rather conventional narratives of familial belonging within American culture. These families, as suggested here, are plagued by secrets that are perceived even if they are not known or understood. In turn, the secrets are due to specific forms of abandonment due to *passing*, and they lead to the desire of the contemporary generation to be reunited with lost family members as they cannot experience fulfillment on their own.

By finding their family on the other side of the "color line," the families portrayed within the genre correspond to the ideal of the large extended family. They are fit to blend themselves into the mainstream, albeit with the limitation that these stories do not come with a happy ending. At the same time, the tribulations and disappointments told of in these texts are likely those that would also appear in other kinds of family narratives—on this end, would they only speak of harmony, there would not be a story to tell.

Chapter 3

Media of Memory
Generating the Family

In their inquiries relating to the unraveling of the family secret, the narrators in the *memoir of the search* emphasize that they feel the need to undertake their research because of a lack in their lives: There is something missing from their family story and family circle, their family is not "whole." This perceived lack or absence is a prime motif in the genre and goes hand in hand with the motif of the family secret, which in turn is the reason for this lack. Upon closer observation, it becomes clear that the absence of an extended family in the *memoir of the search* also means a lack of documentation available to these textual American families, through which they would negotiate and publicly celebrate their identities.

The genre has found its answer to this absence of traditional family media. This chapter shows that the *memoir of the search* is not only characterized by its autobiographical narrative positioning and its thematic content and structure consisting of the exploration of the family in its complex relation to racial mixedness, but that it also features specific ordering devices to construct a genealogical set of data and a visual archive of mixed-race families in the United States since the nineteenth century. The practices employed in the memoirs are well in tune with American families and their processes of identity construction at large. Genealogy is one of America's favorite past times and an ever-growing business; the United States is, as social anthropologist Sarah Abel (2018) claims, "a nation obsessed by genealogy." Genealogical projects take place in churches, in schools, in clubs; for many African American children the encounter with genealogy is a moment when "they first [feel] aware of *not knowing* their family origins" (ibid.; italics in original), when they learn that their family is different because it is not clear where, when, and how exactly their ancestors came to America. By implication, to be a white American commonly means to have this type of information readily available, which places a burden on the African American population: all too often, to be mainstream American means to be in possession of this type of information.

Family memories are not only present in the form of genealogical data, of course. Families often possess family albums, sometimes going back not just one or two, but multiple generations. These albums archive past moments that mattered in the context of the family's identity formation; they are storytelling devices and can be used to introduce others to the family. *Passing* and the breaking of family ties represent a serious disruption of the story, as well as of the family's visual archive. If a part of the family has become isolated from another due to *passing*, these members of the family will not be part of the family tree or family album. The narrators in the *memoir of the search* struggle with these absences and try to complete the available data and material in order to build a more inclusive archive.

DNA testing, which plays a role in the memoirs, is a much more recent technology than family trees and family photographs with their long tradition in the Western world. DNA tests make claims about an individual's local origin and ancestry. Thus, like genealogy and photography, DNA testing contributes to a supposedly more complete idea of the self and to the possibility of reevaluating and reconstructing the family and its multigenerational history.

Certainly, the media of memory included in the *memoir of the search* serve to generate an imagery of mixed-race American families: Unlike common genealogical practice that is often used to silence the racial dimension, these memoirs have developed a set of strategies to include, to narrate, and to visualize mixed-race identities using these devices at the turn of the millennium. In the *memoir of the search*, just like in other texts emerging out of postslavery conditions, in which genealogical media are used in order to deal with the past (Handley 2000, 4).

In the *memoir of the search*, the inclusion of family photographs and family trees aids the establishment of an intergenerational and extended, multibranched family where—due to the previous absence of communication between the different branches of the family—there had been none before. The introduction to an intergenerational and multibranched family leads both narrator and reader to a critical examination of the interdependence of blackness and whiteness in the United States throughout American history. Just like the written text—a narrative about the resolution of a family secret including the encounter with previously absent relatives—the visual media contribute to the process of resolving the family secret and to generating an extended family for the narrator to relate to. Where there used to be a nuclear family, a large circle of cousins, aunts, and uncles emerges through the process of the narrator's investigation. In the case of Ball's text, starting out with a larger family than the others, the white family is confronted with the presence of the descendants of their ancestors who were enslaved, changing the family narrative and family structure previously built on whiteness alone. As family members become newly included in the family story, the family tree and the family album grow. DNA testing then serves to extend the mixed-race legacy beyond the singular family and beyond the national context, as the memoirs also look back to Europe and to Africa, albeit in most cases indirectly.

Photography and genealogy point to the challenges the families constructed in the narratives have to deal with. As powerful transmitters of intergenerational memory, family trees and photographs order family history. With supposedly factual clarity, these media show who is considered part of the family both before and after the narrator's quest. They contribute to the normalization of racial transgression across American history and to steadily locating such complex histories in the middle class, but they also point to existing "anxieties about genealogy, narrative authority and racial difference" (Handley 2000, 5) of their time.

The narratives speak to the intertwining of history and memory: In their physicality, these medial forms connect what Aleida Assmann (2006, 102) has termed the material dimension of memory to its social dimension. In working with different medial realizations—genealogy and photography—the texts analyzed here make a statement about the possibilities and impossibilities of addressing the past and compel their readers to reflect upon the effect of presences and absences of memory for the individual family and the nation. Once again it is claimed, albeit indirectly, that it is possible to create a "complete" family regardless of heritage and socialization and that the supposed completion of the family will simultaneously lead to a resolution of traumas of the past.

The narratives seem to work under the assumption that to be a family, this type of documentation and analysis is necessary. To be oneself in these texts, therefore, means also to document the self by carefully measuring, calculating, and taking stock of all its different layers. The narrator again becomes an explorer and discoverer.

The incorporation of genealogical devices such as family trees and photographs of people from the different families and generations links the past to the present, as do DNA tests that make it possible to locate an individual's origin more precisely in terms of a specific place or region the ancestors are supposedly from. As media, family trees and photographs counteract the notion that to be a family means either being "black" or "white"; indeed, a family can be both. To be a family means to have more than one line of ancestry. This idea of mixedness productively relates back to the titles typically given to these memoirs that suggest that an American family can be both, black and white. The notion of an essential mixedness of course also works well in connection to DNA tests that prove there is no "purity," but that every human being is of mixed descent. For ideological reasons, the United States has been built on the assumption that every person is either "black" or "white," but these texts focus on the distinctive experience of families where this is not the case. Purity is a fiction that can no longer be maintained.

In the *memoir of the search*, "black" and "white" are no longer mutually exclusive categories. Serving as quasi-visual proof that an act of black/ white race mixing has happened and has had visible and/or measurable consequences, family trees, photographs, and DNA tests make clear that the family secret explored by narrators is not a secret because it is invisible, but because family members have benefited from its keeping for ideological and political reasons. While mixed heritage is "visible," for example, in a family member's skin tone or in the results of a DNA test, it is absent from *speech* before the narrator explores it and communication is established between the different branches of the family sharing a common ancestry. The lack of language to address the topic of race in all of its dimensions is a widespread motif in the *memoir of the search*, as once a dialogue is initiated, there do not seem to be any adequate terms to describe what has happened in these families.

As George Handley (2000, 33) states, "knowledge cannot be separated from power any more easily than narrative truth can be separated from narrative authority." When the narrators in the memoirs take up the topic of racial mixedness, they try to attain control and authority regarding the discourse, being well aware that such research also always implies taking into account the role of the current generation and their obligations toward the past in the present (33). The secrecy central to the text is a trope indicating that neither the singular family nor the larger, national family has found productive ways to properly address this past in which they are still complicit. Despite all the available proof, the crossing of supposed racial boundaries still *is* a secret, but one that can literally not be overlooked any longer. Thus, the media included can also be understood as meta-commentaries on this phenomenon. By the same token, the texts and their media help make the past speakable, but in doing so, they simultaneously make it controllable, measurable, and supposedly "knowable." Constructing the self via these storytelling devices is a political act.

FAMILY TREES: FINDING ROOTS

Family trees establish a family's genealogy and, because of their popularity, are often equated with genealogy as a whole. As visual ordering devices they specify origin, times, and locations where people have met, gathered, and loved, where they have been in touch with each other and in each other's lives: "[t]he family tree is a model of genealogical relations through generational time" (Nash 2017). Family trees attest to spatial and temporal connections between individuals. Following a rather simple, tree-like structure to indicate connections—such as marriage or brotherhood—between people, they make the family as a system visible and viable. They can also be part of "an imaginative exercise in considering the place of ancestors within historical contexts" (ibid.). In this way, family trees attest to the "truth" of a birth, a union, or a marriage, and to its (possible) results, for example, the children born in a marriage between a man and a woman. The practice of adoption, where filiation has no biological basis, challenges genealogy and its traditional devices.

The family tree supposedly depicts the family as a whole and across several generations. Generally, if a person is represented in the family tree, they are recognized as part of the family. If absent, then they are not family. White planters routinely denied such connections, for example, when patriarchs had raped and fathered children with their female slaves. Whenever a descendant of mixed heritage was not considered part of the family, this person simply did not become a part of the family tree, and in turn there were no further duties or obligations toward that person. Genealogical methods, and specifically family trees, have by implication contributed to and strengthened the historical unspeakability of race, and how race intervenes in family history in various ways.

That being stated, family trees are not objective artifacts and require interpretation. They are produced by and produce (or disrupt) families in turn. There is no obligation—except maybe a moral one—to include a specific person or a specific branch in the family tree; rather, an active process of selective inclusion lies behind its making. Essentially, the person tasked with constructing the family tree makes conscious decisions about who is represented, what information is included, and what is disregarded. This individual has the power and authority to define the family. The reasons for this person's decisions are, of course, not shown in the family tree. In the case of a family secret—of *passing*, of a relationship outside of marriage that resulted in children, and so on—there will certainly always be absences in the family tree. Consequently, the making of a family tree stresses and even produces families and their genealogies (Nash 2004, 5).

Family trees have often been used to justify or advance one's superior social status. It is no surprise then that royal status is usually hereditary. Julia Watson (1996, 297) argues that genealogy's "fundamental assumption is categorical: Humans are defined by who and where we are 'from'—in terms such as stock, blood, class, race." While certainly this idea of categorizing individuals plays into the use of family trees in the *memoir of the search*, at the same time, the use of genealogy in the genre by and large turns away from such established patterns of silencing race mixing. Instead of demonstrating purity of stock, the family trees in these texts represent a verification of contacts—relationships leading to children—across the "color line." These contacts have been unspeakable before and kept secret in order for the family to remain stable; specifically, in families identifying as white and wishing to keep their white privilege.

Commonly, genealogical methods stand in opposition to egalitarian or democratic visions of American society—genealogy "values origin, stock, race, blood, in an increasingly heterogeneous world" (298) and thus becomes used to focus on purity rather than diversity. These social practices clearly stand in line with conservative, patriarchal, and heteronormative assumptions about what the family is or can be. According to Watson, genealogical practice works as "a necessary fiction" (299) in the contemporary period characterized by complexity and the displacement of individuals. Genealogical practice appears to be a science, and one enabling neutral statements. Thus, it serves as orientation where orientation is lost. It creates stability in a world of supposed chaos.

Despite its claims to neutrality, genealogy's gaze is defined by vested interests; it strongly "mistrusts 'family secrets' as a subjective record that contaminates the preservation and transmission of accurate family history" (299). By this token, the process of making gaps visible in the family tree, and then filling these gaps with previously absent information, is one of the liberating functions of genealogy (Nash 2004, 6).

Through its use of genealogical methods, the *memoir of the search* indicates the specific discontinuities and absences in the family history due to race, and allows for the inclusion of formerly excluded family members. In its incorporation of family trees as they existed before and after the narrator's investigation, the genre at first documents the mutual exclusiveness of blackness and whiteness: It exposes the United States as a society of hypodescent, meaning that children of a supposedly "higher-caste and a lower-caste parent may be assigned the lower-parent status" (Sollors 1999, 249). In the United States, commonly, race is permanent; it is the only social category that supposedly cannot change (257). By using family trees that display the mixedness of families, the *memoir of the search* then effectively ends the exclusivity of the white American middle-class family now and into the past: there is a whole new, more diverse history to be mapped, which includes this knowledge and awareness.

At the same time, the fact that supposedly complete family trees are part of these texts counteracts the notion of a new history, as it suggests that this liberation has already occurred. The previous gaps are rendered invisible, as the family on the other side of the "color line" is included into the family tree without further remarks or explanation. Such a family tree suggests that there is a sense of proximity, that these family members lived alongside each other in the past, and that they do so now. It is important to remember that the existence of the family tree alone says little about the actual quality of the relationships within it. There is no automatic sense of connection or obligation due to the existence of branches on the family tree; it merely documents that the biological connection itself exists.

In the *memoir of the search*, the mixed-race family trees emphasize diversity. However, as documents contributing to a more multicultural understanding of the family, they only become readable in conjunction with the narrative as a whole: They are best studied alongside the reading process. In the written text, the narrators provide detailed historical and social information about their family background, for example, about the cities where their ancestors resided, their income patterns, or society's attitudes toward several issues, including race, during their ancestors' lifetime. The narrators also explain who in the family had children with each other, thereby disclosing the family secret. The inclusion of family trees into these narratives then serves as additional validation of the information and also provides a visual reference point and shortcut for the rather complex and long-winded family histories related in the narratives. As a result of the inclusion of family trees, the narrative as a whole acquires its historiographical, research-oriented quality, as if to show that it is not merely a *memoir*, but rather a sophisticated study which measures up, if not to historical scholarly research, then at least to dedicated investigative journalism, instead of merely personal perception: Genealogy has documentary functions and thus at least seemingly goes beyond personal details (Watson 1996, 299).

The inclusion of genealogical data and the use of its investigative methods including the construction of family trees tie the *memoir of the search* to its time and social context of emergence. The growth of peoples' interest in the topic of genealogy following the publication of *Roots* coincided with the emergence of self-help guides to genealogy that specifically address the African American experience, revealing a need for exploration of the past both within the African American community as well as beyond. In the introduction to one of these guides published around the high time of the *memoir of the search*, Dee Parmer Woodtor's *Finding a Place Called Home: A Guide to African-American Genealogy and Historical Identity* (1999), Velma Maia Thomas explains that "[a]s African Americans, those whom this nation has doubted and discounted, we are pressed to prove, to produce records that validate our existence and history" (Thomas 1999, ix). Apparently, the main assumption behind this is that something only happened if it is properly documented and made to fit into established storylines.

At the same time, the history of slavery and its aftermath is not easy to tell, as often there is no such accurate documentation of facts to rely on because of the institution of slavery itself, and the subsequent system of segregation. The unavailability of records in those terms means that a precondition of mainstream belonging and by implication, of whiteness, is not met. Still, it appears that for oral history to become believable, specific historical information supporting any such claims is necessary—not least because financial or other claims are potentially affiliated with the verification of family stories. The difficulty of finding the "right" kind of proof for sexual contact across the "color line" is documented very well in the case of the Jefferson–Hemings controversy—a family with very high visibility and much at stake in terms of their perception by the public.

Arguably, the *memoir of the search* includes family trees in part because of convention—a "real" family needs a "real" family tree—and in order to speak to the apparently growing cultural need for the resolution of family secrets about race mixing and its consequences. By using codified terms and tools, the memoirs become studies of intergenerational race mixing rather than personal or familial stories. At the end of the twentieth century, the normalization of mixed-race identity begins with its insertion into an existing, rather conventional American model of the extended heterosexual family. This factor severely limits the disruptive and scandalizing potential of the texts. Instead of overcoming the boundaries of conventional family narratives, the *memoir of the search* uses well-known narrative and cultural techniques to make a statement about the existence of mixed-race families, pointing to the laws of speakability at this time.

GENEALOGY AND AUTOBIOGRAPHY

Julia Watson (1996) argues that from the outside genealogical practice and autobiographical narrative share many characteristics. Still, they are very different formats of family representation. Autobiography, generally told in retrospect, is open to the diversity of memories of different people and generations, as well as to changes and reversals, while genealogy resists these tendencies with positivistic detachment (303). In the *memoir of the search*, genealogical methods serve to support rather than to establish the narrative; they are illustrative rather than generative. In contrast to the claims to scientific validity often connected to the genealogical impulse, these devices acquire an affective quality in the *memoir of the search*. They indicate the need for reversing the established story of how the family came into being, developing a decidedly more inclusive perspective insofar as they unite a supposedly "white" and a supposedly "black" family. Instead of excluding personal judgment to underline the scientific qualities of genealogy, the narrator of the *memoir of the search* is telling a deeply personal story, often to the point of "baring all" and sparing (almost) nothing.

The family story is added to by the family trees through which the intersections and meeting points of former generations become visible. The quest for roots and for a more complete family genealogy in the *memoir of the search* signifies more than the desire to find an identity rooted in one's local and familial origins. While certainly "ancestry is routinely viewed as a meaningful, legitimate, valuable and natural source of personal and collective identity" (Nash 2003, 182), the narrators in these texts, consciously or subconsciously, also conduct their research because they feel entitled to a past, to a story addressing the injustices committed by their ancestors, as well as the little acts of heroism that defined their lives.

The impulse "to make the story whole" centrally drives their quest (Ball 1999, 14). This characteristic of the texts ultimately connects back to the ethical dimensions of the *memoir of the search*, as well as to the structure of the family secret itself. Still, the question of what a family is remains—is it a shared family tree or, rather than that, a shared story to tell and a shared sense of obligation to truth?

GENEALOGY WITH A TWIST

At present, African Americans often undertake genealogical research to find more information about the origins of their African ancestors. It is of interest where these ancestors came from exactly, on which ship they were brought to the New World, and on which plantations they may have worked at what time and in what roles. Genealogy serves to build a personal connection to history by exercising these methods, and by creating links to the past not available through evidence or inaccessible due to matters of migration and suppression (Watson 1996, 306–307).

For African Americans, genealogical work goes along with specific challenges inherent in its subject matter because these practices and methods, unsurprisingly, "have been formed around normative WASP subjects who first invaded and ordered the Americas" (308). Descendants of African slaves who had been brought to the country against their will could not have elite status and, in turn, on the basis of the absence of a genealogy, could be denied humanity and their status as family members. These specific absences characterize them as black.

In the *memoir of the search* the expected difficulties of finding personal connections to Africa do not play a role at all. The investigation for actual African ancestors who were brought to the United States during the time of slavery, by and large, is neglected. With the emergence of these narratives highly focused on finding relatives alive and living in the twentieth century, there is an increased awareness that the potentially meaningful connections to the past need to be found, made, and established in the present. This does not mean that slavery is no longer relevant to the narrators or their families, but the focus of the investigation clearly remains within the United States and on the present moment, rather than being an attempt to establish a connection to a perceived ancestral homeland in Africa.

While in the *memoir of the search*, the genealogical project still includes the three dimensions of "time, place, and perspective" (Woodtor 1999, 7), the specific connections to this triad differ significantly from how the genealogical impulse has played out in the past—here, genealogy is used to find symbolic "roots" in the United States. Finding a *griot* in a distant time and place is no longer necessary for the narrators in the *memoir of the search*, since they think of the United States as their home: their "roots" are in America.

Consequentially, they only follow the multiple branches of their "American" family trees. The claims these narrators make about their own situatedness in the United States are radically different from those voiced in *Roots*. If *Roots* is "the story of nearly every *African American* family" (11; italics mine), then texts such as *The Sweeter the Juice* or *One Drop*, texts subsumed under the header of the genre of the *memoir of the search*, are more than that. While these narratives certainly deal with the complex meanings of being black and white in America, their main emphases are on the meaning of being *mixed*, of being both black *and* white in the United States, and of living a life that acknowledges this mixedness. In these terms Ball's narrative stands out, since the narrator identifies clearly as white but is very aware of his family's complicated legacy of slavery. He feels that the descendants of the family's slaves are his own family members in some sense as well. Additionally, Broyard's text demonstrates how a supposedly "white" family can also be mixed without being aware of it.

In his article "Black and White: American Genealogy, Race, and Popular Response," Eric Gardner (2003, 148) suggests that texts such as *Slaves in the Family* or *The Sweeter the Juice* indeed "represent important revisions of the idea and place of genealogy in America" in that they include formerly absent family members, but also in their popularization of the topic of race and genealogy. These texts bring to the forefront issues that are traditionally silenced by genealogical investigations (149). Now, genealogy is used to speak to questions of race and color, as well as to class, and at its very center, albeit within strict genre confines.

In the texts, a mixed-race history of the United States is explicated using the example of one specific family. Unlike average white American family trees that perpetuate hierarchy, the family trees in these texts are more diverse and include "multiple progenitors and multiple descendants" (153). This extends the focus of the family tree and corresponds with the narrative scope of the genre. The use of family trees also makes the texts discussed here different from *Roots*, which relies on the primary ancestor, the African *griot*, as an authority (Watson 1996, 314).

While the multiplicity of ancestors is not a unique characteristic of the *memoir of the search*, what defines these narratives as a different type of text, a genre in its own right, is the shift of focus from the past to the present. The texts all make evident that decisions made in the past—whether distant or not so distant—have shaped and continue to shape not only the people who were alive at the time, but also the current generation. Here, the *memoir of the search* is firmly committed to its nonfictional stance, remaining located in the present at all times.

Their use of genealogy "as a mode to begin representing 'blackness' and 'whiteness' in a dialogue—a dialogue that begins to listen to the cries of critics like bell hooks, AnnLouise Keating, and Toni Morrison to contextualize representations of race and to vocalize how whiteness and power shape such representations" is a defining quality of these texts (Gardner 2003, 154). The notion of a dialogue across boundaries of time, space, and skin color is not only central to the narrators' attempts to come clean with the past.

Implicitly, the question "What makes a family?" is addressed and given one possible answer in the figure of the family tree. A family is like a tree: It is stable, and it has one point of origin and a "root" system that sustains the members and feeds into their stories. At the same time the family spreads out like the different branches of the tree. The branches may not always be in contact with each other, but they are floating on the same air. They share one environment, the nation. Depending on location, the branches will be affected by circumstances in different ways. The tree is a weirdly fitting image to talk about the families in the text and the lives they have led.

RACE MIXING AT THE ROOT

As a genre, the *memoir of the search* extends the meaning of family by crossing the "color line" through the narrator's process of researching the family members on the supposed "other side." In these terms, the family trees are not used to confine the circle of the family or to demonstrate pedigree but to visualize racial mixing and its legacy up to the present. The family trees are inclusive of *Otherness*, as they declare that the supposed *Other* is a family member. In that sense, they speak against the artificial separation between the black and the white communities—they are the same community and the same family.

The family portrayed in this genre comes into being because the supposed "color line" was crossed: There is no purity of origins. The family trees used in the genre for the most part begin with the white ancestor who migrated into the New World, and they do not look back any further. In Ball's *Slaves in the Family*, the manifold family trees included begin with a slave coming to America and settling on a Ball plantation—proof of the Ball empire's origins. Still, in any case studied here, the family trees focus on connections and meeting points between black and white in the United States as instances of building the larger American family: families with American family trees, originating in the country's complex history of race mixing.

The use of family trees in Neil Henry's *Pearl's Secret* is not only the most compelling with regard to the texts discussed here, but also in relation to the genre as a whole, and will be analyzed in greater detail to measure the specific significance of these documents. *Pearl's Secret* includes two different family trees, one in a separate section at the beginning of the narrative, and another at the end of the text. The first family tree is referred to as "beginning family tree" (Henry 2001, 16), the latter as "complete family tree" (314–15). When comparing the two, the family has been significantly extended for the latter tree.

Early on in the narrative, the narrator is not aware whether there are any family members alive on the "white" side of his family—these members cannot be part of the "beginning family tree" that focuses on the African American side of the Henry family, the side of the family the search starts out with, and in which the narrator was socialized. Since this family tree is supposedly not "complete," the reader can assume that there is significant pressure to "complete" the family. This also suggests that the complete family is knowable: It is actually possible to conduct enough research to be able to fill all the gaps. Certainly, this is not generally true for all families, and specifically not for all African American families.

At the root of both family trees in *Pearl's Secret* is A. J. Beaumont as the quasi-patriarch and founder of the family. Even though A. J. Beaumont lived in Europe before he came to the United States as an adult and settled in the South, no European ancestors or relatives are listed in the family tree. These are also not part of the narrator's investigative project, which centers on the United States and the patriarch's life and descendants after immigration. At the root of both trees, in the "beginning" as well as in the "complete" family tree, A. J. Beaumont is shown as the father of children by two women, one of whom is of African descent, Laura Brumley. The other woman is of European descent, Mary Ann Simms. The ancestors of these two women are also not part of this family tree, even though theoretically the narrator could have investigated these ancestors as well. But going further back in time or including any further branches is not a priority.

Rather, this family comes into being at the moment of a union between one person identifying as "white" and another person identifying as "black." This act significantly impacts the family's future due to the birth of Pearl, the mixed child of A. J. Beaumont and Laura Brumley. As is true for the *memoir of the search* in general, in this family tree no mark of ethnic origins, race, or skin color serves as identifiers. These factors only become clear when reading the text. Nevertheless, in conjunction with the narrative itself, the family tree in *Pearl's Secret* is fascinating to look at because it so openly points toward the union of black and white as its point of origin, though it certainly says nothing about the voluntary or involuntary character of this encounter. The union A. J. Beaumont had with Laura Brumley still resonates at the time of writing: There are descendants of the child they had who are alive in the 1990s. One such descendant is the narrator himself. At the same time, there is a second family: the white Beaumonts.

The "beginning family tree," just like the "complete family tree," extends from the nineteenth century into the time of the narrative, but it only includes the contemporary generation on the side of the family descended from Pearl. The other side ends with the children A. J. Beaumont fathered with his later wife Mary Ann Simms. By contrast, the "complete family tree" at the end of the text contains much more information on both sides of the family and shows how many family members the "complete" family actually includes, and, by implication, how many descendants of A. J. Beaumont, the immigrant and Confederate, there really are.

The "complete" family tree supposedly shows all descendants of Beaumont with their own children and children's children, continuing into the 1990s. A. J. Beaumont unites them all; there is a common figure all of them can look back to, independent of their skin color or personal racial identification, as well as other factors from their political attitude to sexual orientation. Beaumont almost appears to be some type of white griot. While the connections established between the different people located on the same family tree might suggest that these are several families living side by side with each other, invested in the same causes, this was not actually the case. The black and white families differ from each other significantly due to the routes taken by the ancestors and the narrators are aware of this.

The paths of the two families already diverged in the nineteenth century, and this separation continues to this day. For a long time, there was no communication between the two branches of the same tree. This only changed because of the activities undertaken by the narrator in the text, who extended his hand to those on the other side of the tree. In the Henry family, the agency comes from an unlikely side. The black-identifying descendant of A. J.

Beaumont could have just as well decided that he wanted nothing to do with his white ancestor or with his descendants on the white side of the "color line." He is not obliged to be interested in them, but instead his own desire (or obsession) drives him to create a more comprehensive family narrative. Certainly, it is helpful that he feels firmly located in the black community and within his own family, because he goes on to be confronted with some painful truths during his research that could otherwise literally "uproot" him and make him feel isolated or even helpless or inferior.

Through this investigative project, both families, black and white, learn that there are more descendants of A. J. Beaumont than they were previously aware of. In effect, the family tree helps render questions of race invisible, because, unless it is embedded in the narrative, there would be no way to tell the reasons for the formation of two different families originating from the same ancestor, A. J. Beaumont. This may also potentially signify that matters of skin color and race do not matter, though this idea is strangely at odds with the memoir's general argument. By just looking at the family tree, one could possibly assume that Beaumont simply married twice and raised families with both of these women. That family loyalties were disrupted, bearing consequences into the time of the writing of the narrative, is not shown in the family tree itself.

In *Pearl's Secret*, the family originates in the American South and only comes into being as an extended family in the act of crossing the "color line." This unifies black and white families. It is also this act that renders this family American. The supposed completeness of the family tree is achieved via the investigation of the past through the lens of the present, through the interrogation of contemporary family members and the study of documents from the past.

The use of genealogy and genealogical methods links the *memoir of the search* to texts George B. Handley has subsumed under the header of *post-slavery narratives*. Handley (2000, 15) argues that these kinds of texts are very much concerned with genealogy. He explains that this is related to the fact that genealogy was used to hide or deny the connections between black and white people, and in order to silence demands for black citizenship. Now this trend is reversed in order to point to the previous absence. This observation is significant for the *memoir of the search* as well: Certainly it can be argued that the patriarchy is dismantled with the deconstruction of traditional notions of the family at large, such as in the idea that a family can only be black *or* white, but not both. At the same time the patriarchal structure of the family is alive and well, as the origin of the family is attributed to a white male immigrant progenitor.

According to Handley, the use of genealogy by postslavery writers serves the purpose of using what was formerly a master's tool against the master in order to expose what the ruling class of the "Old South" or the plantation belt, as well as their descendants, have always tried to hide from view: the "impurity" of the population, and the fact that those to whom they denied humanity, citizenship, and equal rights are their own *relatives*, their children and children's children. In Handley's words, this helps in order "to point to the miscegenated roots of their nations" (16) and to point to the vexed relationship between personal unfreedom and the emergence of a white national consciousness in the plantation belt. This mechanism therefore stands in direct relation to the idea of the parallel emergence of nationalism and chattel slavery—the recognition that American freedom was built on the backs of the unfree.

Significantly, these texts use genealogy "to follow biology rather than ideology" (17), in order to be able to point to issues that were previously unspeakable because they relate to issues considered illegitimate. By taking matters into their own hands, the narrators in these texts attempt to deconstruct the idea of purity. But at the same time, such use of genealogical practice may be less liberating than it may seem at first sight, as genealogy in this use might lead to new strategies of excluding the other (17), becoming evident, for example, in the exclusion of those whose families cannot be made to conform to the traditional shape of the family tree, or those whose family history does not contain the success narrative of the American Dream (see following chapter).

In the *memoir of the search*, the process of Americanization is understood to mean racial mixing, instead of the colonization of the slave body. At the core of this story is always a more or less romantic love story, for example, that of A. J. Beaumont and Laura Brumley, of a young Irish girl encountering a black man and leaving her family behind out of love for him. None of the texts discussed here addresses the subject of the rape of black women by white men. At first this may seem a little surprising, as generally, "[r]ace mixing is acknowledged more readily if it happened in the past and if it is likely that the interaction was forced rather than freely chosen" (Pabst 2003, 191). But acknowledgment of a forced interaction in this case would mean to compromise the idealized concept of the American family constructed via the family trees. The hesitation on the part of the *memoir of the search* to contest established notions of the family and the self becomes further evident when turning to the second visual medium of memory included as a standard device in these texts: family photography.

FAMILY ALBUMS: PICTURING THE FAMILY

Like the family trees included in the narratives, the family photographs form a separate section within the text: They are an addendum to the text, often printed on special paper and commonly in black and white. They are usually placed not at the beginning or end of the text, like the family trees, but rather tend to form a separate section (or several separate sections) within the books. This may not only be due to technical considerations, but also it also literally embeds these media into the storylines as the narrative progresses. The photography sections could even be classified as paratextual features within the genre. The text would be understandable without the photography section, but the photographs would not contain the same meaning without their being embedded into the written text.

Along with the family trees, the photographs are a material and visual manifestation of the family secret explored in the *memoir of the search*. They may also stimulate questions about the family that do not necessarily come to mind when looking at family trees. For example: Was the person in the photograph happy when it was taken? What was this person thinking about? What is the context of the photograph? Photography can trigger storytelling as well as an affective response to the story told in the text: it may even create a sense of empathy in the reader.

The practice of photography emerged and developed alongside the growth and changes of these families—it started in the nineteenth century, when the families originated according to their family trees. Photography and its steady advancement into today is the result of what photographer Stuart Franklin (2016, 5) refers to as the "documentary impulse," meaning "the passion to record moments we experience and wish to preserve, the things we witness and might want to reform, or simply the people, places or things we find remarkable." Photographs provide insights into private moments, but also into public ones.

In the *memoir of the search*, photographs serve as powerful reminders that the "color line" is not an abstract political term, but that it also has a powerful visual dimension. This is true even though the photographs in the memoirs are conventionally kept in black and white, in a sense equalizing all the individuals portrayed: it becomes impossible to tell, for example, where exactly an individual lived, or when. Their reading and understanding is a matter of a racialized gaze that has a long tradition in the United States: "Visual culture was fundamental not only to racist classification but also to racial reinscription and the re-construction of racial knowledge in the nineteenth and early twentieth centuries" (Smith 2004, 3), a legacy that continues into this day and is evident in photographic practice. For the longest time, European and North American documentary photographers used photography in order to document differences between "types" of people. It played a role in the establishment of the colonizer's gaze, has been employed to give proof to difference, and was also used together with other assumptions, for example, about hereditary genetics (Franklin 2016, 32–35).

While the narrators do not directly comment on the family trees, they do specifically address the photographs, considering them in a quasi-ekphrastic way. In some texts, a photograph inspires the narrator's interest in researching the role of race and race mixing within the family history. In *Pearl's Secret*, it is the photograph of the white ancestor A. J. Beaumont, along with his obituary and a letter from 1901 that he sent to his daughter Pearl (also included in the photography section of the text), that intrigues the narrator to such a degree that he finally sets off to discover his family heritage (Henry 2001, 9–11).

In *The Sweeter the Juice*, the narrator comments repeatedly on family photography, for example, when stating that her aunt's disassociation from her past, and, by implication, her blackness, becomes evident in the absence of family photographs in her own home (Haizlip 1995, 244)—photographs that might have made her mixed heritage obvious even to casual and outside observers, and even more so to her immediate family members, who knew nothing about the act of her *passing* and leaving behind her extended family. This narrator also designs a "white corner" (266) in her own home to include photographs of her newly found family members, alluding to the fact that these people are her family, but that they still deserve special designation as "white" because of the complex legacy of *passing* and neglect that cannot easily be resolved. At the same time, she feels they deserve to be permanently present in her own home. She remains connected to them despite these complications.

The use of photographs in the narratives complicates established notions of victim and perpetrator: In *Pearl's Secret*, the inclusion of A. J. Beaumont, the Confederate into the black Henry family album poses complex ethical questions about the meaning and importance of family, as well as about the obligations that come with being a family. Beaumont is not only a white man who left the narrator's great-great-grandmother and their daughter alone; he is also an ancestor, and there is nothing in his carefully photographed face that spells "neglect" or "evil." The understanding that a person's transgressions or mistakes cannot be seen in their face, or in the faces of their descendants, but that these mistakes still have real effects is very much in tune with the interview questions the narrator drafts before encountering his white family members. To deny A. J. Beaumont would also mean to deny himself, as the narrator only exists because of the white man's connection to his black maternal ancestor. His family is a result of that union, whether he likes it or not. To be himself and to accept his past, he cannot deny the man.

Yet, within the genre, the photographs at times also provoke negative or accusatory thoughts. The narrator in *Slaves in the Family*, upon receiving an invitation to a reunion of his formerly slaveholding family—an instance for the members to celebrate their former greatness—describes how he "brought out a photograph of Isaac the Confederate, Dad's grandfather, and the faceless crowd of slaves gathered once again before [his] eyes" (Ball 1999, 13). The immediate encounter with the photograph of a white ancestor and known Confederate conjures up imagery that is threatening to the narrator and, by implication, his family.

The slaves are not present in the photographs, of course, but the narrator knows that there is more to Isaac the Confederate than is apparent in the image he holds in his hands. The image is a trigger for memories or ideas—as suggested in the text, the narrator feels that the slaves may have come to seek revenge, or to claim their place in his life. He is aware that at his family gathering this ancestor's legacy will be discussed, but crucial dimensions of it will remain unmentioned. In effect, this narrator sees a different image than his relatives: there is an unexplored part to the family story, and it is coming to threaten and haunt him.

The photography sections overall are congruous with the texts and the family trees. The individuals listed in the family trees oftentimes also appear in a photograph. But the photographs are also strangely at odds with what the narrators report in the memoirs, specifically when they are understood as comprising a quasi-family album: Again, the collection of photographs suggests that the different sides of the families, who meet because of the narrator's efforts, unite easily and merge into one, larger, mixed-race family that is complete. This suggestion contradicts the story being told. The contradiction is possibly due to the fact that "photographs [. . .] float. They remain untethered unless placed with a text explaining their context" (Franklin 2016, 83).

Just as is the case with the family trees, the photographs from the past as such do not supply any information with regard to the present family. They do not make a statement about mutual care or respect, though they may well serve an appealing function. Once the relatives' faces are known, it is harder for them to be pushed away or denied their humanity, personhood, past. Still, this is an undercurrent in the texts: the narrator in *The Sweeter the Juice*, for example, keeps wondering whether those who would reject a family member might look different, and less human (Haizlip 1995, 96–97).

There is great variety among the photographs included in the narratives, making it rather difficult to sum up what is being shown, and how. The photographs included come from different times and from different settings. They adhere to a multiplicity of photographic conventions: There are portraits of single persons, as well as portraits of families or other groups, for example, siblings. Different styles of clothing attest to different eras, as do different hairstyles and settings—there are more formal portraits certainly taken by professional photographers, at times in studios instead of the home, and more casual ones certainly taken by family members or family friends. People are photographed sitting, standing, and seated in a specific arranged order. The background information available about them is not very extensive. It is hardly ever stated who took the photograph and when, or for what purpose—it is clear, though, that the majority of these photographs could not have been taken by the narrator as part of the investigation, as they were taken at an earlier moment preceding the narrator's life or before they knew this part of the family. Some exceptions are photographs taken during the process of research, showing family members of different generations and different skin tones together. At times the context of an image becomes clear from what is visible—a wedding, a birthday party. Some of them appear to have been taken at gatherings, family reunions, or other more common family events, such as a Sunday outing. This is not too surprising, as family photographs are usually taken for purposes of remembering a specific event rather than to reflect daily life (Ickstadt 2010, 57), such as doing household chores. The individuals photographed in each case seem to have been aware of the camera, as they look into it and/or pose for the photograph to be taken—these are not coincidental snapshots.

Nevertheless, the motifs are still somewhat surprising. These are photographs that would likely be kept in a family album, or put up on a wall, or framed and kept on a desk. In *Slaves in the Family*, in addition to portrait photographs, several drawings are included showing the Ball family members before the camera was invented. These drawings do not only show persons, but also depict the landscape in which the family settled. The book also includes advertisements from the period of slavery. All of these images serve to ground the story in the landscape and social context and fuel the reader's imagination with regard to the circumstances of that time. They expose the slaveholding legacy, which the family is certainly very aware of and which is a source of pride for them.

But by way of the investigation in the text, the images also make a different statement: "This is what my family did," and, essentially, "this is what I do to make up for it." Significantly, the genre often includes photographs of reunions before and after the investigative project. These show how the family has changed and grown, how it has expanded over time. The most generous expansion occurs when different families become reunited across generations and racial identifications by way of the narrative itself.

The photographs are usually accompanied by a rather short descriptive text, sometimes indicating the occasion and time the photograph was taken. In the Henry family narrative, the commentary also occasionally focuses on the emotional life of those portrayed. Regarding the narrator's grandmother Fredda, it is said, for example, that "[t]he daughter of Pearl, Fredda easily passed for white, but she felt that love was far more important." Such comments link the photographs to the ethical questions posed by the text;

the photographs are no longer what Franklin called "floating" (Franklin 2016, 83). At the same time, it is significant to remember that this short text is addressing the photographs from the time of writing the memoir, and not from the time when they were taken. Clearly, the commentary is a reference to the narrative in the memoir. It is the result of an act of interpretation taking place in the present.

In part for this reason, it is impossible to come to any conclusions with regard to the exact circumstances in which the photographs were taken, or what the people portrayed in them might have been thinking or feeling. There is always the danger to read a lot of things into photographs (Miller 2010, 37). While the reader at times may know a lot about them, their history, their attitude, the people shown in the pictures were not aware of what was coming in their future, of the context in which a particular photograph would be published, or that they would become part of a memoir. Of course, those photographed had any knowledge of what was to happen to them or their family members at a later point in time (Hirsch and Spitzer 2010, 18), such as when a family would be disrupted or when it would be reunified, or how they would react to any of the questions posed by the narrators at the time of the memoir's writing. At times, the reader knows for sure that different people did not have any idea of each other's existence either. They are embedded within their own social moment.

Overall, it remains rather unclear why specific photographs were chosen for inclusion in the memoirs, and by whom this choice was made: These might have been the only photographs available, or there might have been a mechanism of selecting these pictures (and not others) for inclusion. There is no way to know, as the photographs form a separate section within the narrative and the selection processes are not elucidated by the author, whom we can only assume is the compiler of the photographs. They might have also been put together by the publishing house and have been included due to conventions relating to the autobiographical genre as such. Because the prints stem from different moments in history, this section of the memoir is likely the only time these very images appear together: a real family album could not, for reasons of format alone, accommodate such different media as paintings, letters, daguerreotypes, and modern-day photographs (Langford 2008, 92).

PHOTOGRAPHS AS EVIDENCE: QUESTIONING THE 'COLOR LINE'

As storage of intergenerational mixed-race memory within the text, the photographs suggest a certain authenticity with regard to the story told in the narrative. A photograph of several people together can only be taken if those people have really gathered at the same place and time, unless, of course, technical alterations have been made. In *Camera Lucida*, Roland Barthes comments on how a photograph changes the perception of an event:

> I remember for a long time a photograph I had cut out of a magazine—lost subsequently, like everything to carefully put away—which showed a slave market: the slavemaster, in a hat, standing; the slaves, in loincloths, sitting. I repeat: a photograph, not a drawing or engraving; for my horror and my fascination as a child came from this: that there was a *certainty* that such a thing had existed: not a question of exactitude, but of reality: the historian was no longer the mediator, slavery was given without mediation, the fact was established *without method*. (Barthes 1993, 80, italics in original)

The photograph, despite being a medium itself, makes the past situation real, or authenticates it—a story can be invented where a photograph cannot, unless one uses techniques such as montage.

Like genealogy, photography is often perceived to be neutral and objective like a science, which of course it is not, as different camera angles can create different versions of the same scene, for example. Photography, much like writing, is a creative act, but when presented alongside nonfictional storytelling photographs are assumed to be more closely connected to the real world than a fictional one (Adams 1999, 11). In the contemporary era, and throughout much of the twentieth century, photography has been fairly accessible to the public: it is not without reason that Bourdieu (1965) circumscribed it as "a middle-brow art."

In the *memoir of the search*, the photographs prove that the family members in the text really existed, even if the narrator's family had not been in touch with them. They illustrate daily family life despite the existence of a secret in this family and despite the gaps in the family tree. In some ways, the photographs situate the families in the mainstream; the visual codes—clothing, hairstyle—place them in the middle class. In disclosing events such as weddings, graduations, or family outings, the photographs render private matters public.

Most importantly, with regard to the family secret explored in the text, the photographs attest to the presence of different skin colors or tones of the family members. They are a visual representation of the "color line" and its different variations. Even though one would be rather hard-pressed to use these photographs for phenotypical studies along the lines of W. E. B. Du Bois's 1900 project *Types of American Negroes*, the photographs do show what people within the same family look like and how much they can possibly differ from one other in their physical characteristics.

In some cases, the photographs included in the memoirs show family members with different skin tones together, openly suggesting that the family portrayed is and has always been "racially diverse." Such photographs powerfully attest to the fact that the racial mixing that could not be talked about was in fact *visible*. By extension, these photographs—both in the present, but especially also at the time of their taking—point to the idea that the supposed biological differences between "black" and "white" did not and do not exist in the way proclaimed by racial essentialists, and that the "color line" as such is ambivalent in its allocation of people as either/or.

The reading of a photograph is context dependent. In more than one instance, the people in the photographs cannot clearly be assigned to either category—"black" or "white"—suggesting that such categorization might not only be wrong but, in fact, besides the point: Who would make such decisions? These photographs, ideally, will lead the onlooker to critically examine and question their own gaze and own use of essentialist categories such as "black" or "white."

In visualizing the family secret, the photographs work in tandem with the family trees. Like the family trees, they represent a palpable repertoire of the legacy of race mixing in the family. For example, it is apparent that older photographs do not show family members who identify as black and family members who identify as white together. There was no contact across the "color line": people did not meet each other, and they did not attend each other's family events. They could have been *one* family, but they were *two*.

They chose not to meet or could not meet because skin color separated them from each other and in some cases, as illustrated in the text, made it virtually impossible to meet or be at each other's family events. *Passing* required a severing of family ties at least in the way these texts depict it. They may not have been aware of each other in many cases. This breakup of one family into two becomes reversed by the narrator's quest: The existence of these different pictures together, and especially visual evidence of family reunions taking place following the exploration of the family secret, represents a record of this investigation. At the same time, even those photographs do not attest to feelings of mutual understanding, or of disappointment.

In their arrangement, in their evocation of a mixed-race multigenerational extended family, the photographs appear to be much akin to an actual family album. As media,

> [f]amily albums structure the images of past, create chronological narratives out of fragments, and order memories. That is, they write, rewrite and erase, affirm, or fake that obscure and polyphonic story of secrets and lies, joys, and traumas, oblivions, and memories that is the history of a family. Proving once again that photography's truth-claim is anything but justified, family albums

look as we would like to see ourselves, often through the images of others. (Berecz 2010, 154)

The family album as ordering device is a medium of communication between different family members. As a medial form, it gives incentive to communication *about* these family members and the family as a whole. It facilitates cross-generational exchange and cultural continuity within a family (Langford 2008, 4).

The family album suggests that there is a meaningful connection to the past (3). As a genre-defining element of the *memoir of the search*, it highlights that the past is important to the narrators and their identity in that it shapes their own and, respectively, their families' present. By ordering the photographs from past to present and commenting on them, the narrative voice in the text gains power over the story as it is up to her to tell it to the reader. Significantly, what is being shown in a family album "is only a fragment of a larger family history" and by implication "freezes the family unit as a moment in time" (97). A family album is subject to change—pictures can be taken out or added at a later point and for any reason. A single photograph, as well as a family album as a whole, is a snapshot in these terms.

In showing moments from an earlier time, the photography sections indicate the intergenerational quality of the family's life, despite its disruptions due to the "color line" and the practice of *passing*. The photographs provide a glimpse of the life of the ancestors by way of (indirect) eyewitnessing. They establish continuity and a coherent story shared between the different generations and different parts of the family living in potentially different locations, all the while from the point of view of the present.

Since the family album as a medium first and foremost helps family members remember and talk about their family members and about how the family came to be, the inclusion of these formerly neglected family members also changes the story in unforeseen ways. It is up to the future generation to find a formula for narrating this story. They can openly address the neglect, or cover it over. To do the latter would in effect restore the family secret in the opposite direction, by denying the shame of having neglected or hidden specific family members. Certainly, whether to neglect or emphasize earlier generation's mistakes also depends upon cultural factors playing into the discussion about "race," about "slavery," and about "family" at large.

In their relation to the text, the photographs point to the absences in the family's life. In relation to the generation of narrators, the photographs show events that have not been part of the narrator's own immediate family's experience. In Ball's narrative there are many photographs of descendants of the Ball slaves from throughout the twentieth century. The narrator in *Slaves in the Family* has not experienced those family events and gatherings firsthand, because he was not in touch with or even aware of these people at the time the photographs were taken. Thus, it becomes clear that the separation of the family also led to missing important events in the others' lives. The inclusion of the images also suggests a sense of regret about missing events that were defining to the family. This is something that cannot be compensated for, not even by talking about these events after the fact. That moment is forever gone—it is elusive. There is nothing the narrators or anyone else can do to undo the past.

However, these visual archives functioning as a type of complete family album within the narrative is still rather problematic, as the album actively counteracts the family's legacy of disruption by race and *passing*. The family album generally idealizes the family, excluding "negative images of divorce, anti-social behavior, illegitimacy, disease, disability and violence" (34). This does not mean that these events did not happen, but rather, that such events "are suppressed, or more precisely, they are not pictured, which is not to deny their latent presence" (34).

There is no way to visualize the familial neglect that was or is a result of processes of *passing*. The inclusion of a complete family album potentially suggests that the wounds resulting from this process can all too easily be healed. The process of unification is a matter of putting together the album. The neglect can supposedly be rendered invisible through the composition of a more inclusive family album. It is suggested that, by taking pictures together as an extended family, the hurt can be undone. The family can become a mainstream American family complete with a family album.

This impression factually betrays the complexity that is crucial to the narratives themselves. More than once, the narrators in these texts emphasize how despite the establishment of contact across the so-called color line, the families remain separate from each other as their histories and legacies, and indeed their very formation, have been so totally defined by race that it is impossible to overcome these differences easily. This would require more time, more conversations, and a different degree of understanding that is not often achieved according to the narrators. It would mean entirely rewriting the family story in a coordinated dialogue in which everyone equally has a say.

One person cannot undertake this task alone, but rather, the entire collective of the family would have to commit to it, which cannot be achieved easily. The narrators are very much aware of these challenges, as, for example, is expressed by the narrator in *Pearl's Secret*, who comments on these historically different legacies stating that family traditions and rites depended on race, even though there is one common ancestor (Henry 2001, 247). The mere fact of sharing same ancestors does not unite the two families who have lived on opposite ends of the "color line" for a long time. Solidarity is not necessarily always the result of a blood link.

It is the very sense of completion alluded to by the photographs that might point to some of these problems. Martha Langford argues, "[a] photographic album formed in a crucible of instability may by intent seem *more* normal than any other family album" (Langford 2008, 97; italics in original). This observation can be made very productive with regard to the family album in the *memoir of the search*: it is because of the contestedness of these kinds of families—as families—that their family albums have to be especially comprehensive and tell a particularly ideal and idealized family story.

Taking this into account, the family album, just like the family tree, while suggesting a sense of completeness that is not factually there according to the narratives, attests to the pressure to conform to established middle-class strategies of ordering and picturing the family that are still present in the 1990s and early 2000s, at the time of the emergence of these narratives.

Finally, there are several points of access to reading these photography sections in the memoirs. To do justice to the photographs as artistic documents stemming from a specific time would require a book in itself. Centrally for this study, the photographs expose America's family secret of racial mixing and provide a visual commentary on the narrator's investigation and findings. Moreover, the photographs serve to locate the family portrayed in the text as within a mainstream narrative of the family, as well as in the American middle class. In these terms, the photographs also work as part of the visual intergenerational memory of the text. Last, they underline the inclusiveness of the narratives as well as the genre as such, demonstrating that very different people can become part of the family album established in the *memoir of the search*, but also point to the complications going along with a family legacy of *passing*.

DNA TESTS: CALCULATING THE FAMILY

While the particular texts discussed in this study only marginally focus on it, a third way to address mixed-race heritage around the time of the publication of these books was, and is to this day, DNA testing. Genealogical DNA tests make claims about a person's "racial admixture," meaning an individual's different strings ("ingredients") of ancestry, as well as an individual's local origins going back hundreds of years. In the early 2000s, DNA testing emerged in the United States as a large-scale industry; and while it was and is also used for medical purposes (e.g., in terms of diagnosing hereditary disorders or illnesses), or in criminology (e.g., to solve murder cases), its prime significance for this study is in terms of the genealogical information that can be gained via the analysis of DNA, "a substance found in the nuclei of cells, [that] contains encoded material that, decoded, can reveal our individual master plan, or genetic code, to put it another way" (Cook 1996, 79).

Just like family trees and other genealogical practices, DNA tests bear special significance for the African American community. Being able to locate one's ancestors in a specific country or even region in Africa through DNA testing can be useful in finding out more about "the traumas and triumphs of one's enslaved ancestors," and it provides the opportunity for one to reclaim "a link to African cultural tradition and kinship community" (Abel 2018). Certainly, the prevalence of DNA testing stems from the idea propagated by *Roots* that "a unique and historically *authentic* lineage [is] waiting to be uncovered" (ibid.; italics in original).

There are different forms of the test: One focuses exclusively on a person's maternal line by analyzing the so-called mitochondrial DNA that is passed on to children from their mothers. The second focuses on the Y-chromosome, giving information about someone's paternal ancestry, and can only be taken by men. While this means that more information can be revealed about a person's ancestry if they have a Y-chromosome, these paternal connections all too often do not point to Africa, but to Europe: many African American women were raped by white men, and so this information is generally not as revealing as one might hope, at least if the goal is to find one's African origins.

Overall, these tests only analyze about 1 percent of a person's DNA, and thus they make available limited information—contrary to what commercials for DNA testing usually claim. It has also been found that generally, most African Americans share genetic characteristics with more than one group in Africa, making it almost impossible to give exact information about someone's family's local origins (Nixon 2007).

For-profit companies such as *AfricanAncestry* and *MyHeritage* specialize in helping individuals find their supposed "roots" by analyzing a swab of their cheek. On their websites, these companies make DNA tests sound like an easy undertaking that will lead to a conclusive answer with regard to the person's local origin—all the way down to a specific African region a person's ancestor came from. *AfricanAncestry* claims to have the largest database relating to Africa and promises support during the emotional experience of finding one's origins. They will also send out information about the place the ancestors came from once this has been found, and have an online community in which people can address the experience of finding "their true identity" (AfricanAncestry). The suggestion here is that knowing one's origins will help an individual find closure and a way to make peace with the past (meaning with slavery and one's family history).

Like genealogy, DNA tests appear scientifically correct and detached, and they assert the ability to make truth claims about the self. DNA tests promise to provide empirically verifiable information; moreover, they promise that this information actually bears a meaning and that a person *is* what is in their DNA—a substance that is singular in every person (Cook 1996, 80). The assumption then would be that once an individual knows the self in its specifics on a genetic level, an individual achieves a status of completeness and gets into contact with the innermost self. An individual would then not be characterized by stories and experiences, but by genetic material and physical substance. In a sense, these ideas feed into the still ongoing nature/nurture debate in disciplines from philosophy to social psychology. At the same time, a DNA test may offer the ability for an individual to establish connections with certain locations, but it does not offer cultural information—not even if a company offers to send along some cultural information about a region of origin with the test.

In the early 2000s, the television show *African American Lives* on PBS (2006–2008) greatly contributed to the popularity of DNA testing. In this show, Harvard professor Henry Louis Gates Jr. helped famous Americans—from singer Tina Turner to actor Morgan Freeman to Bliss Broyard, the author of *One Drop*—discover their heritage using genealogical methods and DNA testing. The participants were interviewed about their family history and about their upbringing, and they were confronted with the results of a DNA test they had previously taken. Often, the encounter with the past in front of the camera was orchestrated as a very moving moment in which, finally, the person reached a new stage of clarity about the past. At times, there are tears, unbelieving looks, and relief about finally having answers with regard to their origins. The show also accompanied the guests to sites where their ancestors had lived so they could physically encounter "the past."

This show, as well as some others with a more or less similar concept (e.g., the BBC's *Who Do You Think You Are?*), made DNA testing and its supposed effects widely visible and helped garner interest in the subject. These shows told and continue to tell stories quite similar to the ones in the *memoir of the search*—stories of disrupted families, stories of *passing*, stories of the transgression of boundaries—and present the idea that the "truth" can be found. In those terms, these series could—in a different study—be read in a very productive dialogue with the memoirs. They certainly respond to the same historical moment and ask a similar set of questions, but do so via a different medium that offers different opportunities for the unraveling of cultural and family secrets.

Since DNA testing made a giant leap after the completion of the Human Genome Project in 2003, and the memoirs discussed here mostly precede this moment, they generally can only indirectly comment on the notion of DNA testing and the importance of genetics to their project at large. The narrator in *The Sweeter the Juice* contemplates at various times how her genetic heritage might shape her looks, her habits, and her ways of perceiving the world. She wonders the same thing about her family members. In the prologue to her exploration, she states about her own genetic makeup that "[g]enes and chromosomes from Africa, Europe and a pristine America commingled and created [her]" and goes on to state that this puts her in a specific, at times vexed, status: "I am an American anomaly. I am an American ideal. I am the new America" (Haizlip 1995, 15).

Here, it appears as if this narrator was convinced that her genetic makeup defines her, or at least shapes her as a person. The narrative makes very clear that she is also shaped by her surroundings, by her experiences, by her upbringing, and so on—there is much more to a person than their genetic fingerprint. The second part of the quote is even more interesting as the mixedness here is declared part of the "new America," the condition she literally embodies: the ultimate form of saying *pluribus unum*. However, this was, as also becomes clear in the quote, a development: from an anomaly to an ideal. This passage clearly pays a tribute to more contemporary ways of talking about the United States as a multicultural nation, rather than one solely built for and by white people. The ideal now, according to the quote, is diversity of the self.

While DNA testing has come under scrutiny in recent years due to false or limited information, a person's DNA can potentially contain mysteries that would otherwise not be solved. DNA tests make racial *passing* impossible, for example. African heritage of any kind would be detected in a test. At the same time, testing could expose that a person does not bear the heritage she assumes to be a central part of her identity: An individual could find out that her parents are not her biological mother and father, but that her heritage is Native American instead of African. A final consequence of DNA testing is that it shows the veracity of a family story and thus also can expose family secrets, and not only those relating to race.

While DNA testing potentially serves to show that race is a genetic fact that can be proven, it also has the significant antiracist potential of "deconstructing older notions of America as made up of biologically 'pure' races" (Abel 2018). DNA results can establish previously invisible connections between people and lead to a wider definition of kinship. Generally, it is assumed that humanity originated in East Africa. By locating all humans in the same geographical region in a common story of origin, it becomes possible to advance the notion of a global humanity in which all people are—however distantly—related to each other. This idea transcends the nation and extends to all people independent of their personal story, any visual characteristics, citizenship, and other forces that may divide people from each other. While the *memoir of the search* as a genre is centrally focused on the American nation and its citizens' experiences with racial diversity around the turn of the millennium, the genre does offer the potential to extend this type of narrative to an even broader context to address processes of exclusion due to difference.

In the afterword to *One Drop*, the narrator in Bliss Broyard's memoir addresses her experience taking a DNA test in order to finally get a clear answer to the question that has haunted her since she found out about her father's African American origins and his passing: *"How black am I?"* (Broyard 2007, 467; italics in original). She intends to use her father's ashes in order to determine his origins, but it turns out that the remains cannot be used and she has to refer to her own as well as to her living family members' DNA (468), meaning her paternal aunt's DNA, her own, and her brother's.

The narrator is a little disillusioned after the process, because the results are not what she had assumed they would be, and they also differed depending on the test: It appears to be a matter of "the luck of the draw" (473). This shows that the results of DNA tests are nowhere near as reliable as is often assumed. Even Henry Louis Gates Jr. has by now stated that there is always the danger that the tests will tell a person what they want to hear instead of giving factual proof of anything (Nixon 2007). Both tests taken in *One Drop* do reveal that the percentage of African ancestry is not nearly as high as the family had originally suspected, leaving the narrator a little disillusioned, but still in a situation where she can claim that, despite her privileged white socialization, she has African ancestry.

At the same time, the results lead her to contemplate the specific meaning of this string of ancestry for her family and its makeup. She tries to place her findings in a specific time and setting, arguing that while the actual percentage of African ancestry in his DNA was likely low like his sister's, "[h]istory, law, and public opinion made the fact of his black blood matter, whether it was 50 percent, 13 percent, or just one drop" (Broyard 2007, 474). This points to the idea that while the categories may matter in different ways to individuals and/or their families and while DNA tests may reveal heretofore hidden knowledge, the interpretation of the different percentages is what counts. Historical and social circumstance, close-cut definitions of who counts as black and who counts as white, as well as concrete regulations to exclude certain populations from specific human and civil rights, are what shaped this particular family's history.

ARCHIVING THE FAMILY

Taken together, the family trees and family photographs as well as the other documents included in the memoirs function as a limited, but still more or less comprehensive mixed-race family archive. As a form, the archive is also not a neutral practice; rather, it "constructs the knowledge it would seem only to register or make evident" (Smith 2004, 7). Here, the family archive attests to the long-term legacy of racial mixing in the United States, as do the DNA tests brought up in *One Drop*.

These practices ground and trace back the legacy of race and the limitations brought on by segregation in daily life into the eighteenth and nineteenth centuries, and in the case of DNA testing even beyond, giving supposedly factual, visible, and thus believable proof of the family secret. The fiction of purity is dissolved. That it takes significant examples of proof makes clear that the stakes are high.

The archive in these memoirs represents a counter-archive of the white American family, with racial diversity at its very root. As such, it attests to the fact that race, despite all talk of a "post-racial" age, is still an important factor in American society at large, not only because it has shaped this society throughout the past centuries, but also because it still resonates in the present day and generates specific notions of purity and mixedness, intergenerational relating, and connections across supposedly fixed boundaries. Race is indeed such a powerful force that it can potentially disrupt and has indeed disrupted the most important American institution, namely, the family.

The *memoir of the search* speaks against the erasure of this complex layer of American history in favor of the "multiracial" terminology, and for the incorporation of racial diversity into the individual families as well as the national narrative and terminology currently in use. The texts reveal medial strategies of how this incorporation can be achieved across several dimensions to make sure the story is heard and cannot be silenced again. In these terms, the texts do not only neutrally store and collect content, but in effect also reverse and regulate how such stories can be structured and transmitted.

As a genre, the *memoir of the search* operates along the fault lines of the discussion around America's legacy of race mixing and racial diversity around the time of its emergence: How to make this—heretofore often excluded—story resonate with other American narratives. It does so from a decidedly middle-class stance that also becomes evident in its incorporation of media of memory and its strategies of archiving the mixed family. By implication, a family with a family album is a middle-class family. The presence of family photography renders the texts subsumed here under the heading of the *memoir of the search* into readable family narratives, relatable to a middle-class audience who will be very familiar with family albums and their ritualistic qualities for the building and strengthening of family identity. This strategy of the genre may also be a way of responding to the worry that to be African American means to be poor or even to be thought of as poor or lacking cultural capital. These families have a long legacy of middle-class standing: they were doctors and lawyers throughout the twentieth century, and are people with the cultural capital to investigate their family history in the present day.

Along similar lines, genealogical research is linked to middle-class belonging: It amounts to a way of counting and recounting one's blessings, ultimately leading to progress and upward social mobility. Just like the other dimensions of the texts discussed here, the social outlook is strongly determined by the middle-class gaze. While the narrators all appear aware of their own status and refer to the challenges encountered by African Americans trying to rise socially in the United States, neither the narratives told nor the media used here linger on these challenges for long. Given the time it must have taken for the authors to compile the photographs and compose the family trees, it is clear that being able to tell these stories is a matter of class as well as of education—it is a matter of access and entitlement. One must know how to find these images, how to deal with them, and how to find a suitable interpretation.

Reading these types of texts by black and white narrators in dialogue, while paying special attention to the media of memory incorporated into these texts, thus shows how a particular set of people—middle-class Americans with a similar educational background specific to their economic status—regard themselves and their family histories, specifically relating to questions of race, and racial mixedness.

By implication, these texts are an exemplary study in how to gain access to the master narrative at the time of their writing: At the end of the twentieth century, the topic of racial difference and diversity in a family can be formulated using conventional media of family memory, under the condition that the material is indeed accessible and available. The way in which the narrators in these texts literally trace the previously hidden branches of their family trees nevertheless signifies the breaking of a taboo on both sides: It is not common for a white great-great-grandson of a slaveholder to look for the descendants of those his ancestors enslaved. It is also not common for an African American to try and find the descendants of those who abandoned her family due to skin color.

The breaking of this taboo, however, takes place in rather established forms using well-known patterns of shaping the family through the use of specific visual media that express the typical, mainstream American family experience. Once more, the liberating potential of these texts significantly complicates established ways of constructing linearity. Nevertheless, the intergenerational family memory put together for the memoirs still appears to be more inclusive of difference and diversity than earlier texts of this kind suggest.

As Catherine Nash (2002, 28) emphasizes, "[g]enealogy is a practice which joins imaginative self-making and guarantees of truth about individual identity. The genealogical quest to know with certainty 'who you are' and 'where you come from' by knowing your ancestors suggests a primordial and predetermined identity that can be simply uncovered." While this does not seem in tune with the postmodern imperative to "be who are you are" and to freely invent yourself, undertaking genealogical research may also lead to a situation where a person can decide to privilege one line of ancestry over another.

Again, the mere fact of biological connectedness, or the existence of family photographs in a shared album, does not signify that people are also emotionally connected to each other. Still, in these texts, genealogical practice, family photography, and reflections about DNA work together to locate these mixed-race families in the mainstream by generating a family archive that fulfills all parameters needed for the family members to be accepted as full members of American society—the existence and inclusion of these media enable a process of *passing* in and of itself. To lead over to the following chapter: the families in this genre have a family tree, a family album, and an immigration story to tell—they are genuinely American families.

Chapter 4

Narrating the Mixed-Race Nation

Beyond consolidating an extended family history disrupted by the "color line," the *memoir of the search* is concerned with a second, larger family: the American nation. By picking up on well-known myths and narratives of Americanness, the memoirs discussed in this study engage with complex issues of national identity and its narration in the late twentieth and early twenty-first centuries—the story of America. In this way, the texts respond to ongoing concerns of their time.

By tracing their families' hidden histories and repressed memories, the narrators reflect on their family members' roles in American society. They also talk about their self-perception not only as people with their particular family history, but also, and possibly most importantly, as Americans with a long history relating to this country. This family story is constantly rewritten and retold in the memoirs, albeit using similar types of narratives and images.

The family stories the narrators uncover during the process of the search, described in such detail in the text, have not only been hidden by their own family members. They have also been unspeakable within the larger American public discourse. These family stories do not cohere with the dominant narrative of the American nation's history, which is by and large an exclusively white account of immigration, Americanization, and social advancement following the ideals of self-realization and actualization perpetuated by the American Dream.

This chapter shows how the narrators inscribe their own family stories into the larger family history of the American nation. This inscription is achieved through the relation of the family to important figures or events, to the popular imagining of the immigration story, and to the concept of the American Dream. In essence, the *memoir of the search* is a genre devoted to addressing relationships of different kinds, including that between the family and the nation.

The state of race relations is pertinent to the emergence of the memoirs, since the texts ask how these divisions in society came to be. By the 1990s, following the development of Critical Race Theory, it had been established that "much of what is broadly associated with distinct racial groups is the result of history, custom, and legalized injustice" (878).

The narrators in the *memoir of the search* understand their family histories as both unique in their specificity, and emblematic of the American story at the turn of the twenty-first century. By and large, the texts show how the experiences of the narrators' families "have mirrored the stresses and strains of our nation's racial history, from slavery to Jim Crow to the integration of the 1960's and on into the complex world of multiculturalism that seems to define the present" (Henry 2001, 11). The *memoir of the search*, then, does not a call for a new story, or contest the concept of the American nation. Once again, this rather conventional narration represents a hope of normalizing the story of mixed race.

Of course, the attempt by the texts to *pass* into the mainstream is still accompanied by strong criticism of how the nation was built and how it has so far dealt with its past, specifically in relation to race. The narrator in *Pearl's Secret* observes that there is still no equality in the United States (5). This understanding makes clear how the narrators in the genre are very aware, and at times also very weary, of the ongoing tensions between the American promise and its fulfillment in terms of social inclusiveness and racial justice.

The narrators' considerations throughout their investigations are reflections not only on their immediate families, but also on the larger themes of access, equality, and integrity in American society. The questions they raise concern how they, or rather their generation, could possibly contribute to building a different society in which the American promise is fulfilled. In those terms, it can be argued that the narrators speak from an activist point of view, though not one that is interested in revolution. Rather, the desire is for full participation and narrative inclusion in the story that made America and shaped their families and them as individuals.

Therefore, the *memoir of the search* stresses the multiculturalism and diversity of the contemporary nation, but still builds on the central pillar of twentieth-century American society—the heterosexual nuclear family. Despite their rather groundbreaking investigation of the family past, these texts are rather "tame" in their approach and in leveling their criticism. They claim that America's mixed-race story has always been part of the nation's narrative, and therefore the larger American story does not require radical alteration or full-scale reversal in order to become more inclusive.

As a genre, the *memoir of the search* examines and imagines how specific constellations and understandings of racial difference in American history; larger societal trends; and also perceptions, regulations, laws, and singular events, have shaped and continue to shape individual persons and families. As one goal of their research, the narrators aim to understand how their ancestors were affected by the specific chapters in American history of slavery and segregation. Their understanding of family members' different roles during these periods in history also leads the narrators to question their relatives' complicity in injustices committed in the past. Which decisions did these ancestors make, and why? How have these decisions and their repercussions shaped the family and where it stands today? How does the past shape the present, more generally? And what should an individual do with this type of knowledge about the past?

The narrators attempt to read American history through the lens of a specific micro-history, namely, their family's story. The idea behind this effort to understand the past is that a "true story," namely, their family's story, can be investigated using historical documents and written down in a coherent way. They therefore attest to the potential of a more inclusive American nation that has always already been there. The idea of rewriting history in a more inclusive manner is connected to the genealogical research methods used in the narratives. Through tracing the ancestors and finding out how and where they lived, a previously abstract history becomes concrete and personal, and also manageable. Genealogy and genealogical research in these terms is, as the narrator in Henry's (2001, 30) text emphasizes, "a way of connecting personally to history and to [. . .] racial and ethnic identity."

The research the narrators undertake serves as their entry point into investigating American history at large and narratives of Americanness, as well as their fulfillment in their own family. The nation's history appears in a different light to the narrator once they realize that their ancestors shaped American history in incredible, even if very small, ways: Through very specific decisions that have in one way or another brought about change or development—mostly forward-looking development. The genre of the *memoir of the search* then points to mixed race as an advancement leading the way toward an inclusive and diverse American future.

At its time of emergence, the *memoir of the search* enters into ongoing discussions regarding what it means to be American, how America should be addressing the past and its trespasses, and whether reconciliation with the past is possible at all. Within the dominant story of America's becoming, slavery for the longest time was "something, like a miracle, that can be denied even by those who witness it or its effects" (Rushdy 2001, 3). Due to a renewed negotiation of the American slaveholding past and its memory as well as its public display, for example, in the country's national parks, the topic of mixed-race families became politically meaningful in the 1990s. The importance of mixed-race identity is immediately relevant in the American South, where the question was raised of how the region should own up to its past, and whether any form of compensation to the descendants of slaves, financial or otherwise, would be necessary or useful. But people also recognized that slavery and its long-term legacy is an issue of national scope, since it has centrally shaped the nation and its definitions of access, diversity, and equality.

Slavery continues to haunt Americans who conceive of themselves as black, and those who conceive of themselves as white. Specifically, the idea of black/white mixing is central to the American imagination as it bears witness and gives proof to what Michelle Elam (2001, 118) has called "the paradox of unequal entitlement in the land of equality." This understanding of unequal entitlement despite the quintessential American narrative of equality also means, by implication, that within the genre of the *memoir of the search*, the narrators identifying as black and those identifying as white must differ significantly in their strategies of talking about the nation. This degree of difference should not come as a big surprise. It is a result of opposing legacies—oppressor and oppressed, perpetrator and victim—and of the different stories and experiences the narrators were confronted with when they were growing up, as well as how they are perceived within their culture on a daily basis.

In these texts, the American story is reconfirmed by way of narrative intervention. For the narrators, at the turn of the twenty-first century, to be American means to be of mixed descent: to be rooted in America and to be quintessentially American *because* of this mixed heritage, and not *despite* it. In some ways, these texts reverse earlier attempts to speak to the meaning of mixed race in the national American context, by attempting to contextualize and root racial transgression within the American national context, instead of outside of it.

The process of questioning and rewriting the dominant American story and its foundation runs parallel to the narrators' struggles regarding their families' becoming. Through their investigations, they are potentially changing the stories their families have known and passed on about their past and their origins. Along parallel lines, the dominant narrative of the United States is the foundational text of the national family. Every challenge possibly leading to change is a threat to the identity of the national family, which is firmly built on such ideas as the American Dream, but also notions relating to slavery, for example. By exposing a different "truth," a more complex layering of the past constitutes a danger to the integrity of the national narrative. By steadily intertwining micro- and macro-history, the narratives attest to the constitutive power of storytelling in both the family and the nation.

The *memoir of the search* by and large reflects an apparent desire to reevaluate the national past in terms of its mixed legacy, and to expose how history has been written up to the present moment—including by whom, and with what agenda. As a genre, the *memoir of the search* suggests continuity between the past and the present by assuming that the present is as it is because it is constituted by a specific past in which specific actors took specific actions in specific contexts. The mistakes of the past will have palpable consequences in the present.

To come back to Rushdy's (2001) observation that assuming a sense of responsibility for past events depends on a collective identity, this would mean that for contemporary Americans to assume responsibility for slavery and its aftermath, slavery and its aftermath must first be made part of the national story. Placing slavery at the center of the national story is one of the concerns of the *memoir of the search*. In building a link between an individual family and the nation, and between the present state of affairs and the long-term consequences of slavery, these texts potentially and carefully contribute to the writing of an updated national story.

Lauren Berlant (1997, 8) argues that "[q]uestions of intimacy, sexuality, reproduction, and the family [. . .] are properly interrelated with [. . .] questions of identity, inequality, and national existence." American public culture has rejected or even negated its mixed heritage for the longest time, while at the same time making this topic central to the question of who could be a citizen. The so-called one-drop rule, which continued into much of the twentieth century, determined who would be considered white, and who would be considered black—an understanding central to daily life in the segregated United States. The importance of race becomes evident when studying, for example, American legal history dealing with such definitions of citizenship.

The *memoir of the search* speaks to established notions of citizenship and personhood by suggesting that to be "American" means to be of mixed descent, rather than to be WASP. Seen from this angle, the texts classified here as *memoir of the search* respond to what Berlant has termed "the nostalgic desire for official national culture" (180). Instead of disregarding the idea of a national culture as such, they rewrite the national story according to their needs—or rather, reformulate it to be inclusive of their own stories of mixed race and its long-term consequences for family, identity, and nation. That this project is carried out within the confines of a specific literary genre presents a complication. What comes across as liberation then amounts to being a weakness, in that these texts do not open up exclusive notions of Americanness for the telling of new stories.

THE NATIONAL STORY AS FAMILY STORY

While not being official representatives of the United States, the narrators in the *memoir of the search* express they feel deeply rooted in the United

States, and in American history. This rootedness gives them agency and also serves as validation of their Americanness. Throughout the narratives, they use different strategies to intertwine their families' stories with the larger story of America, but they also locate themselves in the complexities of the contemporary period.

In *Pearl's Secret*, the narrator expresses in much detail how strongly he feels for his country, and how his attitude, despite the criticism that will follow in his text, is inherently motivated by patriotism, respect, and love for his nation. He is intensely aware that the contemporary period and its culture is full of contradictions, and cannot easily be summed up in one line that would encompass all of American culture. Technological advances go along with opportunities, but the innovations brought to life in the twentieth century do not automatically mean that everyone can live well in this time, or that all these resources are equally accessible (Henry 2001, 33).

The narrators in the *memoir of the search* are, very generally speaking, aware that they have, in that sense, been privileged due to their middle-class background. At the same time, Henry's narrator's privilege as a black member of the middle class is not quite the same as the white privilege his family members on the other side of the "color line" have profited from during their lifetimes in the United States. There are questions they do not need to address in the same manner; instances where they did not have to fight for the position or question themselves the way the black-identifying narrator in *Pearl's Secret* did. In those terms, Henry's narrator strongly relates to the African American experience in the United States.

The genealogical impulse these texts follow stems in part from the recognition of this privilege. Genealogy helps explain why some families are more privileged than others. Skin color shapes opportunity, which in turn shapes perspective. The narrators in the *memoir of the search* reflect about how "their" America, the nation of which they firmly consider themselves a part of, is full of paradoxes. The narrator in *Pearl's Secret* states that African American men face many social and economic disadvantages, while at the same time, they could run for president (33). This idea is made more relevant by the 2008–2016 Obama presidency, when a mixed-race candidate ran for president and won the vote twice, but still repeatedly had to prove his own Americanness, to the extent of publishing his birth certificate.

Much like the narrators consider their family history representative in terms of the larger national story, they view their own lives as representative of their respective generation. The narrator in *Pearl's Secret* remembers that in the neighborhood and community where he grew up, he was "the quintessential poster child of the era of racial integration" and even won the American Legion medal as an adolescent because he was considered "a model American" (38) by veterans of the Vietnam War. At the same time, he was certainly aware of his blackness, and of the fact that *colorism* played an important role in facilitating his social advancement (39).

The narrator in *One Drop*, who only learns about her mixed ancestry as an adult, connects her own story to a story about America she has grown up with, namely, the idea of the melting pot: "I had always bought into the idea of the American 'melting pot,' and now I was an example of it. [. . .] I felt like I mattered in a way that I hadn't before" (Broyard 2007, 17). This idea in turn alludes to American individualism and to the notion that your heritage alone in some way makes you "special" and makes you "matter." Knowing her heritage empowers this narrator and makes her feel exceptional, or at least more-than-ordinary, because hers is different from most Americans' heritage. The notion of mixed race as something exceptional and, indeed, exotic is, of all texts studied here, nowhere as clearly evident as in *One Drop*; still, it is an important feature of the genre as a whole. This observation points to the narrators' position of privilege, social and otherwise in the *memoir of the search*.

TECHNIQUES OF ENTANGLEMENT

One way in which the *memoir of the search* intertwines family history with national history is through the connection to important political and cultural figures or events. In the process of investigating her family heritage, the narrator in *The Sweeter the Juice* discovers that she is related to a woman named Martha Washington Dandridge, who, while not being "the Mother of Our country," is a woman referenced "in Anne Wharton's biography of Martha Washington" (Haizlip 1995, 44). She is the aunt of Martha Washington. That her family is related to the Washington family—to the wife of the first president of the United States—is the foundation of the claim that the Haizlip family history resides at the center of the American national story. This story also places the family at the point of origin of the American nation, and the first manifestation of its unique identity.

The narrator devotes much thought to the personal maid of Martha Washington, a woman named Oney who disappeared when Washington became the first lady. This interest in Oney arises because the narrator wonders whether she might have been Martha's secret half-sister (45). It is not absolutely unlikely that this woman is Oney Judge, an escaped slave formerly owned by Martha Washington and for same time her first attendant. This historical figure did not "disappear," but rather, she escaped slavery in 1796 (Dunbar 2015). Much is known about her life because she was interviewed by abolitionist newspapers following her escape, and since 2010, her escape is being honored on a day of celebration (Salisbury 2010).

By assuming that this woman may have been the First Lady's illegitimate half-sister, in effect, the narrator in *The Sweeter the Juice* reads her immediate family's story into the larger national story, placing a narrative of the crossing of racial boundaries in the political league of the early national period. At the same time, the idea of racial mixing in the White House links the Haizlip family legacy to the case of Thomas Jefferson and Sally Hemings (a controversy rumored, yet unproven, at the time of the memoir's publication), meaning an instance of black/white racial mixing taking place around the White House. In this way, mixed-race heritage is not only placed at the nation's origin, but also within the American political elite, showing how central it has been to the nation from its very start.

The narrator also discovers that she is distantly related to Sir Walter Scott, and so is able to relate to both "a Founding Mother and a Romantic poet" (Haizlip 1995, 46). Interestingly, Sir Walter Scott, while being Scottish, played a major role in the emergence of the "Southern" American mindset—it was Mark Twain who claimed in *Life on the Mississippi* (1883) that "Sir Walter Scott had so large a hand in making Southern character, as it existed before the war, that he is in great measure responsible for the war." It may even be a little ironic that the narrator who feels so firmly located in the African American community had an ancestor who may have, at least in some ways, contributed to the emergence of the system that separated her family.

While none of these discoveries change the narrator's loyalty to her black-identifying family and to the black community, the inclusion of these stories is important in terms of her recognizing that her ancestors were central to the formation and the making of America in different ways than she has previously been able to assume. Her family members matter beyond their own lifetimes; they changed the course of history. This recognition leads her to contemplate how this blood relation is still present in her genetically, and which visual features of these ancestors may show in her own and her relatives' features, thus wondering about the connection between genotype and phenotype (Haizlip 1994, 46–47). At the time these memoirs were published, such ideas were of increasing interest, given the large-scale emergence of DNA testing and its ability to reveal a person's ancestry across generations. The narrator knows, however, because of her own family history, that genetic connections do not necessarily lead to the upkeep of family ties. Rather, as she has experienced in her own family, phenotype is determinative of the roles one is able to assume in society, but also in the family. Her mother's family has *passed*, and her mother was not able to do so—and therefore got rejected by her own kin.

Haizlip's narrator is aware that she owes much to her black ancestors. In the nineteenth century, many of these black ancestors lived in places where slave revolts occurred because injustices committed against the slaves were becoming unbearable, and resistance necessary. These family members thus also contributed to changing the course of history. On the whole, the narrator is keenly aware of her privilege—her family members enabled the Haizlip family to be where they are today in their lives and their careers (106). The narrator does not take this process of social uplift that includes educational opportunities for granted. She knows that her family members undertook many efforts in order to rise socially and to ensure a good life for their children. A black family in which college educations and professional careers were standard is one firmly located in the middle class.

The text passage alluded to above also mirrors the known patterns of an "American success story," a story of rising up the social ladder—albeit with a twist, as these family members are not white and have a heritage of slavery. They succeeded because they did not give up, but overcame the expectations society had of them: They were resilient and thus able to rise socially. The narrator sees herself and her own life as connected by a direct line to these ancestors: "I believe that the independent thinking, leadership and political advocacy in my family are the results of tendencies passed down from those oppressive times through more than six generations" (108).

This powerful statement about the narrator's own activism confirms that she attributes her strength and resilience to her black family members who contributed great things to American history and accomplished these achievements under (in part) dire conditions. The idea voiced here also supports the American notion that it is, indeed, possible to rise "from dishwasher to millionaire" and that hard work will essentially get you everywhere, or at least somewhere. The American Dream is not a concept solely relating to white society. It is also a reality for the persistent black middle-class family encountered by the reader of this memoir.

The idea of leadership and the mind of the entrepreneur—a rather "American" concept in itself—is emphasized several times in relation to this narrator's family. Her paternal grandfather, just like her father, was an important man in his town and beyond, whose actions significantly impacted African American communities at the time. The narrator explains that this paternal grandfather, a man named William, was featured in the 1920s compilation volume of *Who's Who in Colored America* (110), an indication of his extraordinary standing and visibility in the African American community at the time. The fact that he compiled the Standard Baptist Hymnal shows his importance for many Americans all over the United States even beyond his own life, but also his commitment to the church and to organized religion, another factor alluding to his middle-class belonging, his moral standing, and principles. He is a man to look up to, a man with God on his side, and a man deeply politically engaged in the advancement of race relations (111).

During his lifetime, the grandfather liked to be perceived as an intellectual (113). He distanced himself from the image of the servant which was common for African Americans at the time and knew about his privilege (113). Apparently, he could afford not to take a job of this kind, pointing to his high social and financial status. The narrator describes her grandfather—quite fittingly—as a "new negro" (113): a person who has contributed significantly to the flourishing of the Florida Avenue Baptist Church in part because of fundraising capacities (115), a sign of his oratory as well as his economic skills. The grandfather was associated with other formative figures of the black community at the time, internationally renowned intellectuals and poets such as W. E. B. Du Bois, Countee Cullen, and Jean Toomer (116). In many ways he was a true example of the "Talented Tenth."

The family's association with prominent African Americans demonstrates both the social privilege they have enjoyed from the early twentieth century onward, and how seriously they took the obligations that go along with this social privilege. The idea of the "Talented Tenth" makes clear that opportunity was both expanded and restricted: only a very limited number of African Americans could rise to excellence, and those leaders were imbued with specific responsibilities for advancing African American society at large. These classically educated men, according to W. E. B. Du Bois and other Northern intellectuals of his time, were asked to work as teachers and writers, and to support the rise of African Americans (also beyond the North) as progressive activists. Privilege and access to education came with responsibility to work in the interest of those who could not obtain that status. The narrator in this memoir certainly also sees herself as a person imbued with specific responsibilities and the leadership skills needed to take action and refamiliarize her family members with each other. Thereby, she continues a family tradition.

While the narrator takes pride in her family members' achievements, she is also aware of the exceptional status of her family, and that the experiences her ancestors have made are far from common. This recognition of her privilege becomes especially evident to her when she moves to California to direct the National Center for Film and Video Preservation at the American Film Institute. Here, she feels the urge in herself to commit to change but is in no position to truly turn her ideas into reality. She finds that Hollywood is still dominated by whites, and the stereotypes associated with blackness are very painful for her to see (238). She speaks critically of the role the American media and film industries have played and continue to play in perpetuating the oppression of and negative stereotypes about African Americans. The narrator recognizes that Hollywood's preoccupation with the plantation myth, so dominant in classics such as *Gone with the Wind*, is not productive in advancing the position of African Americans in society.

Representation matters, and the absence of positive portrayals of black people leads the narrator to reject her career advancement out of loyalty to her community. This act shows her ethical position and also her persistence in her beliefs and ideals. She resigns from this job because she feels that it is disconnected from the black experience and requires a white normativity that is not in tune with her idea of a meaningful life. As a black woman she firmly locates herself in the African American context, and even though she may likely be able to *pass*, she is unwilling to make use of this career opportunity (13). "Blackness" is not just a matter of skin color or tone, but also one of socialization and cultural experience, and having been told specific stories.

In *Pearl's Secret*, investigating where family members were at a certain point in time and how they contributed to American history at large is central to the narrator's undertaking. He explains that he aspired to put together a narrative that speaks to relations between black and white Americans, and about the ways they have shaped the present (Henry 2001, 58). Here it becomes very clear that the *memoir of the search* is not just the story of one family. Rather, it is a book about the race relations that crucially define the United States, and how race relations play out in one specific family through the nineteenth and twentieth centuries.

As a genre, the *memoir of the search* reflects how the current state of race relations has come to be, and which parties were involved in these developments. It examines which steps could or possibly should be taken in order to better understand why race is still a point of contention in the contemporary United States, and what the role of dialogue between members of supposedly different groups could be. By intertwining the individual with the national family in these terms, the genre locates these struggles for racial and social equality at the center of the American nation. In essence, the nation becomes a family with shared responsibility for the past, present, and possible futures. Essentially, there is not even one defined past or present; both of these, as well as the possible futures, depend on circumstance as well as on action.

The ongoing struggle about racial matters is not an individual "problem" or the result of one particular family miscommunicating, but one that all of society is confronted with. Here, it is important to show that those on the perceived "other" side of the "color line" are firmly located both in the American nation and in the middle class, are people of moral standing, of mainstream political and religious values, and have contributed in important ways to the nation's development. These are people whom potential readers will want in their own families. They are unthreatening in terms of their support for American culture and ideology: The genre would be fundamentally different were the characters in support of, for example, radical splinter groups wishing to separate themselves from mainstream society. Here, however, educated

African Americans are asking for full inclusion as middle-class American citizens.

In *Pearl's Secret*, the narrator's white ancestor A. J. Beaumont, unlike Haizlip's ancestor, was not related to any of the Founding Fathers. But this man is still depicted as a representative of his respective generation. He has experienced important social changes and cultural developments during his lifetime, and the narrator aligns his life with these global political and social developments, with technological progress as well as artistic innovations that occurred during his lifetime (Henry 2001, 35). To the narrator, this period is crucial to understanding the state of the American nation today. Learning about Beaumont's historical background also helps the narrator contextualize his life and social environment, as well as the philosophical and political thought that impacted his personality. In this way the mysterious relative is humanized and made less shrouded in secrecy: he is no longer a mystery man but a regular person. The reader can imagine him as a contemporary of very well-known thinkers and artists, "giants like Darwin, Hugo, Marx, and Lincoln; Tchaikovsky, Monet, Whitman, and Edison" (Henry 2001, 35).

The narrator also refers to his black family members' involvements in the shaping and the making of America. His grandfather, as he explains, worked for the NAACP in St. Louis, founded in 1909, and was honored by the organization for his intense engagement (257)—locating him at the center of civil rights struggles and black political progress. The narrator also emphasizes that his parents and their generation have made extraordinary achievements and contributed greatly to the ability of African Americans to rise socially. He feels that his parents in their activism against repressive zoning laws changed the outlook of America (192) and suggests that his parents' generation as a whole had brought much change to the United States (194). The narrator raises another immediate connection between his family's actions and the achievement of the Civil Rights Movement in the United States, a success that the narrator's generation now certainly profits from.

These examples show that even though there may not be a famous ancestor in the family, or someone known to the narrator's generation for great inventions or achievements, in small but very significant ways family members have played a part in American history. These contributions relate specifically to advancing civil rights for African Americans. The narrator is aware that the stories he knows about the successes of his family members, the people who raised him and made him what he is today, are not representative of the African American experience at large (284). Their successes, and his career as a college professor, mark him and his family as socially privileged.

Significantly, the narrator's family members on the white side of the "color line" actively worked against the civil rights his black family was so strongly trying to advance (263). This factor makes the narrator wonder how much of his story the newly found family members actually understand. While on the surface, he feels that they are having a productive conversation with each other, in which they learn about their respective families and their development, he is taken aback by their different degrees of awareness of civil rights in America and the struggles of the African American family (267). There is no script for this type of conversation about the past and its legacies, and different lives have contributed to a very real sense of difference and separation (263).

A similar feeling of doubt and insecurity is expressed by Broyard's narrator, who assumes that her family members may be wary of her lack of knowledge about black concerns and may reject her. This concern contributes to her general sense of unease following her enthusiasm upon discovering her African American heritage. It is a more complicated process to claim her African American heritage, as she begins to understand. She recalls a conversation with her mother in which she wonders whether meetings with her family members may bring the reconciliation she seeks, and questions her parents' choices—to which her mother replies that some injuries cannot heal—an indication of the complexity of coming to terms with the family's past (Broyard 2007, 456).

History is indeed full of contradictions, and the narrators we encounter in these texts have had at times radically different experiences compared with their family members on the other side of the "color line." These family members have actively contributed to the historical development in very different ways. The narrator in *Pearl's Secret* comes to understand that some family members at least indirectly worked against others—a complex legacy for a family to reconcile. In *The Sweeter the Juice*, the narrator describes this complexity of differing legacies using the image of a quadrille that was set in motion by the first instance of race mixing in her family (Haizlip 1995, 51). This image fits well with her family's story—a quadrille is commonly danced by four couples, rather than one, and is a dance form imported from Europe. At the same time, it is a rather controlled type of dance, where the steps are at times even announced. Premeditation is not what happened in her family: Too many coincidences led to the current situation, including multiple instances of *passing* and crossing of a variety of lines. The word choice in this passage—specifically the term "miscegenation"—also points to the contested quality of racial transgression in the past as well as in the time frame in which the narrative was written: It often remains unclear whether an act was indeed voluntary or not.

In *One Drop*, many of the narrator's reflections about history and famous people her family members may have encountered relate back to the history of the state of Louisiana. While this emphasis on a specific state makes for a slightly different focus compared to the narratives previously discussed, the narrator also still locates her family's experience in the American context, explaining that the family retained a French identity into the 1920s even though they had become Americans by official status in 1803 (Broyard 2007, 158). This is an important observation relating directly to the complex ways in which the state of Louisiana negotiated its Americanness, but the comment can also be linked to her family history. The family's habits and traditions were in many ways different from those of other Americans, as they did not consider themselves national subjects. This self-perception may in some sense have led the narrator's father to take the decision to *pass*; the narrator often mentions her father's "French" upbringing to explain how he became the man he was.

The narrator herself undergoes a transformation through her investigation of her family alongside American history: she understands how her family is "at once ordinary and emblematic" (157). The discovery of many parallels between the stories she hears about her family and the larger American narrative cause the narrator to reevaluate what it means to be an American. She recognizes that being American means that one's family has had a part in some of the major struggles of American history, a comparatively "young" nation.

This understanding of the family contribution to history is also relevant in terms of the narrator learning about some of the successes of her family members who lived as black. Her aunt, she discovers, is married to the former ambassador of the United States to Ghana, a civil rights lawyer (36); and she wonders why her father kept this part of the family a secret in the first place. These are not the kinds of family members that she, or any of her immediate family members, would likely feel ashamed of having. Again, this particular narrative of the black family's success firmly insists on the placement of relatives and family connections within the middle class, almost to the point of cutting out other African American experiences that were also social realities in the 1990s and early 2000s, when these narratives were published, and still are today.

While the narrator in *One Drop* is surprised to find that her family was among the slave-owning black families of eighteenth-century Louisiana, the narrator in *Slaves in the Family* has always known that his ancestors had slaves, and that his family members had once played an important role in the economic development of the Chesapeake area in coastal South Carolina. He, too, throughout his attempts to reconstruct his family history, has to come to terms with his family members' involvements with and participation in different events that have shaped American history at large.

Considering his family background, this approach also means learning about how his forebears fought against the progress of civil rights. In this text, the dynamics of oppressor and oppressed are significantly different. It appears as if the narrator wanted to place himself in the role of a redeemer who wishes to make up for the wrongs committed by his slave-owning ancestors. Once again, *Slaves in the Family* presents a story similar to the other texts but negotiates the topics throughout the narrative from a very different, and still believable, perspective. The narrator cannot leave his background behind but remains firmly located in his own context. This is also true of the other texts discussed here, but plays out in different ways due to the reversed sides of the narrators.

Generally, the narrator is very critical about his ancestors' opinions regarding civil rights and African Americans. He refers to the English settlers in the Carolinas as "colonizers" and is explicit about the cruelty of slavery. He knows much about slavery in America, and much of what he knows is not positive. However, what he hears from his family members contradicts this knowledge. One of his distant cousins, Elias, has worked in the field of historic preservation and is known as a family historian. He is therefore supposedly a good resource for details about the narrator's family members and how they lived before the Civil War (43). However, the cousin claims that while the Ball family owned many slaves, many of them were not forced to work on the plantation, but "were supported" by the Ball family, meaning that they were not on the fields and not being sold away (47). Moreover, the family historian describes how the slaves on the Ball family rice plantations had it easier than the slaves on cotton plantations, and that many of them even owned guns (47) and fought on the side of the Confederates in the Civil War (48). In this particular story about the Ball rice empire, the slaves are described as loyal Americans and loyal Southerners.

In contrast to his ancestors' opinions on the world, the narrator's view of American culture is much more inclusive. For example, he emphasizes that American culture has been significantly shaped by the contributions of African Americans, and specifically refers to music and the multiple genres originated in African American forms (68). At the same time, he recognizes the ambivalence of American history and how his ancestors' actions have contributed to the establishment of an unjust system.

He describes his perception of the rice plantations his ancestors owned as follows: "Rice would become the manna of the Balls and the bane of thousands of blacks" (102). This reference to Exodus, in which "manna" is the bread of heaven offered to the Israelites by God to sustain them on their way through the desert, is very interesting. The "manna" as described in the Bible does if in fact bring to mind rice, as it is described as small, round, and fine (Exod. 16:14–16). The rice, the "manna," secured a comfortable life for the white Ball families even in difficult times. However, the narrator does not understand this situation as a God-given privilege, but rather makes clear that his family's riches were only possible on the backs of those the family enslaved. In this way he pays a tribute to the interconnected histories of blacks and whites with regard to the Ball plantations.

The narrator in Ball's *Slaves in the Family* clearly identifies that what his ancestors achieved was rare, despite the images of Southern plantations spread by popular culture (Ball 1999, 176). While the narrator spends much time explaining what exactly his family had achieved during the time of their rice empire on the East Coast and thinks about which factors may have contributed to their rise, he does not neglect the fact that on the part of the Ball slaves, there were also some remarkable characters who are remembered in the family.

He brings up, for example, a slave referred to as Boston King, who he left the United States for Sierra Leone when it was established as a colony in which many freed former African American slaves settled after they had been given their freedom or had escaped from slavery, mostly during the eighteenth century. Boston King is described as a remarkable man and a "rebel" (216): in the Revolutionary War, he ran away from the Ball plantations and then went to Sierra Leone via Canada, in effect reversing his father's transatlantic passage (215). The story was published, making Boston King a well-known man and the best-known of the former Ball slaves as he is the only one whose life story was written down (215–16).

That Boston King is brought up in the text shows the narrator's general open-mindedness to hearing and passing on these stories, and his willingness to make them part of the family narrative which he is essentially recomposing through investigating what became of the Ball slaves. At the same time, this passage in the text shows the feelings of loss and nostalgia the narrator feels in connection with this part of history. He is aware that there were other stories that would likely be equally worth telling, but that have been lost because they were not documented.

Overall, the narrators in the *memoir of the search* put great effort into giving a more or less balanced account of how their family story was part of the larger American story, and they point out where family members may have even altered this larger national story. The narrators describe "the making of America" as an accumulation of different events, a process evolving over a long period of time, and one shaped by many different people contributing in different places and in different ways. Due to the research-oriented quality of the *memoir of the search*, the narrators refer back to a variety of sources relating to their families' and American history, including personal documents but also historical and sociological studies. It would be very interesting to go through the material cited in these narratives in order to understand better how exactly family history is archived and ordered in these narratives, to see whether an analysis of the archiving process might not provide additional insights into a familial reading of the nation's history.

The research-oriented quality of the narrative makes clear that what the reader is told is not solely the story of one family with its successes, failures, and shortcomings. Rather, the *memoir of the search* engages in a process of inscribing new stories into the national narrative of Americanness. The research and careful documentation prove necessary so that these stories can no longer be denied, so they can move beyond oral narrative or family legend. At the same time, the narrator in *Slaves in the Family* is putting himself into a contested position because as a white person, he is telling the story of the descendants of those his family members enslaved. Something similar can also be said about those narrators who identify as black: The fact that they are looking for white relatives puts them into a contested position. The act of seeking out these hidden layers alone does not change the primary framework of the story, slavery, and its long-term legacy.

REWRITING THE IMMIGRANT STORY

The *memoir of the search* plays with the notion of the quintessential American immigration story. While the classic story of immigration to the United States, mostly from Europe, has usually been denied to those with African heritage, immigration is an important part of the genre. Employing the immigration narrative, the narrators position themselves as Americans from the start. While the narrator in *The Sweeter the Juice* clearly states that she does not desire to be white (Haizlip 1995, 14), she still links herself to white settlers.

In these terms, all narrators are descendants of the settlers who built the country. They describe in detail how their ancestors became American, and how they, like all other Americans, at one point migrated to America and struggled to follow their personal version of the American Dream. Phrasing this experience in terms of an immigration story speaks to the desire of locating mixed-race heritage at the center of the established American story, with its European origins and its mainstream impact. The idea of placing race mixing in the mainstream alludes to the narrators' (and, by extension, the genre's) attempt to normalize slavery and segregation as part of American history and combatting the perception of mixed race as a "problem" plaguing the nation. Once again, it becomes crucial in this process to place the narratives of these mixed-race families not only at the center of the American story, but also at the center of society and the middle class. Again, there appears to be no tolerance within the genre for disrupting this pattern.

Eric Gardner (2003, 149) has noted with regard to the common structures and narrative patterns of these texts that they start with immigration and build on one white, often English, man, who combines attributes "of religious pilgrim, pioneer, patriot and entrepreneur." This immigrant descendant is the human point of origin in the story. He receives special attention as the first "American" in the line of family ancestors, and he therefore matters specifically in the family's process of becoming "American."

Close observation shows that even the wording of the immigration story is very similar in all of these texts and can be considered a defining feature in such narratives subsumed here under the *memoir of the search*. The immigration of an ancestor, the arrival in the New World, marks the beginning of the family story in America. While this observation may not sound very remarkable to begin with, it does make these narratives resonant with other narratives—about the construction of America and of Americans—that were previously denied to those with African heritage, such as European immigrant stories that were studied in detail by Boelhower (1982).

The narrator in Haizlip's text starts her family story with a white Irish immigrant and his family, and their arrival in America following the Irish famine, that has devastated their country of origin (Haizlip 1995, 35). In its focus on the starvation and death of the Irish, the passage stresses the resilience of these immigrants. Their dire situation in Europe fueled their immediate departure, and the description is reminiscent of other narratives of Irish families coming to the United States because of the famine. Despite the desperate situation depicted, her ancestor Maher was an experienced traveler and adjusted to new circumstances easily (35–36).

Maher was unlikely one of the many "undesirable" Irish immigrating to the United States—he was a man of class, someone with money, resources, and access, even before he relocated permanently to the United States. Maher finally settled in Washington, DC, becoming a business owner, and eventually, wealthy and respected (36). The narrator here provides little detail; the story remains set within the established parameters of immigrant biography and the success story.

In her version of the immigration story, the narrator states that the story is not unique, but rather, that it begins like countless other stories of this kind—which indeed it does. The narrator in Neil Henry's *Pearl's Secret* introduces his white forebear much in the same way: He speaks about his English great-great-great grandfather by the name of Arthur John Beaumont, who as a young man left his Kent home for the New World. He built a life in Louisiana, "where he found work as an overseer on a cotton plantation" (Henry 2001, 1). This white forebear later joins the Confederate Army out of loyalty to his new country, a measure that attests to his Americanness. Later, he returns to his hometown where he became an important man, and well respected (2). To this, the narrator remarks that this story appears rather conventional: it is a common immigration narrative (2). The conventionality of the story aligns the ancestor with other white immigrants, instead of isolating Beaumont because he conceived a child with a black woman.

Both these narrators, even though they clearly identify as African American and express their loyalty to African American culture, tend not to talk about their family before the second half of the nineteenth century. Rather, they tell their family story beginning with the immigration of a white forebear to the New World. It is more than likely that their black progenitors had been in the country far longer than that. Certainly, one of the reasons why this is not explicated in detail lies in the fact that not very much is known about their African ancestors (Haizlip 1995, 104). The narrator makes evident that nothing specific can be said about the exact location where the ancestors lived. Unlike in European immigration narratives, there is no definite place these people departed from, only a vague geographical area of origin. Despite these gaps and the apparent lack of information about the African region her ancestors originate from, this narrator *can* trace back her African American forebears to the early nineteenth century. The same is evident from the family tree included in *The Sweeter the Juice*. Nevertheless, the story of these African ancestors is not evaluated in much detail.

In contrast, the Irish immigration to America is discussed as a defining event, and in a rather stereotypical manner—the well-known story of coming from Ireland following the famine. Yet, and this represents a twist to the established narrative, they are not "regular" Irish people—William Maher is depicted as an adventurous man, since he crossed the Atlantic Ocean many times before settling in the United States. The remark of him being middle class once again locates the family, in the grand scheme, within a higher social class than a conventional arrival from Ireland would attest to. The statement also points to the true American spirit of a white pioneer, who is one of the narrator's ancestors.

Pearl's Secret shows a similar tendency to only focus on the European ancestor in detail while neglecting other ancestries. During his research, the narrator in this text learns much more about his family's past than he lets on at the beginning of his story. He describes Beaumont's roots (Henry 2001, 248) and, via statements alluding to his privilege, places the family in a context of political power and agency. A. J. Beaumont, the immigrant, was not the only ancestor of importance. But he was the one who took the step from the Old World to the New, who contributed to the making of America, and who started something new which has persisted, namely, the narrator's family. Along the same lines, the narrator also makes visible in his family tree that for him, the family started with the encounter in Mississippi of A. J. Beaumont and Laura Brumley, and not in Europe.

The emphasis on the immigrant *from Europe* marks a departure from earlier narratives of this kind. The extensive focus on the white ancestor clearly makes the *memoir of the search* decidedly different from *Roots*. *Roots* attests to the resilience of the African American community and gives them a story to circulate about their origins in North America. In *Roots*, Kunta Kinte is constructed as an "immigrant" (Gardner 2003, 151). In its entirety, the text can be understood as an immigration and Americanization narrative. *Roots* begins with a significant part of the story set in Africa, and talks about community, tradition, and ritual. The subsequent voyage of the African, Kunta Kinte, to America is not voluntary: His passage to the New World is the result of being captured and brought to the continent in chains. Significant parts of *Roots* are set in Africa; the capture of Kunta Kinte and the Middle Passage are also described in much detail.

None of these observations can be made with regard to the *memoir of the search*. The newer genre excludes the African story, the capture, the traumatic experience of the Middle Passage, as well as the direct experience of slavery on American soil. Slavery is only present in the texts via the narrators' meditations on the subject; other topics are not really mentioned at all. The *memory of the search* is located in American history, and on American soil. No further "rooting" is needed.

These texts reverse the idea of Haley's *Roots*, because instead of tracing the black ancestors as Haley does in his narrative about Kunta Kinte and his descendants, Haizlip and Henry do not look for their black relatives, but rather for those who are white or have become white. They are not looking for their African roots at all because they are rooted in America and understand themselves as representatives of the American experience: an experience that is, in its mainstream iteration, and almost ironically, shaped by white European migration and not by the trauma of the Middle Passage.

The narrator in *The Sweeter the Juice* reports traveling to Senegal in the 1980s because she was involved in a film project there (Haizlip 1995, 105); that is, she was being asked to fulfill the role of mediator bridging the perceived gap between the United States and Africa. She also had the opportunity to see some of the former slave huts, leading her to think about her ancestors in quite some detail (105).

Chanie Robinson Taylor, her paternal great-grandmother, is the narrator's real-life connection to slavery. The narrator owns a photograph of this woman which was given to her by her uncle. From her facial features, Haizlip's protagonist tries to find an answer as to where her ancestors might have originated, and which different heritage strains may have been involved (106). While the narrator reflects on the influence of these earlier ancestors on her family, she does not express any desire for a prolonged stay in Africa: She feels that her family and her life are in America, and that this national context is where she belongs as well. With regard to her ancestors who came to America as slaves, she emphasizes that these people "would never be African again" once they had set foot on American soil, because their American experience changed them undeniably (104).

Just like the narrator in *The Sweeter the Juice*, the protagonist of Henry's text spends some time in Africa working as a foreign correspondent. He emphasizes that he did not necessarily choose to go there, nor did he know much about Africa when he was asked to work there for a while. This statement of course stands in stark contrast to the (certainly stereotypical) assumption that all African Americans are inherently interested in their African origins and have a special relationship to the continent their ancestors were brought to America from. However, he took the chance and moved to Nairobi (Henry 2001, 86–87). There, he consciously distances himself from the quest for belonging that often leads African Americans to travel to Africa, stating that he has no interest in this (87). His business was reporting, doing his job, and not looking for places where his ancestors had maybe lived at some point in what he perceives to be a very distant past. This statement is almost ironic considering he is—on a different level—so obsessed with finding his ancestors in the United States.

Rather than expressing unity with those he meets in Africa (88), he points to cultural differences between America and Africa, and between American citizens and those of African countries. Despite his African roots, the narrator places himself outside of the African context: He clearly sees himself as an American first and foremost. The time he spends in Africa, dealing with crises, with complex questions of wars, hunger, and poverty, convinces him yet again that he is American, and needs to look for his family's story there (89). Thus, if anything, his time in Africa, which also confronts him with his own mortality since he is living in constant danger of dying in one of the ongoing battles in the locations he visits (Somalia, for example), makes him more American.

He forms no inherent connection to Africa but notes his attachment to the United States. He realizes that the story which he has already spent a lot of time thinking about, that of his family and the story of his family as the story of America, needs to be investigated in order for him to understand himself and his African American identity better in the context of his home of America. It is telling that he refers to his American story as the one the "roots" of which he needs to rediscover—meaning bring back into his family's awareness after decades of not talking about it.

He understands that his effort to reconstruct his family history in the United States is somewhat opposed to how people tend to perceive an investigation of origins—he aims to build stronger connections to the United States instead of finding out what has happened to his ancestors in other parts of the world.

Hence, his undertaking of finding out about his family history in the United States is important to him as African Americans were too long denied such a sense of history, and in their own country, the United States (287–88). Thus, the narrator talks about his research project describing it as a process of building "ties" to the United States. He makes clear that there is significant effort in undertaking this project, as he cannot take his citizen rights for granted.

His being rooted in America represents an important step away from the perception that African Americans are mainly interested in their African ancestors. This understanding is likely a recent development, and one the narrator also alludes to in the text. He describes a letter, now in his possession, that his mother sent to his grandmother. In this letter, written while she was in Heidelberg where her husband was stationed in the 1950s—the time and place where the family first felt really free from the constraints of race—the mother describes that she feels "American" all of a sudden (168). Her statement suggests that the freedom usually associated with being "American" is not part of her daily life experience and routine in the United States. Instead, in Europe she feels much more respected. Her son, on the other hand, one generation later, very obviously feels "American" in America and so does not need to investigate his African roots, not even as a genealogist. This development shows that a generation has passed since *Roots* and indeed, the roots are different now, as well.

Much in the same way, the narrator in *The Sweeter the Juice* comments on her identity as an American in a way that is different from how an earlier generation of African Americans would have addressed the topic of roots and origins. She vividly recalls hearing a speech by Malcolm X at Harvard University and how she reacted to the Afrocentric approach in this speech where he claimed African Americans are still Africans in every way. She remembers how she "had to wrap myself around the African part to make it stick" (Haizlip 1995, 201–202). The "African part" central to Afrocentric concepts is not part of her daily experience in America—by consequence, she feels American.

Instead of looking for their roots in Africa, the narrators in *Pearl's Secret* and *The Sweeter the Juice* are only interested in investigating the part of their Americanness they feel ambivalent about at best because it has given them and their families hardships and caused much pain in the past: the "white" section of their families.

Bearing that in mind, it may be surprising that those narratives in which a narrator actually identifies as white are much closer to the original pattern established by *Roots*, with Broyard's text probably coming the closest to this original pattern. The narrator attempts to find her black relatives despite being unable to follow her family history all the way back to Africa. Moreover, it is the narrator in *Slaves in the Family*, the son of a former slaveholding dynasty, who travels across the Atlantic to meet with and talk to Africans, the descendants of slave-sellers, and to discuss the past with them. These instances show important reversals in how stories of origins are told in the late twentieth century. It appears that, suddenly, African Americans are interested in their "white" roots, while "white" people are compelled by potential African ancestors or family members—likely also in order to have something "extraordinary" to show for.

Placing so much emphasis on the white forebear as in Haizlip's narrative almost contradicts the notion the text starts out with. A poem by the author is placed before the preface to the text, summing up her family's doings in America and emphasizing the many ways in which her family was present basically since the beginnings of measurable time, long before America was settled by white Europeans. In this poem, the speaker builds a connection between the various "strings" of her identity and genetic origins. She names the Native American, English, African, and the immigrant strings, the latter likely referring to the Irish (Haizlip 1995, 8).

Her oldest connection to the country is thus via Native Americans, who were there before the settlers. Her poem critically alludes to the process of Europeans taking claim of the country, as well as to bringing Africans to the New World in chains. She clearly points out the unequal relationships that were established due to these early hierarchies in the colonial and early national period. In the overall context of *The Sweeter the Juice*, this poem makes clear that even though this text in its entirety is oftentimes referred to as a prime example of a biracial biography (e.g., Spickard 2001), it goes further than that: it is a story of America, of how America came to be, of how the different populations who inhabited the land have shaped it, and how all of these groups emerged in a new generation which is *aware* of all of these different ancestries.

The poem makes evident that the family, down to all its different branches, has felt loyal to the land, and that the speaker as a result feels very rooted in America and nowhere else. A family history such as hers is a very American story, and it could be argued that the poem serves to unite all of the different micro-histories of the narrator's family and merge them into one large macro-story of America. One factor tying together all of the different groups represented in the poem—with the exception of the Native Americans—is that they came to America from elsewhere at one point in time, and that they contributed to the building of the new country. Here, to be American means to be an immigrant, specifically, to be a white immigrant or a descendant of one.

Why among all these different strings of the family, the narrator picks the quasi-Anglo immigrant as the prime progenitor whose story is expounded in the text deserves further analysis. The choice clearly represents an instance of privileging white origins over all other possible choices of identity construction. Specifically, when considering the narrator's ambivalence regarding her whiteness, this process of privileging white "roots" raises questions. It can be read as a way of showing that the narrator feels most impacted by her white Irish ancestry, since the white heritage that has complicated her family found originated with this specific Irish forebear. The emphasis on the white forebear alludes to the process of inscribing mixed-race heritage into the mainstream narratives of nation-building. The Anglo root—or rather, the wealthy Irish ancestor in Haizlip's case—is privileged over the others to make it fit.

In effect, focusing on the story of the Anglo immigrant, and doing so in a somewhat stereotypical manner without a detailed evaluation of the reasons for the departure or the exact conditions at the time of arrival, detaches these narratives from both Europe and Africa. It is very clear from the beginning that this is an American story—it begins like many American stories, as the narrator in *The Sweeter the Juice* emphasizes—and it follows the typical patterns such an American story has to follow, namely, immigration, Americanization, and following the American Dream.

Just like the narrator in *The Sweeter the Juice*, the narrator in *Pearl's Secret* looks at his family history as a story that illustrates the American Melting Pot. He grows up with the notion that his family's experience matters in a larger context, and he recalls something that his mother always used to say to him when he was a child: "'We've got America in us [. . .] We've got the story of America'" (Henry 2001, 50). The idea that a single family's story stands representative for the story of America is important to all the narratives, possibly also because these texts may try to contribute to a new collective memory in which past injustices are being acknowledged, and in which the interconnectedness of different stories and different histories is made evident. By inserting the narrative of a conventional middle-class mixed-race family, the descendants of European immigrants to the United States, into conventional stories about America's origin and becoming, mixed-race heritage is normalized and made part of the mainstream.

The narrator in Bliss Broyard's *One Drop* constructs her story of immigration in a similar way. In contrast to the other two examples discussed here, she does not describe the white progenitor as an adventurous entrepreneur who came to the New World from the British Isles, but rather as someone who was taken there involuntarily: Her ancestor came as a French soldier in 1753 (Broyard 2007, 148). The progenitor, Etienne Broyard, did not become a successful businessman, but rather he struggled in the colony (149).

Soon after his arrival, he gets married and becomes a father to eleven children (151), with the narrator's ancestor being the ninth child (152). The passage introducing the great-great-great-great grandfather, of course, does not tell a story of social privilege, but rather one of struggle. The text in its entirety describes a family rising socially since coming to the United States, and especially since embracing an American identity (instead of the French identity the immigrants to Louisiana retained for a long time), but it also intertwines, albeit indirectly, this white ancestor's life with the fate of slaves, who were also brought to the United States unwillingly. The narrator goes on to state that these men and women were not people of privilege but rather, a rejected population (149).

Thus, she finds that not all white immigrants were necessarily part of a ruling class; many suffered hardships (149). She also continues to point out that Louisiana, due its specific conditions, was not so much interested in "segregating the races," but that racial transgression, specifically with Native women, was the norm in the colony (150). Even black-white unions existed to some degree until the introduction of the *Code Noir*, and even then, this practice did not really stop (150). This passage attests that crossing the boundaries associated with race was to a certain extent "normal" in Louisiana society—a society that knew "*gens de couleur libre*, or free people of color" (italics in original).

At the same time her ancestor is atypical, as he does not partake in intercourse with black women but soon after his arrival in the colony got a white woman pregnant (151), whom he also proceeded to marry before the birth of the child. Etienne then became a slave owner, something which "didn't necessarily place them [the Broyards] among the elite of New Orleans" (152). This comment shows that slavery was an ordinary part of the social environment of the time, a practice even accessible to those less privileged.

Edward Ball's immigration narrative begins in Dover in 1669, where the ancestor boards a ship to the New World (Ball 1999, 27), where he also arrived healthy, something that was not granted at the time. Soon thereafter, John Comings' life differed in important aspects from the lives of regular Englishmen and even the gentry in his original home in Europe: His large farm "was peopled by captive workers" (27), in this case meaning Africans as well as Natives. The journey to the New World sets Ball's ancestor apart from his English origins; his involvement in slavery makes John Coming an "American."

He and his later wife, Affra Harleston, are described as "pioneers" (27) and people who got away with things. This emphasizes that John Coming plainly had luck in life. He was at the right place at the right time, leading to him being able to establish himself as a planter, and his plantation eventually became known as one of the most important plantation empires in the South—a mark of his class status. Achieving status here becomes a kind of conquest game, in which the narrator's ancestors become colonizers, explorers, settlers; the narrator even uses the word "invaders" to refer to them (28). At the same time, the narrator explains how his family essentially brought with them a specific mindset that allowed for slavery from elsewhere: "By the time the Carolina colony was founded, all of this [slavery] was already thousands of years old" (30–31). The passage places the blame on Europeans who had by this time "found an easier way of procuring workers, namely, encouraging black clans to fight one another and to sell their prisoners of war" (31). The passage also points to the industrial quality slavery attained at that point in time. In the case of the Ball family's rice plantations in the Charleston peninsula, it was not a matter of Ball family members working alongside a few slaves, but rather a large group of slaves worked on the plantations to ensure their owners' riches and well-being.

These immigration narratives are in some ways much like those in Haizlip's and Henry's text, but they bear less potential surprise for the reader: Immigration stories are part and parcel of white American family stories. The fact that these narrators establish contact with those who have previously not been part of their story is an innovation. These narrators consciously engage with those who have previously been written out of their family trees. This opposite direction of research into the relationship between the family and the nation makes evident that these kinds of texts share the characteristic of how they understand American history, and that they are in dialogue with each other.

REDEFINING THE AMERICAN DREAM

In their rendition of their family stories, the narrators all interpolate different notions connected to the American Dream—the idea that in the United States everybody is able to rise socially by way of hard work. The narrators are able to do so because they speak from a position of economic, social, and cultural privilege, and their family stories prove that it is possible to get ahead through hard work and not giving up on one's dreams. In these texts, the American Dream is also strongly related to the idea of Americanization, especially with regard to first generation immigrants.

By following through with their dreams, the immigrants become Americans. The same is true for the slaves who are neither immigrants nor protagonists in the narratives, but who are referred to as citizens in the texts. Slaves are not construed as Africans in these texts; instead, they are Americans who are in their own ways emblematic of the American story. Their history becomes "Americanized" and is fit into the conventional schemes of established narratives. This process further contributes to "rooting" the genre of the *memoir of the search* in the United States: to be of mixed heritage is a *very American thing* according to the texts discussed here.

The American Dream "fuses private fortune with that of the nation" (Berlant 1997, 4). The American Dream is strongly connected to mobility, to moving across established borders, moving up in social class, and advancing from one generation to the next. Interestingly, in *the memoir of the search* the upward social mobility of the African American branch of the family is usually contrasted with the downfall of the white family. This emphasis on upward social mobility of African Americans reverses the conventional story of white success versus the failure of African Americans. It also places the African American family in the mainstream and the middle class, signifying inclusion and participation in the American Dream.

In *The Sweeter the Juice*, the American Dream as a concept is deeply ingrained in the story of the family. When addressing her African ancestors, the narrator explains that they would actively become American as soon as they had crossed the Atlantic Ocean, and that they would be inspired by the American Dream. They would go through several different stages between discrimination and acceptance, before their story culminates in the present narrator (Haizlip 1995, 104). The transformation from African to American appears to be automatic—in spite of the coercion inherent in slavery—since it is indicated that they would "remake themselves" (104) instead of be passively remade. In this way, the passage alludes to ideas of the American Dream as well as that of the "self-made-man."

Nevertheless, it becomes clear that the process of becoming American was not easy, and it was not full of new opportunities as is often suggested in conventional immigrant narratives. The ancestors could only get access to "drops from the American dream" (104), but these would serve them as inspiration. The process of distillation commonly leads to the purification of a substance, making this an interesting metaphor. These ancestors consumed a purified version of the American Dream that nourished them and made them into "true" Americans, pointing toward their desire for inclusion in the mainstream. However, this desire for inclusion risks erasing the horrors and losses of slavery and does not take into account the collective contributions of African Americans to American national culture.

The arrival in America sets in motion a complex chain of transformations. The narrator considers herself a direct result of these transformations, which go side by side with processes of naming. With each step her ancestors climbed up the social ladder and with each legal decision which opened up new opportunities for them to realize their goals, the way society referred to them changed. The result of these numerous transformations is an *individual* and not a category for an American of African descent anymore. Considering these parameters, the *memoir of the search* plays conveniently into well-established notions of American individualism and self-realization: the becoming of a "self," of "me."

The narrator in *The Sweeter the Juice* makes the connections to the American Dream most obvious by intertwining her family's story with national history in a very complex way. She indicates that her parents' relationship, which included the possibility for the narrator's father to change his life and start anew after a failed marriage, began at Arlington National Cemetery: one of the nation's most important sites of remembrance, erected during the American Civil War, and an important political site, as well as the burial ground of some of their ancestors (Haizlip 1995, 123). This detail signifies their arrival into middle-class society, or even among the national elite.

The American Dream in this text is strongly connected to freedom, self-sustainability, and independence from stereotypes. It also builds on the idea that one can essentially remake and reinvent oneself. By following the ideas of the American Dream across several generations, the abstract "me" that stands for the narrator comes into being. The narrator recognizes that extraordinary circumstances enabled her black family to rise up socially and class-wise instead of being held back by constraints related to skin color.

Some of the most interesting references to the American Dream and its long-term effects can be found in Bliss Broyard's *One Drop*. She suggests that her father, Anatole Broyard, was a typical self-made man who rose from an unimportant Louisiana boy to an important writer, editor, and literary critic. In fact, his move from the South to the North at a very young age recalls the immigration and Americanization story. Anatole Broyard comes from New Orleans to New York, and at one point remade himself, *passing* over into white society and losing the connections to his roots. From then on, he hides his heritage even from his own children. He even seems to understand his own life as the journey of a "self-made man," as the narrator points out (Broyard 1995, 23). The fact that this character can rise by himself, reach a higher status without being dependent on an earlier generation's pedigree as the American Dream promises, enables his *passing*.

He can afford to live without "roots" because this is both possible and accepted within the idea of self-reinvention connected to the American Dream. He can be whoever he wants to be, he does not need anyone, and nobody asks about his background either. As a central character in *One Drop*, the father appears to be a little bit like the Jay Gatsby, a literary reference that is also brought up by the narrator (34). In *One Drop*, America is presented as the country of self-invention, where people can come out of nothing and rise very high socially. *The Great Gatsby*, or rather his own emergence out of nowhere, seems to be the narrator's father's personal version of the American Dream—except that it is a Dream with an edge. While it is possible for him to dissolve almost all ties with his past, his daughter grows up with a deep feeling of incompleteness. Taken to its final conclusion, even *The Great Gatsby* does not end on a positive note; rather, the novel shows the American Dream turning into a nightmare. In these terms, there is a moral lesson indicated in the allusion to Fitzgerald's iconic story.

The rags to riches story that is told in *One Drop* is equally present in *Slaves in the Family*, albeit in a different way. The narrator's ancestors established themselves as slaveholders which enabled them to rise socially (Ball 1999, 154). The text exemplifies how the Ball family rose from being immigrants to being part of the Southern elite within a short period of time. They did not have to commit to manual labor. They effectively turned themselves into royals on American soil despite coming to the country with limited means and having had no such opportunity in the European system shaped by heredity. Their new environment allowed for a social rise unrelated to heritage and blood—this is an American opportunity, the result of the American system of government. While the family is rich and while they own a great deal of land and many slaves, property alone does not amount to much from the point of view of the European elite. Essentially, Red Cap's modest background also likens him to Jay Gatsby, except that historically the Ball family rose a long time before Gatsby had become a quintessential American type.

The narrator describes his ancestor as a "would-be gentleman" (154), meaning that he did not have the pedigree it would usually take to be considered a real member of the gentry. This fact remains the same despite the wealth the Ball family members attain, their quasi-aristocratic lifestyle, and the fact that they are very careful about preserving the "purity" of their blood. The narrator describes the parameters according to which his ancestors, once they had established themselves as planters, measured their success: "land, money, slaves" (177). Later, blood gets added to the equation. Ironically, as history moves on, all these success factors become taboos and family secrets that cannot be mentioned.

The narrator in *Slaves in the Family* describes how his family had originally felt more connected to Europe than to the United States, even though the European elites did not really take the Southern planters seriously despite their riches and lifestyle. While it was only possible for the Ball ancestors to achieve their social status because they were far away from Europe, the family did not become American by way of the earlier mentioned immigration story or because they physically immigrated. Indeed, the ancestors did not believe in the American democratic principles at the time the nation achieved independence (226), which made a part of the family side with the British in the War of Independence. They remained British in the United States, just like the Broyard family held firm to their French identity when settling in Louisiana. The narrator himself attests to his own Americanness, but essentially these slaveholding ancestors, by retaining their Britishness, were not like him, hence isolating slavery from his identity. Not only did slavery no longer exist during his lifetime, but it was also his British ancestors who were in support of it.

The idea of American independence made the Ball family uncomfortable and caused them to fear losing what they had achieved in South Carolina. Once the Civil War was lost, the patriotic South Carolinians spurned the Balls for having sided with the British. Their decision to fight alongside the British even led to their rejection at times. One family ancestor, by consequence, went back to England where he was compensated for his losses in the Carolinas (237). While the Ball story *can* be told as an immigrant story informed by the American Dream, there are also elements that do not conform to the standard pattern. It took the Ball family a long time to sympathize with the American idea and the ideals of freedom connected to it.

The family continued to feel threatened by the historical development America went through at the time the Ball empire still existed. The family feared for their slaves when slavery was abolished in the Northern States (245); the Balls considered democracy a threat; they considered the Three-Fifths Compromise a threat (252); and certainly, the Civil War. In fact the family members, especially the women, appear to be skeptical of the America they apparently celebrated (322). Of course, the feast does not last long because the Confederacy loses, leading to the final loss of the Ball empire as well. Again, these ancestors' essentially non-American identity becomes manifest here.

The loss of the Ball empire is connected to the legend of a curse which the narrator refers to as "the curse of Buzzard Wing" (295). The end of the Ball empire had been in the making even before the Civil War. The social structures on the East Coast had already changed significantly by the 1830s and the family lived an urban lifestyle fueled by their plantation earnings and speculating on the stock market. Moreover, the importance of rice for the plantation economy slowly but surely began to lessen as "King Cotton" took over, and New Orleans became the most important Southern city. Charleston, the home of the Ball empire, on the contrary, became old and outdated (297–302). But the family, especially Caroline Ball, a young widow referred to as "Buzzard Wing," and other young family members, continued to spend money excessively. "Buzzard Wing" even sued the Ball family repeatedly after marrying another man, leading to the loss of yet more wealth (303).

The story of the decline and fall of the Ball empire is at odds with the stories of attaining and living up to the American Dream as described in the other narratives. But at the same time, only the fall of the old empires made it possible for the other narratives to be written—it is the reversal of the common storyline that even leads the narrator to inquire about the past. Time and again, the narrator points out that he personally does not profit financially from the plantations, but at the same time is aware that at least indirectly, all white people in the United States profit from the effects of plantation culture into the present day (14).

The fall of the Ball empire parallels the downfall of the Beaumont family in *Pearl's Secret*, even though A. J. Beaumont never amounted to as much as the owner of an entire plantation empire as in the case of the Balls, and his family's downfall occurred much later and for other reasons. The narrator in *Pearl's Secret* comments on the fact that his black family has managed to live up to many facets of the American Dream, while the white family has been steadily in decline since the end of the Civil War (Henry 2001, 227). The fall of the Beaumont family seems shrouded in mystery. The idea of a white family essentially falling from grace and losing their upward economic status stands in stark contrast to the stereotypical American success narrative. The Beaumont family lost its riches for the reason many Southern families did at the time—because of the boll weevil. The narrator contrasts how rise and fall make each other possible, but how upon looking back they seem unexpected. It seems almost ironic that against the odds, the black family rose up socially while the white family experienced a major economic and social downfall.

The narrator of *The Sweeter the Juice* makes a very similar statement. She also tries to sum up her family's story and the parallel rise and fall of the two families (Haizlip 1995, 16). In contrast to *Pearl's Secret*, where the reader only learns about the Beaumont family's fate toward the end of the story, the summary of the family history is set at the very beginning of the text in *The Sweeter the Juice* and thus functions as a prologue to the narrative. It introduces the reader to the ensuing story in a few lines, using a simple style and short sentences. The fact that this little family story works with very obvious oppositions and contrasts is reminiscent of a children's book. In a very simple and understandable manner, the passage expresses what is to follow in the story. Even though the narrative patterns employed in the rest of the text are more complex, the essence of the story can already be found in the final part of the prologue.

Placing the summary at the start takes away some of the detective work undertaken in the text, of course, as the outcome is already clear at the beginning of the narrative. But it is also not meant to be a detective story as such, but a story of revelation and discovery. What is important is to understand how the narrator undertakes the different steps in the process and how she pieces together the family story behind it.

While the *memoir of the search* productively works with the notion of the American Dream, this idea is rather ambivalent in the genre as a whole. There is a backdrop to the Dream that becomes very clear in these texts. In *One Drop*, the American Dream enables the father to leave behind all of his family connections and become somewhat of a latter-day Gatsby. At the same time, the American Dream makes the father's behavior explicable in a way which does not threaten his authority. His actions can almost be excused: He did not leave his family behind because he was not loyal to them or their blackness; he left them to follow a "Dream" as generations of other men had done before him. Certainly, getting caught up in the American Dream also made it ethically possible for the members of the Morris family to leave the two darkest children behind in *The Sweeter the Juice*. The fact that the black family fared much better than those who were *passing* almost appears to be fate's revenge to them for breaking with the past. For the Balls of *Slaves in the Family*, the American Dream was never an option because their American Dream was already lost when the nation was founded, and then once again when the Civil War was lost and the family empire fell apart. The narrators realize that the American Dream is not only a story of rising socially; it is also always a story of leaving others behind. That in these stories it is mostly the white family that ends up losing their riches while the black family rises adds a degree of irony to the texts.

The narrators all contemplate the fate of those who were not as privileged as they have been, and they are aware that their family members, parents, and grandparents may just have been lucky. This luck is not so much a matter of origin or roots and pedigree, but it also does not appear to be some sort of coincidence. They were able to make good use of the opportunities offered to them at one point in time, through hard work and persistence. The fact that there is an awareness of those who were left behind and those who could not follow the Dream parallels the earlier observation that the narrators also critically interrogate the worthy progenitor, the immigrant, in his authority and his processes of decision-making. The narrators do not take their families' successes for granted but keep alluding to how those successes were possible because American ideals enable them.

The American Dream as a narrative is productive in these texts because it allows the narrators to inscribe their own story of social privilege onto an existing template and to intertwine their family's fate with the nation's fate. At the same time, the narrators open up the possibility of questioning the patterns by pointing out that the American Dream can also become the American Nightmare. Indeed, their own stories ultimately require a revision of the established version of the Dream. This very revision, however, will take place on an ethical rather than a legal or political level. The narratives do not cry out for the establishment of different policies, new racial categories and designations, or different administrative ways of dealing with racial diversity. Rather, they make a point to insert their family's story into existing "American" storylines. The one claim these narrators do make is that racial diversity within a family is neither a rare nor a new phenomenon, but that it has been present since the early beginnings of America and before the nation gained independence.

What would therefore be required is not a new definition of who is officially acceptable as multiracial or mixed race, or even a redefinition of what it means to be American. Instead, what is required is the recognition that to be mixed is to be American at the very core. This conception does call for a redefinition of the family in two ways—in terms of who can be a member of an individual family, and of how the national family wants to narrate itself. The narratives thus do not suggest a "new nation" as is sometimes claimed, but rather a reconsideration of the national story in terms of its origins and its becoming. Including mixed-race narratives of *passing* into the national story does not make this story less "American"—if anything, this inclusion makes the story more complete.

STORIES OF CONFORMITY: NORMALIZING MIXED-RACE HISTORY

The texts subsumed here as *memoirs of the search* are not so much stories of difference, but rather they conform to the national narrative in many ways. Certainly, the narrators recognize that the stories they tell about their American roots are strikingly stereotypical. There is just one deviation: the start of a mixed family. By including the race mixing into a story of immigration and Americanization, this story of race mixing is both normalized and included into the mainstream American story. It is at the center of the story, but at the same time this story is not exceptional: it is "American."

Writing issues of race into the white story of immigration seems unlikely, yet these narrators very consciously pick up the established forms in order to write themselves as supposedly true Americans. The detailed evaluation about how their ancestors became Americans, how they (like all other Americans) at one point immigrated to the country, and how they struggled to follow their personal version of the American Dream can be read as a response to the widespread presumptions that in one way or another "the only viable model for nation-building is a process of 'Americanization'" (Berlant 1997, 192). This factor is clearly evident in the genre, which alludes to all conventional processes subsumed under the idea of "Americanization."

The notion that earlier generations, the narrators' ancestors, played such an essential role in the shaping of America and in what it meant to be American counteracts the idea that mixed-race heritage poses a threat to national integrity and especially to whiteness. The narratives do not counteract this notion by stating that whiteness should be preserved in one way or another, but do so by stating that to be American means to be mixed, and has always meant to be mixed. The melting pot has existed since America's beginnings, and by implication, it has also always included the mixing of black and white Americans.

The story about the centrality of mixed race for the United States is being foregrounded in the form of the mixed-race memoir and investigative autobiography that is the *memoir of the search*. This should not be very surprising overall. Autobiographical narratives, their citation, and their recitation have historically been one means through which the imagined community that was and is America constitutes itself as American on a daily basis. As a potent means of testimony through which identities are constituted and critiqued, autobiographical storytelling has played a major role in the making of Americans and the making, unmaking, and remaking of "America," as Smith and Watson (1996, 4) claim in their introductory chapter to *Getting a Life: Everyday Uses of Autobiography*. Smith and Watson further explain how the writing of an autobiography signifies "arrival in 'America' and the achievement of an 'American' identity" (5). The fact that autobiographies or memoirs are generally only written by or about people whose lives are representative enough to stand as examples has contributed to establishing "the conformity of individuals to new notions of identity and normative concepts of national subjectivity" (5).

While the genre of the *memoir of the search* shows that in the 1990s stories about race mixing could both be made public and be combined with conventional narratives of Americanness, the memoirs also make evident that notions of citizenship are still closely intertwined with questions of conformism to cultural and societal norms. The narrators in these texts establish themselves at the center of American culture by showing—and actually documenting—how they are connected to others, and how their story has remained true to the American ideal. While this feature is not unique to stories dealing with generationally mixed narrators, such as Barack Obama's own "story of race and inheritance," *Dreams from My Father* (1995), there is something to be said about the memoir's establishment of racial mixing at the center of narrating Americanness from early on. The genre emphasizes that to be mixed is not to be member of a new group of people in the United States, nor that being mixed race means to be in some way "Un-American" or less American than someone who is "pure."

In fact, purity has been done away with in these narratives, since everyone—even the stereotypical Anglo immigrant—could be mixed and probably is, because race mixing has been part of America's early beginnings. The family is no longer ethnically or racially homogenous. As these texts make evident, family membership becomes an issue of telling the same story, even if it is the same story told from different vantage points. Moreover, family members do not have to all belong to the same social class and—most importantly—skin color is no longer a guarantee for a specific class status.

The genre also shows it is also possible for formerly established Southern families to lose their privileges and for African American families to rise dramatically in social status. While these facts are not new, the specific way the genre exhibits the possibility, independent of skin color, of rising and falling socially makes this narrative quite remarkable.

In the *memoir of the search*, the complex interdependencies at the heart of American culture of black and white, freedom and bondage, and social rise and fall are depicted at the center of the story. The master narrative is not only rewritten, but implicitly also shown as failing to capture the essence of America's becoming. This realization represents an important shift from emphasizing the heroism of ancestors toward the critical discussion of the decisions they made and how they shaped the immediate as well as the national family.

Additionally, there is a strange contradiction at the center of the narratives. While the narrators each acknowledge the abandonment and the disruptions of history, they try to establish their families as adequate national bodies who have always believed in the American Dream, and who have believed in this Dream despite these gaps. The text which least exhibits this tendency is the one which would at first sight probably be most obviously connected to the American Dream, namely, Edward Ball's narrative, in which the narrator is a white Anglo-Saxon male with a rich family history to look back on. But much to the contrary, in *Slaves in the Family* the American Dream turned nightmare long before it became Republican.

The way national history and race relations are presented in these narratives appears in some ways to be "cleansed." While the narrators refer to issues such as the high incarceration rate for black males (Henry 2001), the racial unrest in Los Angeles (Broyard 2007), or economic inequalities along racial lines (Haizlip 1995), these references merely point to the awareness of these deficits by the narrators. The narratives simply move on from there. The existing, and worsening, inequalities do not have any real impact on the narrators' perceptions of America; they do not represent an impetus for change. The narrators all speak from a rather sheltered point of view, as established members of the middle class and as academics. They provide an idealized version of recent history that is nonthreatening to the average (white) American citizen.

Their demand, the inclusion of their story into the mainstream narrative of America, can easily be fulfilled because these stories pick up the established motifs and patterns by which the nation narrates itself already. When addressing history, the narrators speak as scholars, knowledgeable but detached, using specific sources. They speak from a rather mainstream perspective— often, so it seems, consciously addressing an educated middle-class audience sharing such views: an audience that probably has ancestors who immigrated, who became American, and who followed their dreams and rose up the social ladder. In short, in narrating the nation these texts do not address an audience needing to be convinced that society should be inclusive, that society should be tolerant, and that society should assume responsibility for the wrongs previously committed.

One major dilemma these texts face is that in order to establish themselves at the center of national narration, they have to cite and to refer to those patterns by which the nation has previously narrated itself. They remain tightly within the confines of an established genre instead of finding new strategies for rewriting the story. They construct a linearity that does not exist and has never existed because of the disruption their families have experienced due to race and due to the patterns of abandonment they experienced. Despite the narrators' acknowledgments of their own feelings of inadequacy and incompleteness, they essentially describe how their families have gone through the same process of Americanization that seems to be required in order to become adequate national subjects.

BLENDING INTO THE MAINSTREAM

The various interactions of these texts with established patterns of narrating the nation clearly demonstrate that on a meta-level these texts are narratives of quasi-*passing* themselves. The *memoir of the search* as a genre represents a strategy of blending into the mainstream by picking up the established stories by which the nation has narrated itself since its inception. The memoirists represent race mixing as the root of their family and their family's Americanization. However, inclusion into American mainstream society and into the master narrative depends on whiteness in these texts.

At the same time, by inscribing the racial diversity into the story of Americanization the narrators normalize it, making it part of the process of Americanization—possibly a precondition. The memoirs show that a certain degree of conformity with regard to established family stories seems necessary in order to make them legible within the master narrative. By the same token, the master narrative by the 1990s seems to allow for other stories to blend into it. The *memoir of the search* thus contributes—through the inscription of family narratives into the master narrative—to the normalization of racial diversity and interracial relationships in the national public. This is not only true for the individual story these texts are telling, but also for a normalization on a larger scale.

Along the same lines, these texts are not only palimpsests in that they speak from the present while allowing the past to be visible, but also in that they use the master narrative as the template upon which their story is inscribed.

The master narrative is still legible in the background, but new factors can be made visible against this backdrop. Thus, while conformity is given, these texts arguably also represent a variation on the theme in that they show that the master narrative was previously incomplete because it left out families who can define themselves as "quintessentially American."

It remains to be said that these narratives are not opposing the mainstream in the same ways as other texts which deal with the long-term effects of slavery on the individual and on society at large—texts such as Toni Morrison's *Beloved* (1987) or even Edward P. Jones's *The Known World* (2003). This is not only a matter of stylistic devices, experimental narrative methods, or narrative perspective, but also one of resisting the mainstream tools of documenting the past when addressing topics which are unrepresentable as such.

The major accomplishment of these texts is that they establish a new platform for public conversation about the past, one that is more inclusive of those who do not consider themselves directly related to these questions. They tell a story that is everyone's business as it is the national story. Everyone is implicated: there is no way to deny one's involvement once these texts have made the reader a witness to the past and how it shaped the present. In their own way, these texts point at the gaps left behind by history in a manner that makes them visible to people who may never have thought that they had anything to do with it: those who have managed to live the conventional American Dream and suddenly become aware that their freedom was built on the backs of others, and that the history of slavery and race is their history because it is part of their own story. In this way these texts insert the repressed story into the mainstream narrative. Once the story has fully arrived there, it may generate different kinds of conversations about white privilege, racism, and white power, as well as the police violence the black community is still confronted with in the twenty-first century.

Chapter 5

The Past in the Present
Encounters with the South

In Toni Morrison's novel *Song of Solomon* (1977), the protagonist, a young African American man called Macon Dead III and nicknamed Milkman, engages in a process of discovering his family's origins. He experiences the discovery process as one of awakening, spiritual healing, and coming to terms with the hurts of the past. In making his inquiry, Milkman—who has grown up in the industrial North, an environment shaped by the Great Migration—undertakes a journey to the Southern United States to discover his lineage and make sense of important family conflicts, for example, the difficulties inherent in his relationship with his father and ongoing contention between his father and aunt, a witch-like character named Pilate. Being caught in a complex net of competition and rivalry turns Milkman into a person who is essentially unfree.

Having encountered several difficulties along his path, among them a failed hunt for gold buried by his ancestors, Milkman eventually arrives in Virginia where a woman named Circe is able to point out several connections to his ancestors. The encounter with Circe leads him to come full circle regarding his family history, upon which he returns to Michigan. Later he brings his aunt Pilate to the South with him so that she can finally bury her father and find ways of dealing with the past, as well. At this point, Milkman has learned to "surrender[. . .] to the air" and "ride it" (Morrison 1998, 337), meaning he can escape his perceived imprisonment, the conflicts he is surrounded by at home, and be free—whether in life or death is not clear.

Morrison's novel is a fictional text including many elements of magical realism and employing a unique language addressing the African American experience and its Southern legacies in the urban North. In the novel, a quest to the sites of origin in the South needs to be undertaken by the Northern protagonist, a process of discovering his "roots" in order to free himself ("fly," "ride the air"). The protagonist can only find freedom after he found steady ground to walk on, after he discovered his origins, and become able to address the trauma of his heritage.

The *memoirs of the search* discussed here, while aiming at national inclusion by reciting and inscribing themselves onto central narratives of the nation, undertake a similar turn to the American South in order for their narrators to (re-)discover their family origins and come to terms with the past. While The narrators all live in the Northern or Western States of the United States—a legacy of the Great Migration also central to *Song of Solomon*—and with the exception of Ball's narrator, who spent his childhood in Charleston they, have also grown up outside the South. They all undertake a trip to the sites where their families originated, either during their process of discovery or immediately after. While the Southern United States is the site of origin for the families in the text I am discussing here, what is crucial for the *memoir of the search* as a genre is not so much the South as a location, but rather the quest as leading the narrator to a different site, one defined as a person's "origins." If one were to define Barack Obama's *Dreams from My Father* in those terms, the site of origin would not be the American South, but Kenya, where the narrator travels to understand his father's background and culture.

In the *memoir of the search*, the American South is present both as a region to which the family history is intimately connected, and as a specific location against which the narrators weigh their expectations and their experiences during the process of investigating their origins. Throughout the text, the narrators address several conflicts which originated in the South. These concern their own lives and can be subsumed under questions of racial and social identity, family, and different approaches to dealing with the past. Their concerns are strongly related to the ethical inquiries posed by the memoirs at large, as well as to the idea of finding a coherent self that is aware of its origins. In addition, the texts also comment on larger historical conflicts in the American South that still carry an impact in the present time, for example, slavery and the Civil War. Here, the South is presented as ambivalent both in terms of its (former) politics which contributed, directly or indirectly, to the status of the narrators' families, and in terms of its contemporary meaning(s) for the families being discovered through the narrators' investigations. Hence, the memoirs invite the reader to think about the South's role for the nation and its position in relation to America at large.

At the same time, the narrators do not reduce the South to a site of conflict alone: They also establish the region as a place of contact and encounter with people, documents, and locations that lead them to a deeper understanding of the region's meaning(s) for their families in the present. Their careful explorations of the Southern landscape, both in its physicality and in its showcasing of memory, turn the region into an archive of the past, a storage of memory, a resource for survival in the present. Depending on a narrator's upbringing, family history, and current racial identification, their negotiation of the South has multiple meanings, which I will explore in this chapter.

The lingering importance of the South is clear in the chapter titles chosen for the memoirs: *Pearl's Secret*, for example, has a chapter titled "Jim Crow's Shadow"; *Slaves in the Family* begins with "Plantation Memories" and, linking the chapter titles to the family's heritage, also has chapters called "Masters from England" and "The Making of a Dynasty," all of which refer to slavery and the American South. While these specific chapters that already refer to the region in their titles are explicitly linked to the region's history and culture, the South is an important undercurrent throughout the narratives in general. The narratives could not exist if it were not for the South.

A SITE OF SEGREGATION: CHILDHOOD MEMORIES OF THE SOUTH

In all cases, the family secret discovered and resolved in these texts originates in and relates back to the South; the South is where the family came into being, and where black and white family ancestors first encountered each other. The trips the narrators undertake to the region enable them to conduct research at the site where a particular event happened, or where its memory is kept or documented, for example, a public archive. The narrators also use these trips to meet up with people connected to the family in order to interview relatives, specialists, or others who may know something about the family's past. In this context, they report on previous trips to the South and refer to their feelings as children as well as in the present.

For Henry's narrator, the essential role of the region for the process of resolving the family secret is clear from the outset. In the course of his investigation, he suggests that the South is central to the family's identity (Henry 2001, 108) and crucial in order to solve the riddles associated with its history (112). To the narrator's family, the region is at the heart of the story and every other story relevant to the family members, even though they are far removed from their Southern origins. In *Pearl's Secret*, the family history is firmly associated with particular places in the South. St. Joseph, the site of the plantation where the narrator's white ancestor Beaumont worked as an overseer, as well as Natchez and Vicksburg are crucial.

Among the memoirs discussed here, three include the childhood memories of the narrator: *Slaves in the Family*, *The Sweeter the Juice*, and *Pearl's Secret*. In *One Drop*, the narrator grows up aware of her father's Southern origins, but only travels to New Orleans, where his family is from, when she is an adult and seeking more information about her father's past and about black Creole culture. The text does include a variety of childhood memories of encounters with her parents' acquaintances. She finds it particularly striking that the Broyards do not visit family members and live a rather isolated life. Her father claims that these family members do not interest him at all, that liking people has nothing to do with blood ties (Broyard 2007, 24). Since he hides his heritage from his children, there is no way he could travel to visit family in the South or elsewhere. The family's isolation is thus enforced by the father's *passing*.

Still, in *One Drop* there are "stories, artifacts buried in closets, photos tucked into old albums" that "kept their [the family members'] spectral presences in the air" (25). These childhood memories are mainly linked to the idea that there is a truth about her and her family that is hidden from her—the family secret already discussed. The narrator wonders how it is possible that her father moves so securely among African Americans they encounter, for example, a man who comes to their family home with a cleaning crew every few weeks (42–43). Since these childhood memories are mainly linked to her life in New England, to summer vacations in Martha's Vineyard, and to childhood trips to New York City where her father had lived before moving to New England, they will not be discussed as part of this chapter. To the narrator in *One Drop*, for the longest time, her father does not have Southern origins; rather, he comes from "nothing" (23).

The childhood memories in the memoirs help create a bond between reader and narrator. They also show that the South has always been a part of the narrator's life—unless it is entirely kept "closeted" like in *One Drop*—through stories or trips taken when they were children. When the narrators address their childhood memories, their social positioning becomes very clear. Narrators who grew up in an African American family had experiences different from narrators coming from a family of slaveholders. These memories bear witness to different socializations of those growing up as white compared to those growing up black.

The narrator in *Slaves in the Family* is the only one who grew up in the South. Most, but not all, of this time was spent near the place where his family used to have their plantation in coastal South Carolina. He is aware that his family was, at one time, part of the 'haves' in society (Ball 1999, 13). Even though he claims that he did not feel his family's previous riches during childhood or beyond, and underlines that to attend college as a young man he had to take out loans, there is much to say about the cultural and white privilege he gained due to his family's past. That he "remember[s] feeling an intangible sense of worth" (13) clearly points to the privilege his Southern white family attained. The idea of "lords" (13) links them to royals—especially from the perspective of a child.

He has many fond memories of his childhood, during which his family history and the intergenerational transmission of a special status seems to have been rather uncontested. The Ball family has an unusually long history with the South; the first ancestors arrived before the American Revolution. Even for a Southern white planter family, having such a long period of time to look back to is somewhat rare (176). In some ways, the Ball family history is the case of a history written by winners, even though the family experienced a variety of difficulties over time.

By and large, positive images of slavery and segregation were crucial to the narrator's upbringing and his family's stories which were passed on from one generation to the next. In the first chapter of *Slaves in the Family*, fittingly titled "Plantation Memories," the narrator addresses the role of his background for his life and for the investigation undertaken in the memoir by coming up with several ancestors who had participated in the fight for US independence, or fought in the Civil War (8). This narrator grew up in a household where Southern history crucially mattered to the family's identity. The emphasis was clearly on passing on the memories of the planters and fighters to the younger generations. The history is also very male oriented, though the text does focus on some women. The plantation heritage affects him not only from his father's side of the family but also his mother's. She came from a New Orleans plantation (10–11), and her legacy is not further explored in *Slaves in the Family*. Still, this points to marriage taking place in the same social class, even long after the end of slavery and the plantations.

This narrator is less distanced from the South than the others. He feels a deep personal connection to Southern history because of the largely celebratory stories he grew up with. He understands that his family members played important roles in society and had power. Their standing is not contested: they were part of a small elite and have much glory to look back on. This understanding of his family shapes his ways of moving through the world, his ways of understanding and of reading the past.

The family ancestors had attained cultural capital because of their slaveholding background (7–11), and those the narrator grows up around are also aware of it (8). Stories about slaves "passed as a children's story" (9), meaning they were part of the children's socialization. As a child, this narrator was openly told that his ancestors were slaveholders, that they owned people. This fact is passed on to him as a positive and identity-shaping narrative in which the young boy can take pride.

The stories of the Ball family's riches and their loss in the Civil War are kept alive by being passed on at family reunions, which retain a mysterious quality to the narrator. On the one hand, this quality is derived from the lush landscape of humid South Carolina with which he was not familiar as a young boy (12). On the other hand, he recalls memories of racial division

(12). At one point during the narrator's childhood, his father orders him and his brother to stay in the car while he gets out and has an exchange with a black man named George. This encounter familiarizes the narrator with the meaning and consequences of racial difference (12). It also indicates to him the codes of behavior. A different set of social codes is at work when the father speaks to a black man. The narrator never finds out the subject of the exchange between his father and this African American man. This adds to the secrecy of his family's encounters with African Americans.

As an adult, he feels haunted by the actions of his family members, even though they took place long before he was born. This recognition triggers the narrator's research process. He aims to reframe his family narrative and seek a different "truth" about what the plantations signified both for his own life and for the life of the descendants of his family's slaves. This long-term goal is why he decides to relocate to the South, to Charleston, in order to undertake his research (17–20). He can make the decision to move to the South because even though he feels a certain discomfort about his family's past as slaveholders, he still holds white male privilege and does not associate any feelings of pain, trauma, or fear with the South. He does not expect to experience any aversion or open confrontation on moving there.

This is different for the African American narrators. Their families have left the region. Their fear of the South is certainly also related to their socialization and the stories they were told as children. These narrators at times hold positive ideas of the South, though generally a degree of bitterness remains. The South will always be linked to painful experiences of their ancestors.

The narrator in Neil Henry's (2001, 134) *Pearl's Secret* spent the first two years of his life in the South. Then the family relocated and built a life in the Pacific Northwest. Despite leaving the South at a young age the narrator recalls experiencing segregation, though these memories are few and far between (134). When his family traveled across the South in the car, he recalls that his mother always kept a jug with her under her seat (134), since the African American family could not use public restrooms. Traveling is not an enjoyable activity, but represents a series of obstacles to the boy. Still, the parents try to keep their children entertained instead of alarmed.

The Southern past is an occasional topic of conversation while the family lives in Seattle. The narrator describes how his mother at times talks to people about the South, and about how the family had wanted to leave it behind, and accomplished this (134). The narrator assumes that his parents have made bad experiences in the South at a time he does not remember (134). It thus becomes a dark and inaccessible place—a place one does not want to confront but rather prefers to forget. The region is associated with the negative experiences of his parents. From what he is being told, he knows that the family had left in order to provide a better future to the children, and to get from its institutionalized racism (182).

The narrator is aware that the reason for his family's oppression is race and nothing else. His father is a doctor and already worked in the medical field while the family lived in the South. But his professional opportunities were limited at the time, and the health care system for African Americans was not well developed. Hospitals were segregated spaces. In the Pacific Northwest, the narrator and his siblings can finally live up to the ideals of Martin Luther King and gain equal opportunity and educational privilege (195). Far removed from the South, it becomes possible to live a life characterized by freedom and personal choice.

While *The Sweeter the Juice* is first and foremost set outside the South, the narrator's ambivalence about the region is already evident in her childhood. The text contains several accounts of her family travels there as a child. The pleasant recollections concern mostly her explorations of the places her family visits and the stories she hears about haunted houses (Haizlip 1995, 175). She emphasizes the sense of freedom that comes from the experience of playing with others (175). Here, the South is a site of imagination, a rural place where childhood fantasies can run free.

In the South, her family's regular visit is a spectacular event. Relatives celebrate their yearly return, making them feel welcome and letting everyone know they had arrived from the North (175). Their return is special to the whole community. The visits create a bond and lasting connection between the Northern and Southern homes of the family, but they also instill a sour feeling in the narrator as she grows up.

Because of the childhood trips with her parents and siblings to the South, the narrator becomes very aware of the cultural differences between the South and her home in the North at an early age. Even as an adult she recalls that her family members behaved differently in the Southern setting. She talks about the Southern dialect which is not like her own, about food and drink, the weather, and the fact that her father, a pastor, preached in a more emotional manner (175). At home, by contrast, he is very reserved. In this way, the narrator understands from early on that in the South habits change, and that in this case the father preaches in a radically altered manner such that he appears like a different person.

While very well respected in the North, the family does not automatically receive this type of respect in the South outside the black community. Rather, there are different rules the family members have to obey to when visiting the South. The narrator understands that these different rules are related to skin color. She spends time in Highland Beach, a community only open to the better-off African Americans (172), where she feels increasingly uncomfortable as race and people's looks are an important topic of the conversation (173). This sense of discomfort is something she is not used to experiencing in her native Connecticut, where these topics seemingly do not matter. The South is where she encounters segregation based on skin color, despite her family's middle-class standing and good reputation in their hometown, and even though her parents have a strong desire to shelter her from such prejudice.

Her ambivalence grows as she realizes the degree of discrimination against African Americans inherent in the region before the Civil Rights Movement (173–76). She relates in detail her experiences with segregated restrooms and other segregated places over the years (165). These experiences make the South feel foreign to her, as though it were another country (175). Since her parents guard her from experiencing segregation at full force, she can accept the differences in behavior she encounters in the South as a child. There are several situations she recalls where, even at this young age, she began to understand the threat the segregated South could pose to her black family.

One such situation is an encounter with the police. She remembers how her family was stopped on their car ride across the region because her (dark-skinned) father was driving her (light-skinned) mother and his (light-skinned) children across a segregated region where marriage between African Americans and whites was illegal. For reasons she cannot decipher immediately, her father is taken away by police. When he comes back from being questioned in the local police station, he does not give exact information about the content of this conversation. The situation becomes unspeakable in more than one way and contests the family's unity in the face of segregationist public policy. After his encounter with the police, the father asks his wife and children to get into the back of the car as though he were their chauffeur. Later, the narrator understands that such a request is not unusual in the South (175).

While the narrator's perception of the South is related in some detail, there is little account of how her family members addressed these issues in the home after returning to Connecticut. This omission is very interesting, because it is not only the long-ago past which becomes unspeakable in the text, but also the—at the time—current encounter with the South that also needs to be repressed, though as a holiday, it is supposed to strengthen family connections. The experience of not being able to talk about segregation and discrimination openly creates a lack of trust within the intimate circle of the family.

A second situation that exposes the "true face" of the South to the narrator actually occurs when she is in the North. The Emmett Till incident leads her to feel an intense hatred of the South. She relates the moment in detail (177). It transforms the young woman: "When I saw Emmett Till's pictures, my chest was full of water" (177). She describes an experience of drowning, her "chest full of water"—linking her own feeling directly to Emmett Till's lynching, his abuse, and subsequent drowning in the Tallahatchie River. She feels physically attacked, overwhelmed, and drowned like the young boy. An act of injustice done to him is also an injustice to her. At the same time, she is fully aware that the threat of racial injustice is everywhere, and that it is not restricted to the South as a region (178). The narrator's own engagement with the struggles against segregation and discrimination is evident throughout the text and is a long-term result of her experiences in the South as a young girl.

The narratives do not project a unified image of the American South when addressing these childhood memories. Rather, these descriptions make clear that the narrators were aware of differences even during their childhood and that their perception of the region depended both on their experiences and the stories they were told. If anything, the inclusion of childhood memories in the texts shows that such experiences or concepts do not disappear but exert a continuous influence on the narrators. Even before they start researching their family history and traveling to the South, they have mostly a clear idea of what to expect and which challenges they will have to face in the South. In all cases, skin color determines where they place themselves in relation to Southern history.

NEGOTIATING "SOUTHERN HISTORY": CONFRONTING SLAVERY

In the course of the narratives, the texts educate readers in Southern history to a certain extent. The Southern events in the different texts are not identical but refer back to the narrator's social location and racial identification. The events also depend on the local context. In order to offer a frame of reference for their family's experiences and current state of being, the narrators explore the particular micro-history in which they locate their families' origins; and much of this history is part of Southern history.

The memoirs discussed in this study each link up to a different part of the South that is relevant to that family's past and present. While *The Sweeter the Juice* mostly focuses on the Atlantic South, and specifically North Carolina and Virginia, Ball's text is predominantly set in South Carolina, and Broyard's narrator encounters the clues to her family's secret in Louisiana. For *Pearl's Secret*, the state of Mississippi is most significant (129). The roots run deep in this state that he also calls "the front line of the battle over equal rights" (130). Thus, Mississippi is crucial not only in the context of his family history, but also in terms of the advancement of civil rights in a national context.

The passage quoted above shows how family history becomes intertwined with local Southern history and specific sites across the region, and how family members are placed in relation to historical events—in Henry's case, the Civil War. The strategies used here are strikingly similar to the negotiation of national narratives in the memoirs. Possibly, this similarity points to the idea that these historical events are to be understood as events of national importance as well. While the South is a specific region—a fact the narrators acknowledge—the decisions made and laws adopted in the South matter in a larger-than-regional and -sectional context—another moment to contemplate their complex relationship.

At the same time, the narrators' elaborate inclusion of the South, and the very detailed discussion of local Southern historical events, may actually seem rather unusual because of the texts' overall strong focus on narrating the nation. Due to its military defeat in the American Civil War, the South is the only part of the United States that has experienced loss on its own grounds. This history makes the region more like other countries along to so-called plantation belt (e.g., Brazil), and even more like European countries than like the rest of the United States. Because of its experience of defeat in the Civil War and its segregationist policy in the aftermath, too often the South has had an exceptional status in American popular culture as supposedly the only region with racial problems. The American South is frequently portrayed as a region at odds with mainstream America, and the *memoir of the search* by and large aims at national inclusion and at pointing to similarity instead of difference.

Still, the texts crucially depend on the narration of Southern history as it provides the context for understanding how that family came into being, and how it became separated, or how the members became separated from each other. From the battle of Vicksburg to the Great Migration, from slave rebellions to segregation, from the status of African Americans in French Louisiana to the Southern cuisine at the heart of family life, the reader is introduced to a region that at times feels foreign to the narrators as well. In order to evaluate what has happened in the families portrayed in the memoirs, it is necessary to understand the politics and policies that shaped them.

The narrators' introduction of the South requires them to challenge official Southern history and to contest what they were taught as children; it means confronting the pain and neglect their family members have experienced in the South or because of the South. The narrators' encounters as adults with Southern history and the South as a region lead them to have a decidedly ambivalent attitude toward their origins and the region as a whole. While the South as a region has strengthened family relationships and friendships, it has also caused much pain to the families in these texts. Thus, it is difficult for the narrators to determine the meaning of the South with any finality.

The narrator in *One Drop* gives a quite detailed description of how her evaluation of documents leads her from one source to the next. Due to what she calls an "infinity of traces" (Broyard 2007, 135), she recognizes in her story the postmodern truism that all history is a construct, and that it is very difficult to find out anything about ancestors who lived regular lives and were not famous by any definition. During her archival research, she is eager to find direct connections of her family to slavery (265), and to learn more about changing definitions of servitude and the varied history of slavery itself (263). She hopes for these connections to be rather obvious but is disappointed. It is difficult for her to understand how family members had passed back and forth again and again, how the family's status changed over time, and how they lived as African Americans (268). Her strategies of combining a variety of archival and other resources to find the "truth" add a quasi-interdisciplinary angle to the genre. In order to get a hold of the past that has been withheld from her (131), it is necessary to look at the past from different perspectives; especially since she feels a story like hers, while not unique, has not yet been written.

In both *Pearl's Secret* and *Slaves in the Family*, the narrators have access to earlier family narratives and other private family resources referring to Southern life. The narrators use these materials in addition to other public records. The availability of these records makes it possible for them to learn something about their ancestors' ways of viewing their surroundings and the world at large. Again, it is clear that Ball's and Henry's narratives approach the South and Southern history from opposite directions, though both narrators have to come to terms with difficult truths about their white family members. They occupy different positions: While Henry's narrator wants to incorporate these white people and chooses to engage with them to find out about the past, Ball's narrator does not have a choice. He must include them.

Ball's narrator comments that his ancestors were collectors and collected people like one would collect things (Ball 1999, 18). Being a descendant of a planter family provides the narrator with a wide variety of records available for his research, ranging from letters to memoirs to account books in which the ancestors took careful stock of their land and the people they owned. The Ball family papers, serving as main resource for his study, are held in public archives and comprise more than ten thousand pages (18). He also receives the family history book from his father, the 1909 collection *Recollections of the Ball Family of South Carolina and the Comingtee Plantation* (8). All these sources provide him with plentiful material.

However, these sources mostly center on the lives and experiences of the white elite. They give information about the Ball slaves, but the narrator recognizes that there are many gaps that he has to fill throughout his research (8). Despite the plentiful material, his findings regarding the situation of the slaves are based on just a few accounts, likely addressing exceptional situations or personalities. The narrator is aware of this limitation from to the lack of material. His ancestors owned hundreds of slaves at a time and thousands over the years—the Balls were among the larger American slave-dealers of the eighteenth century (190)—and it is difficult to make any general statements about the situation or the treatment of the slaves. Relative to the material about the white family members, very little is available about the slaves, and the material that is accessible to him is also written from a white perspective.

In *Pearl's Secret*, the narrator gets access to an account written by a white relative in the twentieth century. This historical account proves decisive for him. It is not a record of slavery—in contrast to some of the sources available to Ball's narrator—but rather, a reflection of Southern life and history by a white Southern man about ninety years after the end of slavery, after his family has lost much of their money and social standing. Reading this historical text is painful for the narrator; he has to recognize that his ancestors were supportive of the Confederacy and of white supremacy more generally, and he had wanted to believe the opposite was true.

Reading the account from 1941 by Arthur W. Beaumont, Pearl's half-brother and Rita's father, the narrator understands that this text takes exceptional pride in whiteness (Henry 2001, 247), even though the author of the account had a mixed-race half-sister, and despite the Confederacy's glory days being long past. The family still takes pride in the "old days." The document does not contain a single contestation of the celebratory attitude. Pearl's existence is entirely left out of the white Beaumont's family narrative, while at the same time the text looks back three centuries and relates information about how the family became English (248). The entire content of this 1941 document, to the narrator, clearly represents an instance of whitening the past, of taking pride in it without admitting past mistakes, or even just ignorance. Pearl, it seems, did not matter to the family. She did not change Beaumont's mind about race, and she was not considered a family member. Still, gaining access to the historical manuscript helps the narrator add some more details to the family history (250). In order to complete the picture, painful recognitions are necessary: he cannot live in a dream but has to confront his family's reality.

In their approaches to slavery, very generally speaking the memoirs run against what could be called the popular imagination of the South—that of *Gone with the Wind* or other Hollywood films showing a region of "cavaliers and cotton fields" (Fleming 1939). By contrast, the memoirs emphasize that in order to understand the current state of race relations in the United States, it is necessary to engage with Southern history beyond its romantic portrayal in popular culture (Haizlip 1995, 107). Addressing slave revolts, the narrator in *The Sweeter the Juice* calls for a more careful approach to actual historical sources and an attention to detail, rather than a glossing over of what happened. This narrator is unmistakably certain that violence was exerted in case slaves stood up for themselves (107). Yet, the slaves kept on resisting their dehumanization by whites, who feared the revolts. She links her origins to the sites of many different revolts (108). This understanding instills a degree of pride in her. Here, a legacy of having survived slavery and having finally gained freedom stands for power, and for an activist mindset in the context of which the narrator can productively locate her contemporary self.

The narratives all reject the image of happy slaves working on the plantations and the cliché of the benevolent white master. Still, in Ball's *Slaves in the Family* the narrator is told by a family member during his process of investigation that the Ball slaves basically led a happy life. By suggesting they carried arms, he points to the idea that they may have had similar status to free people and citizens, at least since the late eighteenth century (47). He reports that the slaves even fought on the side of the Confederates in the Civil War because they were proslavery, and recognized how beneficial slavery was to them (48). This is exactly the type of attitude about slavery the narrator tries to contest in the context of his family narrative.

Like other white slaveholding families in the South during the Civil War, the Ball family also experienced loss: the loss of their power and their land. *Slaves in the Family* explicates that even before the Civil War, the Ball empire had been confronted with difficulties as the time of rice planting ended and "King Cotton" took over. As is generally known, the invention of the cotton gin contributed to changes in the Southern economy that ended in the gradual decline in rice production and trade. Certainly, this economic development also affected the Ball empire (260).

The Civil War was the final nail in the coffin of their rice dynasty. The narrator's white relatives do not contest the meaning of the war or their memory of it. The story of the war is another intergenerational storyline passed on among the Ball family. The narrator knows stories of his father's grandfather, Isaac the Confederate, through his father. Isaac the Confederate attained his name because he had fought in "the War between the States," with the text adding in brackets that "[t]he War between the States is what the Civil War has been called in the South" (260). This addition is clearly speaking to a non-Southern audience and addresses the differences in perception of the war. The propagandistic expression "War between the States" is more common in the Southern United States and is often used by those still mourning the "Lost Cause." It suggests that the United States was not a unified nation either before or after the end of the Civil War. According to this idea, the North violently took over the South.

Isaac the Confederate never got over the South's loss of the Civil War. As a very old man, almost blind due to glaucoma, he would go out to the Charleston peninsula, as the narrator is told, and aim his cane toward Fort Sumter (10). These types of stories are essential to the Ball family identity and maintain their family narrative of the "Lost Cause." They also make it possible for the family members to take pride in their history. Essentially, they were robbed of their belongings and attacked on their own grounds. They were honorable people who had done nothing wrong—or at least that is their perception.

Having grown up in this family context and been regularly confronted with stories about his family's glorious past, the narrator feels that his family's past still shapes him and his thinking (13). This is still true in spite of his college education and his settling in New York. To him, slavery is not as distant as for most other Americans; he feels as if researching this time is "like doing psychoanalysis on myself" (13). He assumes that slavery is a part of him, locating himself in the Southern context even though he left the region as a young man. The idea of needing to "do psychoanalysis" suggests that he may not be aware of this memory and legacy in his daily life; it is an invisible and inaccessible part of him, located in his subconscious. Slavery's presence in his subconscious may explain why he makes certain decisions, even if the reasoning behind them is not clear to him. By exploring his family heritage, the narrator opens himself to inconvenient truths about himself and about his ancestors.

That the plantation past lives on in him also clearly links the Southern past to the contemporary United States. Essentially, the narrator claims that however invisible it may be by his time, slavery still matters. Even though his life is not shaped by slavery on the outside, this particular past has an impact on his individual life today. He cannot overcome the past without working through it—an idea guiding his research. He admits that slavery was a criminal act, and that the injustices of today clearly relate back to this time. He assumes guilt for his ancestors' actions in these passages, even though he recognizes the seductive feeling of looking back to the past in a more sentimental manner (14).

For the narrator in *Slaves in the Family*, the nineteenth century signifies the loss of an empire, a traumatic experience that shapes his family through to today. In *The Sweeter the Juice*, the narrator also considers the nineteenth century crucial to her family's formation and the obstacles the different members encountered. In a brief passage explicating the events of this time, the narrator refers to the year 1830 when black preachers were no longer allowed to practice and to 1864 when Field Order 15 when land was offered to freed

African Americans to the time Andrew Johnson revoked this order back (Haizlip 1995, 106). She addresses the onset of the Great Migration to the North in the late 1870s, and the situation from 1890 onward under Jim Crow (106). She relates how the conditions first improved following abolition but did not remain that way; worsening and finally culminated in the system of segregation she remembers from her childhood.

In *Pearl's Secret*, the narrator explains the downfall of his white family by linking it not only to the Civil War, but also to the emergence of the boll weevil, a plant-eating beetle, in the early twentieth century. He introduces the boll weevil infestation to the reader by referring to it as a central factor in the end of the reign of "King Cotton" and the onset of the Great Migration (Henry 2001, 238). The white Beaumonts experienced decades of decline, with family privilege ending in the loss of all riches due to the boll weevil (239).

The narrator's white cousin Rita suggests that in addition to the beetle, alcohol had played a part in the family's downfall. She looks to the period before her own life with a sense of nostalgia, exclaiming "'Dust and memories. It was all gone'" (239). The passage is distantly reminiscent of the opening of William Faulkner's *Absalom Absalom* (1936), and unmistakably makes clear that in the white family the narrative of the Lost Cause is still prevalent. The black and the white descendants of Arthur J. Beaumont built their identities on opposing narratives about the South. These different narratives represent a major challenge in the narrator's attempt to bring the family together.

In essence, the narrators in the *memoir of the search* contest existent narratives about the South, but each responds to and accomplishes this challenge on different terms. For the white narrator in *Slaves in the Family*, the confrontation with his family members about the past is crucial to changing the existing narrative. The black-identifying narrators do not need to convince their immediate family about how slavery and segregation have had a negative impact on their families and, by implication, on the nation at large. Rather, their strategies of openly contesting the persistent image of the "happy slave" are directed at the reader.

Southern history in these texts is not limited to the nineteenth century, slavery, the Civil War, and segregation. *Slaves in the Family* also includes the American South's colonial origins. This narrator is able to locate his family origins in colonial times, while, by contrast, the other narrators come to the conclusion that their families did not really "start" before the event they became mixed. This factor places these other families' origins in the nineteenth century rather than in colonial America. The narrator in *Slaves in the Family*, by contrast, alludes to how the settlers brought a specific mindset from Europe to the American colonies: While they were rather simple people in Britain, they quickly adopted a quasi-royal lifestyle in the colonies. He explains how his family's empire grew into one of the largest slaveholding dynasties in the region. Knowing these colonial origins makes it easier for the reader to understand how the "Old South" came to be as it was, especially how its economy became so dependent on slaves. This information, while not essential to understanding the *memoir of the search*, helps a reader locate the texts in the larger context of America's growth into a nation.

In contrast to the other memoirs discussed here, this colonial information is vitally necessary in *Slaves in the Family*. This is not so much because the memoir serves as a quasi-apology for slavery, but rather because it explicates the life conditions of the narrator's ancestors and makes their decisions and desires understandable for the reader and the narrator. The context provided makes it easier for him to formulate strategies for addressing the past. Ball's narrative also refers to changes in the system of slavery over time, and thus contests prevalent perceptions of it.

One such explication of the exact circumstances of a decision taken in *Slaves in the Family* is when the narrator provides detailed information about the so-called 1740 Negro Act. He gives this information with regards to a child conceived between a Ball ancestor and an enslaved woman. This black-identified child, he explains, was born after the Stono Uprising (Ball 1999, 187). Before this slave rebellion it was easier to attain freedom for such children (187), but the South Carolina Negro Act made it impossible for the planters to free slaves after this incident. The legislation made it much harder if not close to impossible to free one's own children without having to expose one's sexual liberties as a slaveholder, which these men certainly refrain from (187).

While this explanation does not apologize for the ancestor's actions, it does make understandable to the reader that it was not possible to simply free a slave, not even if they were the slaveholders' own offspring. The reader is aware that the Ball family had to keep up a certain reputation and could not simply file a petition to free a slave. The Negro Act, as the narrator explains elsewhere, also severely limited the possibility of slaves to move about because it introduced slave passes. If a slave was to be found moving about without a pass, the consequences could be severe (141).

The narrator addresses his ancestors' past mistakes unsparingly. He talks about the cruel treatment of slaves that is never mentioned during family reunions celebrating the Ball family's plantation heritage. He does not hide from the reader, for example, that he finds records attesting to slaveholders amputating toes of supposedly misbehaving slaves, meaning those who did not obey or tried to escape (141). He also reports on instances where food was withheld from slaves in order to make them obedient (235). He openly confronts the meaning of slavery, using words that are in stark opposition to the ideas he was brought up with—to be a slave means to be property (136). This understanding clarifies that slavery is a practice running against the United States Declaration of Independence and Constitution. The narrator also places slavery in a global context and discusses its philosophical foundations as established by John Locke for the revolutionary period (30–31). He recognizes that the type of slavery his ancestors practiced was especially cruel and dehumanizing. He makes clear that American slaves could not testify in court, were not allowed not learn to write, and could not own property (136).

Ball's narrator reveals that his family's empire could be maintained and expanded because the slave owners at first did not pay their slaves enough to buy their own freedom and then, following the American Revolution, did not pay them any more at all, except for extra work (138). This income "was a way to snatch a bit of comfort" for the slaves (137). Only later, when faced with Northern abolition, did the Balls begin to treat their human property in a more paternal fashion. They utter some concerns about the slaves' health, for example, and offered medical care on the plantations carried out by black doctors (246).

The particular cruelty of American slavery, both before and after the revolution, was also a reason for slave uprisings, which regularly took place across the South from the 1730s on. In contrast to the narrator in *The Sweeter the Juice*, who talks about slave rebellions to make a statement about her ancestors' and her own persistence, the narrator in *Slaves in the Family* addresses the topic to make clear how determined the Balls were to keep their plantation business running. While some British slave masters left the Carolinas and returned to England following the confrontation with violence, others remained to keep adding to the family empire (144).

Later on the narrator mentions the conspicuous absence of further information about slave uprisings from the family papers. He comments that this was not because the Balls no longer feared them. Oral history available in the family makes evident that they had an enormous impact on the family's behavior. Slave revolts greatly worried the Balls (268). This suggests that the family members may well have been aware of their maltreatment of the slaves. The narrator certainly makes clear that slavery, and nothing else, made his family rich (154). He explores at some length how it is possible to expand a small colonial settlement into a giant dynasty, showing that building a rice empire at the time depended on slave labor (137).

Once the North had abolished slavery and the Three-Fifths Compromise was issued, the Ball family became worried about their social standing (252). In the text, the narrator does not pass any direct judgment about his ancestors, but by clearly naming their crimes and pointing out that they did not believe in the American principles of equality and democracy, he accuses them of committing an injustice, even if this happens belatedly, at times centuries after they have passed away.

In his process of investigating what became of the Ball slaves following the Civil War, the narrator finds that some of the slaves founded their own community, a place called Sawmill, located very close to the Ball plantations though nobody he talks to knows exactly where. The existence of Sawmill is one of the few pieces of information the narrator can get from his relatives about the whereabouts of the slaves in the aftermath of the Civil War (50). He finds that his ancestors were not interested in keeping track of the people whom they had forced to work for them.

Following this mindset, his ancestors certainly did not put up any memorial plaques remembering the slaves. This is not only true for his ancestors, but for the city of Charleston and much of the South. It is only much later during his investigation that he tracks down the former site of Sawmill (157). Only then is the narrator able to find someone who can answer at least some of his questions (157). The lack of public memory of slavery is conspicuous to the narrator, who describes colonial Charleston as "the Jerusalem of American slavery, its capital and center of faith" (89), and is aware of how many ships loaded with slaves entered American waters via South Carolina, and specifically Charleston (89). Many of them landed in a place called Sullivan's Island, where they first stayed in the pest house, and then, if they had survived both the Middle Passage and quarantine, were sold into slavery (89).

Yet Sullivan's Island, at the time of narration, did not bear any visual marker of slavery. As the narrator explains, even buildings that have been taken down, such as the pest house, still loom large in his conception of the place (90). This utterance—on the continuing presence of a thing, a structure, or an event despite its physical absence—strongly recalls Toni Morrison's concept of rememory, which she established in her 1987 novel *Beloved*: "If a house burns down, it's gone, but the place—the picture of it—stays, and not just in my rememory, but out there, in the world. What I remember is a picture floating around there outside my head. I mean, even if I don't think about it, even if I die, the picture of what I did, or knew, or saw is still out there" (Morrison 2007, 43). Toni Morrison stated in 1989 that she wrote *Beloved* because of the large-scale absence of the memory of slaves across the United States:

> There is no place you or I can go, to think about or not think about, to summon the presences of, or recollect the absences of slaves. . . . There is no suitable memorial, or plaque, or wreath, or wall, or park, or skyscraper lobby. There's no 300-foot tower, there's no small bench by the road. There is not even a tree scored, an initial that I can visit or you can visit in Charleston or Savannah or New York or Providence or better still on the banks of the Mississippi. And

because such a place doesn't exist . . . the book had to. (Quoted in McKay 1999, 3)

It may or may not be a coincidence that in 2006, the Toni Morrison Society placed the first of more than twenty benches referred to as Bench by the Road on Sullivan's Island to offer a place for contemplating slavery and its meanings, and to honor the memory of the slaves who built America.

In contrast to remembering the slaves by putting up a plaque, the Ball family found different ways to keep the slave past alive using the actual words of slaves. These strategies may seem strange to the reader and at odds with the family's disinterest in what had become of them after slavery. The family collected slave songs. The narrator explains that his grandfather, a man named Nathaniel Ingraham Ball, had grown up listening to the songs of slaves, which inspired him to establish the Society for the Preservation of Spirituals, a group that continues its work into the narrative's present (Ball 1999, 383–89). Together with other family members, the narrator's grandfather had collected the songs going from field to field, asking people to sing their traditional music, writing it down, compiling a collection of these songs, then performing them for white audiences (389–90). This passage does suggest, however indirectly, that an interaction occurred between the narrator's grandfather and the slaves, even beyond slavery. With changing strategies of addressing the past and with more open negotiations of slavery, the Society has obviously come under scrutiny today (390). The performance of the slaves' songs by white people to white audiences represents an appropriation of the cultural heritage of African Americans.

This practice of collecting and performing slave songs may be one reason why the narrator becomes so invested in the fate of the former Ball slaves. He had probably grown up around the music. One might even say that indirectly, all Balls, no matter how proud of their Southern planter heritage, must have been aware that life was generally not very good for the slaves on their plantations. As the narrator quickly realizes, the lyrics of the collected music make evident that "there were no songs from the plantations about love" (388), that life was indeed harsh and painful. The narrator's process of unraveling these pains is connected to the preservationist work his grandfather had already done. Not knowing anyone in person who had experienced slavery, and having established his life in New York rather than in the South, the narrator has enough distance to be able to unpack such a difficult legacy for his family.

In Broyard's *One Drop*, the narrator also can trace back her family's origins to the eighteenth century when, in 1753, her forefather came to New Orleans from France. As a French colony, Louisiana had its own regulations relating to skin color. While the first Broyard ancestor who landed in

Louisiana was a white man, within the first century of the family's presence in the colony, the family had changed their identification to "free people of color" (Broyard 2007, 142). According to family lore, this change happened because a Broyard man sweet-talked a woman with Caribbean origins into dating him and "changed sides" out of love (142–43)—a story the narrator is not entirely sure she believes.

The narrative on the whole does not center as much on slavery as Ball's *Slaves in the Family*, but remains firmly rooted in Louisiana's French rather than English context. The narrator mentions categories such as *gens de couleur libre*. Hence, it is difficult to compare the two texts in this way. Rules and regulations were different in Louisiana, where it was possible, for example, for a slave to be freed if certain preconditions were met (150). These regulations were true for slavery in Louisiana both under French and under Spanish rule.

The *Code Noir* gave rights to slaves that they did not have in the American colonies, such as the right to marry. This legal background is different from the action enforced by the Negro Act that Ball's narrator references. In Louisiana, people of African descent could, if they were free, learn a trade and thus make money for themselves (154). Taking free blacks and slaves together, white society was in the minority in late eighteenth-century Louisiana and depended on these people's (paid for) labor, which was very different from working in the rice fields of coastal South Carolina. The narrator explicates these differences as they represent a lesser-known regional history.

She explains how her ancestors certainly owned a slave at the end of the eighteenth century, which was a time in Louisiana when slaves could be bought rather cheaply, and rebellions in places such as St. Domingue made people fear unrest in the state of Louisiana (152). Due to the *Code Noir*, relations between free and unfree people were handled much more flexibly by the colonial government, and once Louisiana had been sold to the United States, the contact between people of different origins even intensified (156). Hence, this narrator does not have to address slavery in the same manner that Ball's narrator needs to. Her family owned slaves, but they did so under very different conditions than the owners of a rice dynasty, as depicted in *Slaves in the Family*.

In *One Drop*, the narrator explains how the Louisiana Purchase negatively affected the situation for free blacks in New Orleans, as did the changing economic structure in the South: Whites were under more pressure and the more they felt slavery to be under threat, the more their disrespect of free blacks rose (198). Pressures increased with the incorporation into the United States and with Americanization. Her mixed-race great-great grandfather Henry Broyard joined the militia, but on the Confederate side (199). The troops he fought for, the Native Guard, were not taken seriously by the Confederates, and were not even equipped for the war (200). A few years later this same ancestor, who lived as black but looked white, joined the Union troops under Joseph Follins (201). The experience of fighting together with other soldiers and being recognized as a member of the Native Guard leads him to encounter racism and stereotypes of black inferiority, the narrator assumes, for the first time. He appears to have joined the efforts for freedom (204), as the narrator interprets his behavior. This passage alludes to her own way of working through the past. By investigating the past and composing her memoir, she makes owning up to the past her own business as well.

Unlike Ball's narrator, the white-identifying narrator in *One Drop* has her great-great grandfather to look back to. Despite looking white, he fought for the freedom of African Americans in the Civil War. This recognition about her ancestor places her in an overall different position. Her earliest relative to come to Louisiana from France passed for black. The family mostly lived as black from then on (which does not make them slaves in the New Orleans context). She actually learns during her research that her black family members had owned slaves, not *been* slaves. This finding is a great disappointment for her (268), as this is not the reality she had expected from her family and from her research in and about the South.

Despite the Broyards' European origins and their (however small-scale) involvement in slavery, unlike the Balls, they were not an important slaveholding dynasty but a more-or-less regular nineteenth-century family in New Orleans. Instead of directing anger or disappointment at long-deceased relatives, in the course of her research the narrator rather comes across family members who blame her father for leaving his family and all his obligations behind (181). The question of obligation and loyalty to one's people here becomes personified in her father, the person who *passed* for white, who did not join the fight for freedom, but who ran, and turned his back on the South and on his family.

SITES OF ENCOUNTER

In some of the memoirs, the South is a central setting in which the narrators encounter a different culture and set of traditions. In the South, Broyard's narrator tries on her newly found "blackness" and first establishes ties to the Louisiana Creoles. For Ball's narrator, as has been demonstrated, the South is the site of confrontation with the family's past. It is also mostly in the South where the narrator forms friendships with the descendants of those his family enslaved, and where he confronts his family members with the realities of slavery. He also has the chance to visit sites that were of importance for his family's history. As I have discussed in the context of the resolution of family secrets, Neil Henry's narrator also encounters his white relatives during his visits to the South. In *Pearl's Secret*, the South's history is most explicitly connected to the Civil Rights Movement and to specific places in which local and family history collide.

Following a business obligation in Atlanta, the narrator in Henry's text makes use of the opportunity to travel around the South more extensively and to conduct some of the research necessary to finding his family members on the other side of the "color line." His feelings about the region are ambivalent, even though he has not really spent any time there except during his early childhood (Henry 2001, 112).

All this narrator's associations with the region relate to him being African American (112). During his trip from Atlanta to Vicksburg, he passes Birmingham, Alabama, the site of violent attacks during the Civil Rights Movement and of George Wallace's speech on segregation. He also passes Philadelphia, Mississippi, the site of the murder of three civil rights workers in the 1960s (113). He has been aware of these struggles since boyhood, meaning that even though he did not grow up in the South, he caught a glimpse of its violence. He witnessed these incidents from far away, and characterizes the South as different from Seattle, where he encountered more subtle forms of racial prejudice (113) rather than violent outbursts or physical attacks. Additionally, he is aware of the South as a site of black protest and courage in times of struggle (113). The region, and specifically Mississippi, relates to both good and horrible times for his family (129).

The narrator finally travels to Vicksburg where he conducts research at the Warren County Court House, a place he describes in vivid language, and claiming that this "building seemed to throb with history" (199). Conducting research in Vicksburg is important to him not only because of the materials stored in the building. The building itself bears historical importance as it was a symbol of defiance during the siege of Vicksburg (199). It is also significant to the Henry family being the site where his great-great-great-grandfather's unit had fought Grant (199). To the narrator, his own symbolically taking control of the building is of great importance. The siege he achieves now is one the Old South had probably not expected: he contests its purity by seeking documents about his white family, and thus, proof of race mixing.

He also finds the grave of his white ancestor A. J. Beaumont at the cemetery in Natchez. The narrator is lost at first, then sees the first four letters of his ancestor's surname flare up on a gravestone (153). In this emotional moment, his search reaches one important goal and he feels some contentment (154). This instance is his opportunity to address the ancestor, to stand in front of him (or rather, his grave), and let his thoughts wander free. While this "encounter" with Beaumont is not the end of the narrative—the meeting with his white relatives is still to come—the search finds one important conclusion here. The narrator contemplates all the steps his family members had taken since A. J. Beaumont had conceived Pearl, finally arriving at the following recognition that his family has indeed made it far from the South (155). The passage shows that he can begin to make peace with the past, but also that his present family, the people he can actually communicate with, matters to him. The quotation also points to the advances his family has made in striving toward a better life. The South has thus become a part of the past. The narrator has moved on, literally and physically.

Meeting some of the descendants of the Ball slaves enables the narrator in *Slaves in the Family* to visit some of the locations important to the slaves and their families. One place is the former old slave cemetery at Comingtee, one of the former Ball plantations. The narrator was aware of the site from family records; he even has a photograph of what it looked like (171–72). The site does not belong to the Ball family anymore but has become corporate property. It has not been very well taken care of by the new owners (170).

At first sight, the area does not bear any resemblance to what it used to be: The narrator sees that even the paths between the black and white communities have become overgrown over time (171). This passage can also be related to the more general storyline of the black and white paths no longer intermingling, of contact having been lost for almost two hundred years, and of grass growing metaphorically over the past. Grass may cover a path but usually does not entirely erase it. The narrator's work centers on locating the traces, rediscovering the connections that were lost, in order to find the paths again, and ideally, to create a new path together.

The narrator visits the site with a search partner named Stanley Richmond. This African American man is married to one of the descendants of the Comingtee slaves (170). After some searching, the two men finally find what is left of the cemetery. In this moment the narrator is confronted with the passage of time, but also with the feeling of finally being connected to the slaves his ancestors kept (172). Visiting the site gives him the chance to personally encounter history, and in some ways also to pay a tribute to the Ball slaves, however belatedly. He stands on their graves, pointing to his still existing power to determine the relationship and make statements about it.

A second site he visits is St. James Reformed Episcopal Church, a church whose parishioners come from Sawmill. The church relates all the way back to the plantation era (173). The building had been taken from the plantation and brought to the town after slavery, and existed until Hurricane Hugo took it down. Then, a new building was erected, including the original bell. This newer building is the one the narrator visits (174). The visit is special to the narrator because he travels to the site together with descendants of the Ball slaves. This is a most unusual constellation of visitors to the site: a descendant of slaveholders and descendants of slaves, visiting the original place of worship of slaves, brought from the slaveholder's family's plantation. Attending a church service together puts them into the same context, and into a similar position. Metaphorically, this moment shows that a bond exists between these two families—something the narrator is not able to achieve with all of the descendants of the Ball slaves whom he meets, and something which he does not take for granted at any point in the text.

The narrator uses the opportunity to contextualize the church's denomination—Episcopalianism brought from England (173)—and its location and history. That the slaves take over the master's religion is another example of the coercive power of slavery. At the same time, the church has been a source of inspiration for slaves. Still, the black and white communities do not typically attend church together. Church is commonly and until today a segregated space.

Following the service, the narrator goes to see the church bells (174). The bells represent a physical connection to the past, all the way back to the time of slavery. The bells have been there since the 1840s; they represent what survives the passage across generations and across locations. The description of their ringing as pleasant alludes to a situation of making peace, and of remembering the endurance of the families, both the Ball family, and the families of those they enslaved. Traditionally, church bells ring to indicate a special occasion, such as a liturgical event or a death. Church bells call the community together, as this narrator calls his family members together in the course of the memoir. In this case, the bells ring a sound that lasts and that unites: a connection has been established.

For the narrator in *One Drop*, the South is not so much a place where she visits sites relevant to her family history, but more a space where she engages with New Orleans and Creole culture, and where she tries out her supposed "new self" following her discovery that she is mixed race. She had engaged with the meaning of the term "Creole" before, ever since her mother described her father that way, but her findings lead her to more questions relating to her family legacy. Upon arriving in the city, she explores New Orleans's history of segregation. She discovers that an urban renewal policy in the 1960s led to the segregation of the city quarters where her family had long resided, the Seventh Ward (206). Her black-identifying Southern Creole relatives welcome her into the family, making her feel happy in turn (208).

At the same time, these family members make certain assumptions about her, for example, that her family must be rich (210). The narrator does consider that life was probably easier for her as a white girl in New England (211), though she does not say this to the family. When one of her family members explains her family's activism for civil rights, she is confronted with the accusation of having been passive, having been raised white in the North (214). This accusation links to her father, who "ran," and it explains why the narrator now desires the acceptance of her black family members. In some ways, it appears she wants to make up for her father's mistakes. She seems to feel inclined to take some responsibility for his mistakes and own up to them—whether this is something her relatives welcome is another question.

She also explores racial differences further by examining data from sociological studies that explain how white families managed to keep larger amounts of money thus attained economic privilege (212). This understanding leads her to recognize that up to that point, she had not really been aware of the role race played in people's lives, how it shaped their view of the world and their possibility to rise economically. Her visit to the South and her encounter with segregated neighborhoods provides her with a more layered understanding of what it means to be either white or black in America (213). This is a line of thought she had already begun during her education at the University of Virginia.

This family, deeply rooted in black Creole society, does not contemplate their black heritage; they do not even consider themselves black or white at all (209). That is a big surprise for her also shows that she, as well, makes assumptions about her family members that they have to work against. The ambivalence between blackness and whiteness is not generally true for all Creoles, but as family members make clear, race mattered more after than before the Civil War (300). Among those Creoles who were assigned as black, French culture was gradually lost. The US racial system entirely changed New Orleans society and its values (300). The state of Louisiana more and more became part of the segregated South.

During her stay in New Orleans, the narrator has the possibility of attending a Mardi Gras ball, a traditional carnival event in the city. The event she attends is not one for tourists, but is supposed to give her an authentic insight into what is going on in the city's Creole community. She also hopes to find relatives at this event. To attend, she has to dress up in what she calls "'plantation attire'" (287), the type of dress slaves would wear to a party. When she first enters the party she feels displaced (288). Only later does she begin to feel a little more familiar with her surroundings. Attending a second party, she has a transgender woman named Cherry dress her up as "'Egyptian Princess'" (291). In a conversation with Cherry, the narrator understands that while both have gone through transformative experiences, Cherry definitely feels female, whereas her "attachment to [her] blackness felt tenuous": She feels that in contract to the trans ladies she meets, who do not expect any permission to identify as female, she wants someone to tell her that she can be something other as has been suggested to her during her upbringing (291).

Once more, her experience of coming to terms with being mixed race is contrasted with the coming out process of an LGBTQ-person; but for her, there is seemingly greater difficulty involved in "coming out." Possibly, as she concludes, she is afraid of stigma (296). She needs to confront her own assumptions about race. In this text, the idea of the narrator not living truthfully to herself is an important undercurrent. Time and again, she struggles with "finding herself" and "defining herself."

The encounter with Creole culture, while it helps her understand the "gumbo" that emerges out of the cultural mixture (297–98), also instills her with a sense of grief because of the vibrant culture she did not get to experience during her childhood (299). Her grandfather had been described by her father as a "'displaced person'" living in Brooklyn (299), where the family took residence. Visiting New Orleans, the narrator comes to understand what leaving behind one's home really means, and what absence the Great Migration has forced into her family's story and identity (299).

For the narrator in *The Sweeter the Juice*, making peace with the South is only possible after she has resolved the family secret and helped her mother reencounter her sister. Following the revelations about her family history, the narrator travels to her father's birthplace in North Carolina with her husband. Her renewed encounter with the region is part of the book's epilogue, meaning it is not part of the story about her family's reunion but an addendum to the text. This is the first time she visits the rural South in thirty years (Haizlip 1995, 261), and also the first time she can appreciate the Southern landscape.

She is still ambivalent about the region and its complicated heritage (263), which she is trying to make sense of. While the experience is not entirely a reversal of her earlier feelings, it shows that the narrator feels much more comfortable with the region she encounters at the end of her search. The region she encounters is no longer the segregated space of her childhood; rather, it is the South after the Civil Rights Movement. In addition, she is more comfortable being in the South after having confronted her own family history of neglect due to skin color. The narrator can let go of her original perception and experience the South from a new perspective.

Still, the narrator and her husband are rather nervous about staying in rural North Carolina overnight and get advice from a minister, who suggests a place to them where he supposes African Americans have stay before (262). That this point matters at all shows the difficulty of overcoming the past, and the ongoing existence of separate spheres. The bed and breakfast they arrive at is a former plantation home (262). The hostess, as the narrator explains, reminds her of "Blythe Danner playing Blanche Dubois in *A Streetcar Named Desire*" (262), a play and character central to the narrative of the fall of the

Old South. The hostess speaks with a Southern dialect and has a casual way of talking about the past. She relates that her family owned slaves but that some of her ancestors were also Quakers like many people in the region, and that Quakers did not support the institution (262). She claims her family freed their slaves, who then immigrated to Liberia, aligning her family history with a narrative of freedom and resistance, to then turn the conversation toward their travel experiences so far (262).

The hostess's intermingling of serious topics with casual conversation is hard for the narrator to get used to. The weight of history is quite heavy on her. This white woman, unlike the narrator, apparently does not have any difficulty talking about her family history. She looks at it from a positive point of view and does not mention, for example, the long-term consequences of slavery both in the South or in America at large. Clearly, this woman has also been raised under white privilege, and unlike Blanche DuBois, she is not in a desperate condition. She has not lost her plantation home but inhabits it, takes pride in it, and hosts guests there.

The narrator, by contrast, does not feel as confident. She does not sleep well in a bedroom where she feels haunted by images of the hostess's ancestors who are looking at her from their picture frames (262), reminding her of overseers. At night she gets up in the hope of encountering a ghost of a slave, a relative (262). She automatically positions herself vis-à-vis the slaves, while her hostess links her own story to that of the slave owners. The narrator's unease with the situation remains present throughout her stay, even though she recognizes that her own white ancestors shared some characteristics with those of the hostess (262).

The narrator's skepticism may not be without reason: She later hears from one of the domestic workers at the bed and breakfast that they had not hosted African Americans before. At the same time, she feels the presence of her father and grandfather when, during breakfast, the white woman serves her and not the other way around (263)—a complete reversal of roles. She finds this to be an unexpected and "life-changing" experience, one difficult to digest, but still overall victorious for her. One way she works through the experience is by writing it down.

MAKING PEACE WITH WHAT WAS

During their trips to the South in the course of their research or afterward, the narrators all encounter situations in which they struggle with what they see and cannot always immediately make sense of. These moments of struggle include confronting traumatic childhood memories, but also situations in the present, from the constant state of insecurity that results from undertaking a quest for family members to the incorporation of new layers of history into one's family narrative and one's individual identity. The family secret cannot be solved unless the narrator travels to encounter the past, which in these texts means traveling to the South.

All narratives suggest that a personal encounter with history is needed in order to come to terms with the past, and that this encounter has to happen on site. The encounter is not only needed in order to see a specific site, or to talk to a specific person, but rather, in order to be able to reach completion and get in touch with one's truest self. Still, the reflections the narrators undertake are often provoked and fueled by a particular location, a specific memory, a particular conversation in which they have to reverse their earlier concept of their family, or their image of a particular family member. The narrator's lengthy analyses regarding the intersections of Southern history and their family's story are often therapeutic. Saying something out loud, or writing it down, can help with finding ways to deal with it.

In many ways, the narrators here revise the stories they grew up with and the way history was likely taught to them. The narrators and protagonists of these memoirs make clear that the past and the present are inherently interlinked, and that what happened during slavery, the Great Migration, or the Civil Rights Movement still has an impact on the family at the time of narration, and implicitly, beyond. The narrators inscribe their stories into Southern history and, by implication, American national history. In their family stories, North and South are inherently connected. Their families brought the Southern legacy to the North—its stories, its cultures, its traditions. By stating quite openly how their family's story relates to the past, how legal and social conceptions shaped their process of becoming, the narrators revise the idea that "Southern history" only means slavery, or something that is solely limited to the past. Locating oneself in a Southern context in these memoirs also means recognizing transnational connections and building the endurance to consistently work toward freedom.

Since the texts lead the discussion about the past in the present, and the South in the nation, in relation to a specific family—instead of, for example, an institution, and what it could potentially be or become—the reader gains personal access to the story and feels touched by it, even involved in it. Potentially, the reader will not only understand that history is much more multilayered than might be assumed, but also that political and other decisions have a real impact that it takes a long time to unpack and respond to. In this way, the reader also becomes a witness of this history and this history becomes their concern. These narratives call for a more affective approach to the past, and for looking at the consequences of the past. They suggest that the region, and by implication, the nation, can grow together by way of personal encounter, and by way of addressing historical harm. Thereby, they play into late twentieth-century ideas of leading dialogues across boundaries in order to find ways of addressing past injustices. Looking at this phenomenon from a transnational angle then becomes a productive setting in which to place these texts beyond their local, regional, and national contexts.

Conclusion

Making History at the Turn of the Millennium

At the onset of the twentieth century, the African American intellectual W. E. B. Du Bois ([1903] 1994, 1) predicted that "[t]he problem of the Twentieth Century is the problem of the color line." Already in the Forethought to his seminal work *The Souls of Black Folk*, Du Bois suggested the forthcoming age would be shaped by racial conflict between blacks and whites in the United States as well as globally. Certainly, his statement is firmly rooted in the specific context in which it was made. At the turn of the twentieth century, the system of racial segregation was firmly in place across the United States and European colonialism was by and large still intact. The Voting Rights Act was in the distant future, as was the Civil Rights Movement. Martin Luther King and Malcolm X were not yet born, neither were Angela Davis, or Toni Morrison, or any of the authors whose works I discussed in this book. But already in Du Bois's time, African Americans were seeking their place in the larger national context and looking for ways of attaining a higher social status and entering the mainstream.

The Souls of Black Folk was first published in 1903, at the onset of the first Great Migration, in a period of intense social change, technological progress, and rapid urbanization. The text laid important groundwork for the development of African American thought throughout the twentieth century but especially for the intellectual and artistic formation that would later become known as the Harlem Renaissance, in which Langston Hughes, whom I quoted at the beginning of this study, rose to fame.

The Souls of Black Folk points to several unresolved issues in the lives of African Americans that would accompany them not only through the Roaring Twenties, the Great Depression, and World War II, but also through the Civil Rights and Black Power Movements, Urban Renewal, the emerging neoliberal capitalist system, and finally into the new millennium. From today's perspective, the book still poses large-scale questions of access, public perception, political power, cultural identity; it also addresses and negotiates history and remembrance. While the contexts have changed almost entirely, even in the time of the *Black Lives Matter* movement, many of the book's points have remained critical. When a young black boy is killed in the streets because he is suspected to be a criminal due to his skin color and clothing, one cannot but be reminded of Du Bois's notions of the double consciousness and the veil—the psychological manifestation of the "color line" in people's minds. His reflections about a nation grappling and wrestling with race, class, and the social system anticipate many future developments. It is not a coincidence, then, that historian Ira Berlin (2004, 1251) has claimed that the late twentieth-century attempt to newly engage with slavery and its aftermath was a result of an ongoing quest for social justice. In the course of one century, much has changed, and yet so much has remained the same.

In the foreword to their volume *Names We Call Home: Autobiography on Racial Identity* (1996), published almost a century after *The Souls of Black Folk*, Becky Thompson and Sangeeta Tyagi (ix) insist that

> [t]rying to understand race in the United States is like putting together a three-dimensional 1000-piece jigsaw puzzle in dim light. Given the vicissitudes of historical amnesia and the elusive quality of communal memory, it is unclear if we even have all the pieces to begin with. Race is about everything—historical, political, personal—and race is about nothing—a construct, an invention that has changed dramatically over time and historical circumstance.

Like Du Bois in *The Souls of Black Folk*, the editors of the volume argue that race, as constructed by the dominant group, shapes every dimension of American life. It is central, and yet it is elusive. Thompson and Thyagi point out that even at the end of the twentieth century race continues to be a problem for the United States. Piecing together a puzzle in dim light is a huge challenge for those involved, be they private citizens or institutions. It requires the right pieces being available at the right time; it requires patience and the insistence not to give up. It also requires sensitivity and the ability to locate those pieces that fit together. It requires an understanding of the work to be done.

In the texts discussed in this study, the narrator is the person working on completing the puzzle. This character starts with just a few pieces, with an old photograph, with an incomplete family story, a narrative that poses more questions than it provides answers. Gradually, the narrator fits more pieces into the puzzle. Sometimes a piece is missing, or it does not seem to fit. Sometimes the narrator has to accept that a piece is undeniably gone, and still keeps working on the puzzle, proving her perseverance. But even if the pieces can be found, there are significant complications. Sometimes it seems as if two or three pieces fit, except that they do not. Sometimes a piece is unexpectedly found, and then someone else claims it. The narrator in the *memoir of the search* struggles with race, with the "color line," and with the veil, with what the past means for the present at large.

The process of combining and recombining the pieces of the puzzle of race requires patience, endurance, the willingness to find different solutions, and the serenity to acknowledge that the whole story will probably never be known. It takes empathy and the ability to approach problems creatively and with sensitivity. The narrator must ask difficult questions and be focused and precise, so as to not miss a piece, or to lose it to somebody else. And still, at times, they will have to cope with such loss.

The *memoir of the search* is a literary negotiation of the "color line" and its implications for and reverberations across several generations into the twenty-first century. From the point of view of a first-person narrator, the genre reflects how family history, local history, and national history are intertwined, and how they can be recombined in the present in order to "make the story whole," as the narrator in *Slaves in the Family* so fittingly puts it (Ball 1999, 14). These are the central claims the texts make: that the past has a lasting effect into the present, that earlier wounds still hurt today, that the past has intergenerational consequences on individuals and families, and that there is indeed a story to be told and to be made whole. This motivation enables the narrators to find the strength and the willingness to persevere in order to gather all resources toward finding the missing pieces and making them fit. There is also a risk involved in this process: Life may be forever changed once a story is known. As becomes evident in the texts, for the narrators, it is at times deeply troubling to engage with their ancestors' sins, and with the consequences of this engagement for themselves as well as their families.

In a sense, the texts make evident that we are, indeed, the stories we tell and that in essence, "[t]o be a person is to have a story" (Isaac 1999, 114). The *memoir of the search* represents one strategy of talking about racial mixing and its public "discovery" that powerfully emerged on the book market at a specific point in time, when a new generation of writers decided to engage with the idea, to maybe contribute yet another few pieces to the puzzle of race. In essence, my study is an analysis of the cultural interpretation and mediation of mixed race in the late 1990s and early 2000s—the years immediately preceding the Obama presidency.

This period saw the introduction of a more open census form allowing, for the first time, to opt for more than one race, ending the mutual exclusiveness of "blackness" and "whiteness"—at least with regard to self-identification on the census. It was the time of a broad debate around multiracialism and multiracial individuals as a distinct population group with special interests and in need of support. It was a time of shifts in the regional and national consciousness due to new groups of migrants arriving in the United States, including from Africa—individuals of color, but without a history of enslavement on American soil. Finally, the public at large began to recognize and then to acknowledge that past injustices shape the American nation in the present, that the country has economically, and in part socially, profited from slavery. During the Clinton administration, there was significant pressure by the public, and especially in the black community, to issue an apology for slavery—an apology that has not been provided by the US administration until today. It was the time when DNA tests and the emergence of epigenetics—the idea that traumatizing experiences may not only be passed on via processes of storytelling, but also genetically, meaning you may physically inherit your ancestors' traumas—contributed to different ways of reading the past and its long-term consequences. Arguably, all these factors that came together in this constellation brought forth the discourses picked up by the *memoir of the search*, and then, by consequence, the genre itself.

The memoirs start with the assumption that the family stories the narrators have grown up with are not "complete." To be able to understand race in America, and their own family, and how the family was shaped by race, the story needs to be extended and include more layers—more pieces of the puzzle. The *memoir of the search* argues that an individual needs to be "grounded," "rooted"—that identity should be built around how exactly one came into being, which historical decisions led to this specific family, this specific family structure, to emerge. This incentive, a postmodern version of "know thyself," urges the narrators' at times obsessive investigation for a supposed "truth" in the memoirs—the idea to make all pieces fit and arrive at some deeper understanding of the self and the past.

All the while, the quest for truth is also a struggle for control, for agency over and containment of the past. If these narrators tell the story, they also save the family from potential harm that can come from others telling it. Thus, the narrators try to write their families into a larger (national) story. In its entirety, this process of telling their story leads them to ask crucial questions: What shapes the self? What is truth? What is family? What is race? What *is* the past? What does the past mean now? How has the past become for us what it is? Is it somehow engrained in us? How do we create meaning from past wrongdoings? At the end of this study, it remains to be asked what these texts contribute to and what they tell us about the state of memory at the turn of the millennium and possibly beyond.

In this concluding part I suggest that there are two ways to evaluate the *memoir of the search* in terms of its arguments and central claims about the self, the family, and the nation. The first is essentially an ethical reading. This means understanding these texts in relation to a global tendency of approaching trauma and reading the *memoir of the search* as an attempt to establish more inclusive narratives about the past for a diverse future shaped by more acceptance and less inequality, more social justice and the end of racial oppression. The genre, then, is much in tune with the global efforts to form, for example, Truth and Reconciliation commissions or issuing apologies for wrongs committed in colonial and postcolonial contexts. Here, the genre becomes one possible tool of working through the past and establishing dialogues where there used to be silence. Considered from this perspective, the genre is connected to strategies of building new interracial, transnational networks based on mutual respect and rooted in the idea of a common humanity. Essentially, these texts make an argument about opening up the exclusive structure of the family in order to include others who previously could not be part of it.

The second is a much less open and less optimistic interpretation of these texts. While equipped with much potential to disrupt existing narratives of Americanness dependent on whiteness and upward social mobility, as well as pointing to more complex patterns of identity creation, this reading of the *memoir of the search* argues that these texts are part of a neoliberal humanist undertaking. In this context, certain stories about racial and national unity are promoted in order to brush over the fact that race is a matter of ongoing contention in the United States and beyond and that the key problem of the twenty-first century is, to invoke W. E. B. Du Bois, still the "color line." These texts would then direct attention away from what is really at stake: social justice, access to resources, equal rights, respect and care for, however abstract, the Other. Instead of confronting sexual violence, oppression, gun culture, and the lack of agency that were and are ongoing issues in the black community, these texts use discourses of a global ethics not to make them productive for the domestic context, but rather to keep at bay contentions about the meanings of blackness, whiteness, and social privilege. This reading is much in tune with what Te-Nehisi Coates has claimed in his 2014 essay "The Case for Reparations" for *The Atlantic*, namely, that "[t]he idea of reparations is frightening not simply because we might lack the ability to pay. The idea of reparations threatens something much deeper: America's heritage, history, and standing in the world." Similarly, the idea of revising the past in terms of America's treatment of African Americans may lead to contestations that are much larger than just the question of who can be a family: It also tackles serious questions of oppression, of agency, social structure, cultural memory, and of the possibility to make up for mistakes. Perhaps it would mean that the stories by which America constructs itself will require significant revision.

Both these approaches to or readings of the genre underline that the *memoir of the search*, as well as the cultural memory it transmits and builds on, is a performance firmly rooted in its time and culture of emergence. As Rocío G. Davis, Jaume Aurell, and Ana Beatriz Delgado (2007, 17) suggest, autobiographical writing—and certainly also the writing of memoirs—mediates the past by way of careful curatorial practice that can only take shape in the present. As is true for all life writing, this type of narrative then "affirms as it performs identity" in a specific moment (12). The texts point to the constructedness of all history as well as of the self at the turn of the millennium—again, a puzzle. As the different approaches by the narrators unmistakably make clear, positionality is crucial in this regard. Privilege enables different ways of seeing, of understanding, of writing.

At the time of their emergence, the recognition that mixed-race families exist in the US-American context was not new at all. It was not even new when W. E. B. Du Bois wrote *The Souls of Black Folk*, or during slavery. Rather, what was new in the 1990s was that this suddenly became a topic of public discussion once again (Elam 2011, 15), rather than an open secret and a topic not to be mentioned in casual dinner conversation. As Michelle Elam has argued, at the turn of the millennium, the large-scale conversation about mixed race contributes to both change and stillstand, it challenges as well as contains (29). The *memoir of the search* is a prime example of this phenomenon. While at least on the surface the text begins the process of "airing family secrets, a settling with old ghosts," it remains doubtful or at least open whether this type of narrative can indeed provide what Coates terms "a healing of the American psyche" (Coates 2018).

APPROACHING PAST ATROCITIES ON THE GLOBAL SCALE

The memoirs studied here are firmly based in the United States. The narrators make clear how, despite all the connections of the issues they discuss to Europe and to Africa, they are seeking a truth in the United States and consider themselves and their families quintessentially American. They even claim they have become more American due to their engagement with US history and their family's specific role in it. Still, in their taking issue with the past and its negotiation and mediation in the present, these texts can be read as part of a more global undertaking to confront the past and its transgressions from a more open stance. The late twentieth century has been shaped by the emergence of discourses of memory around the world. Often, this particular moment is referred to as *memory boom* by cultural historians.

At the turn of the third millennium, there has been, and to this day continues to be, great public interest globally in exploring how the present became what it is, what shaped it, which decisions and mistakes were made, by whom, and how these played out on the larger scale and into this day. Since the memoirs' emergence, a variety of other textual formats have addressed these concerns from a diversity of perspectives. These texts have been published in different contexts and different countries. They share questions of accountability for the past in the present moment as well as the attempt to understand why certain decisions were made, and at times led to atrocities, disasters, or oppression of an individual or a group. While they may focus on institutions, organizations, or political parties, they steadily keep in mind that people are accountable first and foremost. They ask, for example, what mindset moved people to neglect their family members in order to advance socially, or why it took so long for some injustices to come to light. Texts asking questions of this kind come in a multiplicity of formats and include autobiographies and memoirs, but also formats such as novels, films, and TV series.

One example of this idea to investigate the past from a present stance and interrogate how it was shaped by individual processes of decision-making is the German genre of the *Generationenroman* ("generational novel"). This type of text focuses on exploring, from a fictional or at times also nonfictional stance, the continuing impact of the Holocaust, and at times, the GDR regime, on German families. In the *Generationenroman*, much like in the *memoir of the search*, a contemporary investigator-type central character starts inquiring about the past in order to be able to tell a supposedly more complete story about a particular family, a particular group of people (e.g., the inhabitants of a village), and, by implication, the nation (for a more detailed study of this phenomenon see, e.g., Eigler 2005). The *Generationenroman* is also characterized by the inclusion of intense ethical questions and, in these terms, can easily be related to the American *memoir of the search*.

In the German context, this genre has gained special importance in the aftermath of reunification, which asked for the renegotiation of national history at large following a period of separation and the establishment of different narratives about the past and its legacies. This type of text gained additional meaning in the context of Germany's increasing diversification due to migration, as well as because of the fact that the German nation—as well as the rest of the world—needs to find approaches to address the Holocaust as those who witnessed it pass away. The *Generationenroman*—broadly speaking—is interested in practices of memory, memorialization, and in the investigation of family secrets.

It would be interesting to conduct a dialogical study of, for example, family constructions or the use of media in these nonfictional, memoir-type texts of the genre of the *Generationenroman*, such as Wibke Bruhns's *Meines Vaters Land: Geschichte einer deutschen Familie* (2004), in which the narrator, a journalist, investigates her father's involvement in the resistance against and his execution by the National Socialists in 1944, or the more recent *Wie kommt der Krieg ins Kind* (2018) by Susanne Fritz, in which the narrator explores her mother's family history in the context of German-Polish relations, and the memoirs discussed here. Both types of texts, the *Generationenroman* and the *memoir of the search*, address and try to come to terms with what has previously been unspeakable. They each make use of archival material and ask complex questions about guilt and responsibility in the narrators' families and in the nation at large; both lead to different understandings of national identity and the present's impact on the interpretation of the past, and on its memorialization.

Much could be gained from an extensive dialogic reading of these two types of texts using concepts from Trauma Studies—this would enable a better understanding of the intergenerational transmission of memory, and of pain an individual has not experienced on their own body. It might also lead to larger recognitions about the functions of the past in the present, and about how to communicate experiences that are essentially unspeakable. The texts discussed here use some motifs that are similar to the ones the reader encounters in the *Generationenroman*—for example, the idea of inheriting a parent's pain, or the concept of feeling an undefinable absence in one's life—that could be very productive for a future study.

My study has shown that some ideas from the study of Holocaust and post-Holocaust literature, for example, the notion of postmemory, work well to understand the *memoir of the search*. This also triggers the larger question of whether the experience of learning to speak about the Holocaust and its long-term consequences may have helped along the ability of speaking about slavery and its legacies. This is not to say that the Holocaust and slavery should in any way be compared to each other, but rather, that Holocaust literature has helped give birth to a critical language and vocabulary to talk about the heritage of slavery, as well.

The *Generationenroman*, like the *memoir of the search*, points to the idea that while the present is the result of past decisions, people struggle, fail, listen to the wrong advice, and make mistakes. Still, any reconciliation with the past needs to be reached in the present, by addressing what either achievements and successes or mistakes and failures actually mean, how to interpret them and how they have led to the current situation—a process that can only take place with careful retrospection. Though set in the past, history is written in the present. The process of interrogating the past becomes crucial when it comes to depicting, exhibiting, representing colonialism, genocide, and other instances of violence and oppression, but also family legacies more generally. When investigating history, its representation must also be examined and at times be revisited and revised. This transcends one national context—it is a global undertaking.

The late twentieth and early twenty-first century are not the first moment in Western history where memory was central to understanding and approaching present issues (Winter 2008, 97). In his 2008 essay "War, Memory, and Mourning in the Twentieth Century: Notes on the Memory Boom," Jay M. Winter (97) lays out how the period between the 1890s and the 1920s was characterized by a similar phenomenon. Located at the intersection of national identity and collective memory, as well as rooted in experiences such as urbanization and the invention of motorized transportation, this earlier *memory boom* was based on the feeling that the world would never be the same (101–103). It aimed to preserve the past for subsequent generations. This process occurred in the form of memorials as well as in the newly emergent "practices of cinematography," especially after World War I (104). This earlier *memory boom* was by and large a celebratory and nostalgic movement. It was characterized by the desire to record the past before it would be lost or become unrecognizable.

In contrast to this earlier *memory boom* characterized by a longing for the past, where supposedly everything was better, the contemporary *memory boom*, as Winter continues to argue, builds on the recognition that all understanding of past is created in the present (112). It engages with commemorative practices, as well as with the idea of witnessing a particular moment in the past and passing on its interpretation, often from the point of view of the victims or the losers. It is centrally concerned with mourning and with events "about which it is impossible in any straightforward sense to pose questions of historical context or meaning within twentieth-century history" (109): violence, genocide, acts of human cruelty that are not easy to understand or communicate and that are not ethically justifiable. Still, they are part of the human experience.

The current *memory boom* can be understood as an "ongoing meditation [. . .] on war and its victims" (98). Since memory has been ascribed moral value in contemporary society (108), the debate around memorializing very consciously includes questions about the ethics of mourning with regard to the perpetrators and their descendants, and the possibility of reconciliation with the victims and their descendants. Hence, this *memory boom* takes into account intergenerational questions of coping with the past as well; it understands that different generations may have different strategies of approaching past atrocities and different ways of talking about the past, of naming and addressing the unspeakable.

All of the above is exemplified in the ways the global community approaches the Holocaust and its long-term aftermath, including but not limited to the *Generationenroman*. The complex tension and interrelationships between the memories of victims, perpetrators, or their descendants that can be observed in negotiations of the Holocaust also become evident in the *memoir of the search*. This tension is directly alluded to when the narrators in the texts I analyzed in this publication address their difficulties communicating with their newly found family members, or when expectations from both sides clash with each other. The legacy of a victim is decidedly different from the one of a perpetrator, even generations removed. Still, in contrast to earlier moments following the end of US-American slavery, there may now be the space (and possibly, the need) for conversations and shared practices of commemoration between descendants on different sides.

Memory, individual as well as collective, "is active and it is set in the present" (Bal 1999, viii). Memory speaks to questions and anxieties central to its time. According to the German sociologist Ulrich Beck (2002, 20), the ongoing attempts to reevaluate the past in terms of its ethics from the United States to South Africa to India hint at important questions relating to identity and our dealings with the past: "Who questions, who decides, who justifies and who defines who 'who' is?" Working with these questions instead of taking for granted who is meant, and who is taking the necessary decisions "opens up discussions to include groups that have been excluded, to redistribute the burden of proof and exclude some principles as illegitimate, or to questioning their legitimacy" (20). In the US context, this process of inclusion is important to the African American community, but also to other minorities that have yet to become accepted as part of the American mainstream and master narrative. Globally, questions of inclusion can be extended to include colonized populations, but also, for example, religious minorities or the LGBTQ[+]-community, who have been denied their place in history and in society.

While the *memoir of the search* certainly relates to issues of nation-building and national identity, I would argue that there is also an ethical dimension to these texts. This dimension speaks to the crossing of boundaries of race and class in the text, but also beyond it. One central focus of the *memoir of the search* is to establish new dialogues and build new connections, to reestablish paths that have been obliterated or blocked, and to find strategies of communicating about the wounds that have been committed in the past, and their long-term consequences from a standpoint of mutual respect. The narrators constantly cross borders in their efforts to understand the past: They try to overcome stereotypes, fears, the roles their ancestors have played, their established family scripts. They are also confronted with the limits of such processes, for example, when trying to bridge the gap between the different "sides" of their family. While it is often assumed that people of mixed descent are ideal mediators, the *memoir of the search* shows that the narrators encounter a variety of difficulties when meeting their family members on the other side of the "color line." They struggle to find a common language and to find ways of establishing a productive pattern of communication.

At the same time, these texts and their central characters' actions point to the possibility to talk about history differently, to show how history is the result of specific and at times seemingly random, coincidental acts of decision-making. The desire of white-identifying narrators to engage with blackness and with their relatives on the other end of the "color line," the active listening to and engagement with those who did not profit from the American promise the way they did, complicates the presupposed whiteness of American national identity. At the same time, the strategies of black narrators in these memoirs to identify the origins of the family in the moment whiteness enters into it is a double-edged sword. Certainly, it is useful to point to the specific wounds that were inflicted: to the neglect of and to the lack of loyalty toward one's own children.

But these texts may also be read to suggest that Americanness still depends on whiteness, as well as on other factors relevant to these texts at large: on middle-class status, on heterosexuality. In that sense, the *memoir of the search* does nothing to revise the status quo—it does not, for example, speak to the idea that the supposed, oft-lamented pathology of the black family is rooted in "the torture of black fathers, [. . .] the rape of black mothers, [. . .] the sale of black children" (Coates 2018). Rather, the genre points to the possibility of establishing all-American families *despite* the experience of an earlier generation of the family being violently torn apart. Potentially, in the long run, this may open up new paths.

INVENTING MEMORY IN THE PRESENT

Continuing along these lines, while finding strategies to dialogue about past achievements as well as wrongdoings is one of the *memoir of the search*'s major concerns, these texts can also be approached in an arguably more controversial way. They can be considered contributions to a neoliberal tactics of distraction from the continuous absence of social justice in the United States, a nation built on the idea that "all men are created equal." In their strong allusion to narratives of nationhood and nation-building, these texts claim that in order to be heard, one first needs to attach one's story to the mainstream narrative to make one's story readable according to convention.

Even in this context, the *memoir of the search* can be contextualized globally. For South Africa, Kerry Bystrom has studied texts that emerged in the ongoing process of nation-building following racial and ethnic conflict and, specifically, apartheid. She characterizes this type of fiction, for example, Zoë Wicomb's *David's Story* (2000), as "genealogical fiction" (Bystrom 2009, 227). Bystrom describes how these kinds of texts essentially tell "family histories" in an attempt "to create order and guarantee ownership (literal or metaphorical) in a time of social flux" (227). Much like the memoirs discussed in this study, these texts "return to central tropes of nineteenth and early twentieth-century social organization—tropes, such as the 'bloodline,' that links family, science and nation—and pose traditional genealogy as a language of working through the material, emotional and political dislocation created by the democratic transition" (227). While *David's Story* is certainly different from the *memoirs of the search* in commenting on colonial and postcolonial times in South Africa, there are many relevant parallels in the allusions to nationhood and to genealogy. In the attempt to construct larger families, both these types of texts, the *memoir of the search* and this type of *genealogical fiction*, speak to central questions of social justice and belonging in the aftermath of racial conflict and through a period of radical political and social change. They appeal to inclusion, but also do so without having to provide central revisions to the existing story of national becoming. Instead, they make a seemingly belated argument about bloodlines, building on established notions of the family and its formation.

For the American context, Thulani Davis, in her own 2006 *memoir of the search*, *My Confederate Kinfolk: A Twenty-First Century Freedwoman Confronts Her Roots*, expresses her claims to inclusion, social justice, and equality as follows: "It may take the recognition that some of the unnamed actors of American history from traditional heroes shot by the British in the revolution to nameless lynch victims, are our kinfolk—the relatives of black and white Americans—for all of us to act when black votes are not counted" (4). In a sense, the *memoir of the search* appeals to this process of familial inclusion by pointing out that the sons and daughters of slaves and of slaveholders (and in many cases, descendants of both) are related to each other; they are part of the same family. Hence, they are called to take an interest in each other, as one ideally would take an interest in a family member.

The recognition of the *Other* as "kinfolk," as suggested by Davis, requires for slavery and its aftermath to be recognized and established as part of the master narrative. Thus, it is not a side story or an aberration that can be, for example, located solely in the US South; rather it needs to be acknowledged as part of the dominant American story. Since it is difficult to integrate the ultimate form of unfreedom—slavery—within a powerful national narrative of freedom and progress, in the long run, the dominant story would require reversals. Two different histories would need to merge into a more inclusive story taking a step away from the idealization of the nation's becoming. Reconciliation with the past would have to be more than token forgiveness and more than a renewed investigation of the past—it would have to be an active attempt to challenge the dominant narrative about freedom of the self and the community, an attempt that can only be undertaken in dialogue between the different communities affected by it in different ways.

Here is where the memoirs fall short in some sense or prove problematic. They do not provide an alternative approach to reconcile with the past, but write themselves into an existing and established story. They speak to the ideal of the large family being able to trace its genealogy, equipped with a family album and a history that can be told in terms of the (white mainstream) American Dream. They do not question these traditions or these narratives. They also do not ask for legal changes or revisions, not for an open confrontation of slavery, segregation and its ongoing legacy, but solely for narrative inclusion. Considering the pressing social problems and ongoing racial divisions, this appears to be a token act rather than an undertaking propelling long-lasting change and the development of resilient communities.

These texts make mixed-race heritage controllable and knowable. In its copying of and learning from established patterns of telling the story of national becoming and inclusion, the *memoir of the search* can enter the mainstream by way of normalization but cannot live up to its subversive promise to mediate to its readership a story yet unheard. Thus, it only symbolically breaks a long-established silence about America's past. That does not mean it does not use motifs of breaking silences, of reestablishing connections, or solving secrets about "unspeakable things." Neither does it fail to talk about coming out of the literal closet. But the genre lives up to its radical promise only on the surface level.

By proclaiming that these mixed-race families have essentially gone through by-and-large identical experiences as prototypical white American immigrant families, that they have always been quintessentially American, and that all it takes is to look back and recognize this, these texts may also contribute to limiting the impetus for effective change. To build a comprehensive agenda toward social change depends on the ability to recognize injustice, to see that some may not have the same possibility as others to rise to the top, that skin color, social class, and other reasons crucially factor into who gets what opportunity, and when, and at what price. The narratives tell a story of liberation, but this is a liberation that has essentially already been achieved. Thus, they play into the upkeep of the status quo.

In this way, these texts allude to the limits of speakability of their time and at the difficulty of undermining, subverting, and changing existing and well-established stories of nationhood and familial becoming in the United States. They clearly show that the present generation still feels the consequences of their ancestors' actions. At the same time, their agenda appears as one of political containment instead of one leading to question the master narratives and their validity for the early twenty-first century altogether. The *memoir of the search* is part of existing discourses about personal, familial, and national identity and preformulated scripts of racial mixedness and its legacies in the present. For the subjects represented in it, it is impossible to step beyond the boundaries of the existing narratives.

By drawing heavily on the memoir and its genre conventions, these texts invite specific acts of reading and writing, as well as defined reader expectations. In his study *Frames of Friction: Black Genealogies, White Hegemony, and the Essay as Critical Intervention* (2010), Carsten Junker speaks to the memoir and its importance for African Americans gaining narrative and political authority throughout the twentieth century. He argues that as a genre known to be concerned with the mediation of personal memories and the creation of a pronounced personal, albeit also political, standpoint, these types of texts can only make use of "a language that renders the world thinkable in ways that compromise the agency of particular speaking subjects" (Junker 2010, 22). Along the same lines, however, by uttering their reflections in an accessible narrative form, the narrators make it possible to link "experiences of social marginalization to their larger contexts" and, by implication, to communicate these matters and the responsibilities going along with them to a broader audience, even toward raising "ethical questions of social accountability" (22). The potential of these texts in paving the way toward a more open conversation at least should not be neglected despite their obvious weaknesses.

In *The Souls of Mixed Folk*, Michelle Elam (2011, 37) builds on Roderick Ferguson's ideas and argues that the picture of the African American family that has been propagated by sociology has contributed to the idea that these families undeniably deviate from the mainstream. In the memoirs discussed in this study, the narrators then contribute to inscribing the supposedly lacking—heterosexual and patriarchal—African American family model into the mainstream, and in that sense make "race mixing palatable under the cover of conservative 'family values'" (37). Thus, their way of narrating mixed race becomes a step toward both: national social reconciliation and acceptance of the (limiting) conditions, such as they are.

THE FUTURE OF THE PAST

Nationally and globally, these narratives clearly show that working through past atrocities takes more than one generation, more than a few decades, more than a century. By placing essential questions of the lingering consequences of slavery and abuse in a mainstream context, the narratives demonstrate how even middle-class families are affected by the past in ways that might not always be visible or even expected in any way by the outside image these families project. The memoirs interrogate the ethics of remembering and forgetting in relation to individual families as well as the nation at large.

By placing these questions in front of a (supposedly middle class) mass audience, they can, despite all their limitations, be useful to initiate a public conversation about such issues as race relations, racism, heritage, family, responsibility, accountability, and the present state of the above in the United States in the late twentieth and early twenty-first century. This is taking place at a time when all those who experienced slavery are long dead, and even the memory of the Civil Rights Movement has in many ways become tamed, turned into a story of peace and love and inclusion instead of segregation and violent conflict.

It is certainly easier to talk about traumatic disruptions such as slavery in ways that ensure a distance from the event: by way of scientific detachment, by addressing *it*, but not addressing *how* people may be affected, what privileges they may have gained through the event, or what gaps exist in their lives because of it. Possibly, the narrators in the *memoirs of the search* provide such deeper insight into US history not only because they are trying to inscribe their family history into the nation or because they feel the need to educate the reader about the facts and facets of history. For them, too, it becomes impossibly painful to confront the failures of earlier generations, one after the other.

Reading these narratives as part of a global undertaking to speak a truth, not necessarily an objective or measurable truth, but rather one that considers the wounds, the gaps, the failures, and the pains across generations, may facilitate a better understanding of the dynamics of guilt versus responsibility and compensation versus forgiveness at large. The narrators all feel disappointment and disillusionment when they find out their white ancestors supported slavery, supported segregation, made racist statements, used force, and did not support their own relatives. This is a hard realization they need to contextualize to be able to accept it, even if it is past and cannot be changed anymore. These earlier actions shape the current state of the narrators' families, and these families' internal dynamics and entire ways of relating to the world.

Certainly, the texts talk about many injustices which cannot be apologized for or forgiven because nobody alive today is in any position to apologize or forgive. When Ball's narrator travels to Africa and tries to reach some final sense of reconciliation, it is hard for him to understand and come to terms with the fact that there is no one there to forgive or to accept his apologies. Still, the texts discussed throughout this study point to the past indeed never being dead, to allude to William Faulkner's famous quote from *Requiem for a Nun* (1951), not even four or more generations removed from the actual event. Its consequences still exert power in the present, even in families where the past is denied or idealized. But at the same time, these texts also show that later generations have their own ways of relating to and dealing with it.

The *memoirs of the search* point to the potential contribution of literature to cultural memory at large—a dimension of literature that is often neglected (Crewe 1999, 76). They also expose the possible hardships of negotiating and reevaluating the past at a time when the last living witnesses have passed away. In these terms, they can assist reflection on the future of Holocaust Education. Soon, there will come the point when even the last remaining survivors of the Holocaust are no longer there to give a first-person account of what has happened and how it happened. This complicates notions of witnessing and of relating to the past by way of personal accounts and personal dialogue.

A meeting with an eyewitness and/or survivor of a concentration camp, for example—as has often been part of the educational process in schools and other settings in Europe as well as other countries—affords a personal relation to a human being by way of dialoguing, addressing questions, and understanding: "It is no accident we express it this way: *embodied* history, *bearing* witness. For now, and who knows for how much longer, the telling is a physical thing. A living presence transmitted in real time, entering the bodies of those who are listening. Something entirely *un*bearable that must, somehow, be borne, and then passed on" (Rosner 2017, 32). In terms of a value-based education, students should learn in such meetings that even injustices that might not affect them or their families directly have something to do with them for the sole reason that a fellow human being—the person sitting across from them—has been harmed. In a sense, the participants of the conversation become witnesses themselves via the act of sharing the same space and listening to the story. Being familiar with such an approach building on the personal transmission of memory, it is difficult to imagine what will happen when the generation that has experienced the Holocaust is no longer there to tell their story. At that point "we will all experience the threshold where the Holocaust becomes as haunting and as secondary as an echo" (134)—the situation the United States has already experienced with regard to the last personal witnesses of slavery.

When the memory of the Holocaust will be passed on to subsequent generations, it needs to open itself up to different strategies of addressing the unspeakable. There are new challenges that add to the passing of the last witnesses, such as the ongoing migration that is bringing new populations into Europe and causing an increase in anti-Semitic sentiment. It can be argued that future Holocaust Education requires a twofold approach: first, in tracing history back in order to understand how the Holocaust could happen the way it did, and in terms of a projection into the present and future "so that it enlarges the capacity of students to make (and keep) political commitments" (Karn 2012, 225). Holocaust Education has to be connected to contemporary society even though the Holocaust itself is unique in its qualities—something that the witnesses to the event mentioned above have been able to transmit in a singular manner.

The pressures associated with the last witnesses passing away affect Holocaust Education especially in Germany, a country in which, despite the wide canonization of the events, descendants of perpetrators and bystanders alike still tend to idealize the past. In their study *"Opa war kein Nazi." Nationalsozialismus und Holocaust im Familiengedächtnis* (2002), Harald Welzer, Sabine Moeller, and Karoline Tschuggnall have explored that the memory of the Holocaust in German families can indeed be very different from what is transmitted in public institutions from schools to museums to memorials. In family conversations, all too often the Holocaust is removed from the family. While factual knowledge is available, youth have difficulty understanding that their grandparents or great-grandparents were alive during National Socialism, for example, and that they were in whichever way involved in it: as soldiers, as members of political organizations, as people who stood by when neighbors were taken away. By contrast, stories of heroism circulate in families despite the extent of Holocaust Education in schools and other public institutions; and if it is not a story of heroism, it might be the idea that the grandparents or great-grandparents were not aware of what was going on.

This makes even clearer that the Holocaust will not lose its relevance in the educational system, especially not in the face of new migrants coming from countries that have no direct relation to the Holocaust, but who will have to understand this part of history if they want to remain in the country and, possibly, attain citizenship. Even in families where the Holocaust is not brought to the dinner table, children and young adults will certainly become aware of allusions and omissions—"family secrets"—and will grow up with a perception of this lack.

Certainly, the American *memoirs of the search*, dealing with a pre-Holocaust genocidal situation, show that dialogue about the past is possible even without the original witnesses of the event. This is an important realization because it enables new ways of thinking about how to the subsequent generations can learn to understand how the past has shaped the present, and how they can deal with it in a more open, dialogic manner, but also be aware of the dangers of its commodification. "To be sure," as Daniel Levy and Natan Sznaider (2002, 90) have worked out, "face-to-face interaction is different from mediated interaction [. . .]. But there is a fallacy in thinking that impersonal representations are somehow fake and not connected to our real emotions and real identities." Teaching the past and the Holocaust via textual representations turns the media—that can range from memoirs to recorded interviews with witnesses to a variety of art forms—into "a mediator of moral affairs" (91), and thus places much responsibility on those composing and choosing the material.

As value-based education in the present, the "mode of inquiry [of Holocaust Education] should be geared toward uncovering and interrogating the cognitive structures of the historical actors" (Karn 2012, 230). This is a goal that can be accomplished using memoirs and other textual material in the case of Holocaust Education, as these texts show the views and engagements of common people who may not have been in a situation or location from which it was possible to anticipate the outcomes of that situation (231). The encounters portrayed in the memoirs also point to the importance of meetings between members of subsequent generations after the passing away of the last witnesses, meaning between the children and grandchildren of victims and of perpetrators to discuss the present, but also to recall the past.

My study of the *memoir of the search* has made clear that these *types* of texts enable, and in fact suggest, an approach that takes into account such ideas and continues to build on them. In their mediation of family legacies from an individual as well as national perspective and in their use of media ranging from photography to family trees, they enable the reader an identification with the narrator as the character posing a complex inquiry of the past. They make evident how the legacies of the past—those of perpetrator and of victim—become intertwined in the present, and that despite all difficulties, a process of working through the past can only be accomplished by way of dialogue, even if such dialogue is to happen between members of the subsequent generations. They can also serve as preparatory material to open up a dialogue between previously isolated groups. Lasting peace and the recognition of a global humanity is a daily process. Both require constant engagement with past atrocities in a dialogue in which all voices are heard equally and in which differences are recognized, accepted, and acknowledged.

References

Abel, Sarah. 2018. "Of African Descent? Blackness and the Concept of Origins in Cultural Perspective." *Genealogy* 2, no. 1 (March). MDPI. doi:10.3390/genealogy2010011.
Adams, Timothy Dow. 1999. *Light Writing and Life Writing: Photography in Autobiography*. Chapel Hill, NC: University of North Carolina Press.
AfricanAncestry.com. Trace Your DNA. Find Your Roots. Today. 2018. Accessed 23 Dec. 2018. http://www.africanancestry.com/.
Ahokas, Pirjo. 2007. "Ethnic Life Writing in an Era of Postethnicity: 'Maxine Hong Kingston' and 'Alice Walker' at the Millennium." In *Ethnic Life Writing and Histories*, edited by Rocío G. Davis, Jaume Aurell, and Ana Beatriz Delgado, pp. 240–56. Berlin: LIT.
Appiah, Kwame A. 1997. "Cosmopolitan Patriots." *Critical Inquiry* 23, no. 3 (Spring): 617–39. JSTOR. https://www.jstor.org/stable/1344038.
Assmann, Aleida. 2006. *Der lange Schatten der Vergangenheit: Erinnerungskultur und Geschichtspolitik*. Bonn: Bundeszentrale für Politische Bildung.
Astor, Maggie, Christina Caron, and Daniel Victor. 2017. "A Guide to the Charlottesville Aftermath." *The New York Times*, August 14, 2017. www.nytimes.com/2017/08/13/us/charlottesville-virginia-overview.html.
Bal, Mieke. 1999. "Introduction." In *Acts of Memory: Cultural Recall in the Present*, edited by Mieke Bal, Jonathan V. Crewe, and Leo Spitzer, xii–xvii. Lebanon, NH: University Press of New England.
Ball, Edward. (1998) 1999. *Slaves in the Family*. London: Penguin.
Barthes, Roland. (1980) 1993. *Camera Lucida: Reflections on Photography*. New York City: Vintage.
Beck, Ulrich. 2002. "The Cosmopolitan Society and its Enemies." *Theory, Culture & Society* 19, no. 1–2 (Spring): 17–44. SAGE. doi:10.1177/026327640201900101.
Berecz, Agnes. 2010. "Please recycle! On Agnes Eperjesi's family album." In *Exposed memories: Family Pictures in private and collective Memory*, edited by Zsófia Bán and Hedvig Turai, pp. 153–68. Budapest: CEU Press.

Bergland, Betty Ann. 1994. "Representing Ethnicity in Autobiography: Narratives of Opposition." *The Yearbook of English Studies* 24: 67–93. JSTOR. http://www.jstor.org/stable/3507883.

Berlant, Lauren G. 1997. *The Queen of America goes to Washington City: Essays on Sex and Citizenship*. Durham, NC: Duke University Press.

———. 2008. *The Female Complaint. The Unfinished Business of Sentimentality in American Culture*. Durham, NC: Duke University Press.

Berlant, Lauren G., and Jay Prosser. 2001. "Life Writing and Intimate Publics: A Conversation with Lauren Berlant." *Biography* 34, no. 1 (Winter): 180–87. JSTOR. https://www.jstor.org/stable/23541186.

Berlin, Ira. 2004. "American Slavery in History and Memory and the Search for Social Justice." *The Journal of American History* 90, no. 4 (March): 1251–68. JSTOR. doi:10.2307/3660347.

Boelhower, William. 1982. *Immigrant Autobiography in the US. Four Versions of the Italian American Self*. Venice: Essedue Edizioni.

Bourdieu, Pierre. (1965) 1990. *Photography, A Middle Brow Art*. Translated by Shaun Whiteside. Stanford: Stanford University Press.

Bradley, David. (1981) 1990. *The Chaneysville Incident*. New York City: Harper Perennial.

Brown, William Wells. (1853) 2003. *Clotel, or: The President's Daughter*. London: Penguin Classics.

Broyard, Bliss. 2007. *One Drop. My Father's Hidden Life—A Story of Race and Family Secrets*. New York City: Little, Brown and Company.

Bruhns, Wibke. 2005. *Meines Vaters Land: Geschichte einer deutschen Familie*. Berlin: Ullstein.

Butler, Octavia E. (1979) 2003. *Kindred*. Boston, mA: Beacon Press.

Bystrom, Kerry. 2009. "The DNA of the Democratic South Africa: Ancestral Maps, Family Trees, Genealogical Fictions." *Journal of Southern African Studies* 53, no. 1 (March): pp. 223–35. Taylor & Francis Online. doi:10.1080/03057070802685668.

Carpentier, Alejo. (1962) 2001. *Explosion in a Cathedral*. Minneapolis, MN: University of Minnesota Press.

Celan, Paul, and Barbara Wiedemann. 2004. *"Todesfuge" und andere Gedichte*. Berlin: Suhrkamp.

Coates, Ta-Nehisi. 2018. "The Case for Reparations." *The Atlantic*, June 22, 2018. www.theatlantic.com/magazine/archive/2014/06/the-case-for-reparations/361631/.

Cook, Kay C. 1996. "Medical Identity: My DNA/ Myself." In *Getting a Life: Everyday uses of Autobiography*, edited by Sidonie Smith and Julia Watson, pp. 63–85. Minneapolis, MN: University of Minnesota Press.

Crewe, Jonathan V. 1999. "Recalling Adamastor: Literature as Cultural Memory in 'White' South Africa." In *Acts of Memory: Cultural Recall in the Present*, edited by Mieke Bal, Jonathan V. Crewe, and Leo Spitzer, pp. 75–86. Lebanon, NH: University Press of New England.

Cross, June. 2006. *Secret Daughter: A Mixed-Race Daughter and the Mother Who Gave Her Away*. London: Penguin.

Daniel, G. R. 2009. "Race, Multiraciality, and Barack Obama: Toward a More Perfect Union?" *The Black Scholar* 39, no. 3–4 (April): 51–59. Taylor and Francis Online. doi:10.1080/00064246.2009.11413499s.

Dash, Julie, director. 1991. *Daughters of the Dust*. American Playhouse, Geechee Girls and WMG Film. DVD, 113 min.

Davis, Rocío, Jaume Aurell, and Ana Beatriz Delgado. 2007. "Introduction. Ethnic Life Writing and Historical Mediation: Approaches and Interventions." In *Ethnic Life Writing and Histories*, edited by Rocío G. Davis, Jaume Aurell and Ana Beatriz Delgado, pp. 9–21. Berlin: LIT.

Davis, Thulani. 2006. *My Confederate Kinfolk: A Twenty-First Century Freedwoman confronts her Roots*. New York City: Basic Civitas Books.

Drake, Kimberly. 1997. "Rewriting the American Self: Race, Gender, and Identity in the Autobiographies of Frederick Douglass and Harriet Jacobs." *MELUS* 22, no. 4 (Winter): 91–108. JSTOR. doi:10.2307/467991.

Du Bois, W. E. B. (1903) 1994. *The Souls of Black Folk*. Mineola, NY: Dover Thrift Editions.

Dunbar, Erica Armstrong. 2015. "George Washington, Slave Catcher." *The New York Times*, February 16, 2015. https://www.nytimes.com/2015/02/16/opinion/george-washington-slave-catcher.html.

Eigler, Friederike. 2005. *Gedächtnis und Geschichte in Generationenromanen seit der Wende*. Berlin: Schmidt.

Elam, Michele. 2007. "Passing in the Post-Race Era: Danzy Senna, Philip Roth, and Colson Whitehead." *African American Review* 41, no. 4 (Winter): 749–68. Research Gate. doi:10.2307/25426988.

———. 2011. *The Souls of Mixed Folk: Race, Politics, and Aesthetics in the New Millennium*. Stanford: Stanford University Press.

Elliot, Stuart, creator. 2004–present. *Who do you think you are?* Wall to Wall.

Faulkner, William. (1936) 1991. *Absalom, Absalom*. New York City: Vintage Books.

———. (1951) 2011. *Requiem for a Nun*. New York City: Vintage Books.

Ferré, Rosario. 1996. *Sweet Diamond Dust and Other Stories*. New York City: Plume.

Fitzgerald, Francis S. K. (1925) 2000. *The Great Gatsby*. London: Penguin Books.

Fleming, Victor, dir. 1939. *Gone with the Wind*. Selznick International Pictures and Metro-Goldwyn-Mayer. DVD, 238 min.

Franklin, Stuart. 2016. *The Documentary Impulse*. London: Phaidon.

Fritz, Susanne. 2018. *Wie kommt der Krieg ins Kind*. Berlin: Wallstein.

Gardner, Eric. 2003. "Black and White: American Genealogy, Race, and Popular Response." *The Midwest Quarterly* 44, no. 2 (Winter): 148–60. Questia. https://www.questia.com/library/journal/1G1-97331157/black-and-white-american-genealogy-race-and-popular.

Gates, Henry Louis Jr. creator. 2006–2008. *African American Lives*. Kunhardt Productions, thirteen WNET and Inkwell Films.

Gavrilos, Dina. 2010. "White Males lose Presidency for first time: Exposing the Power of Whiteness through Obama's Victory." In *The Obama Effect: Multidisciplinary Renderings of the 2008 Campaign*, edited by Heather E. Harris,

Kimberly R. Moffitt, and Catherine R. Squires, pp. 3–15. Albany: State University of New York Press.

Gerima, Haile, dir. 1993. *Sankofa*. Channel Four Films et. al. Film. DVD, 125 min.

Haizlip, Shirlee T. (1994) 1995. *The Sweeter the Juice: A Family Memoir in Black and White*. New York City: Touchstone.

Haley, Alex. (1976) 1977. *Roots: The Saga of an American Family*. New York City: Dell Publishing.

Handley, George B. 2000. *Postslavery Literatures in the Americas: Family Portraits in Black and White*. Charlottesville, VA: University Press of Virginia.

Helmore, Edward, and Lois Beckett. 2017. "How Charlottesville became the symbolic prize of the far right." *The Guardian*, August 13, 2017. www.theguardian.com/world/2017/aug/13/charlottesville-white-supremacists-far-right-donald-trump-confederate-statue.

Henry, Neil. 2001. *Pearl's Secret: A Black Man's Search for his White Family*. Berkeley, CA: University of California Press.

Herweg, Nicola. 2005. "Die Biographie als paradigmatische Gedächtnisgattung." In *Gedächtniskonzepte der Literaturwissenschaft: Theoretische Grundlegung und Anwendungsperspektiven*, edited by Astrid Erll and Ansgar Nünning, pp. 197–210. Berlin: De Gruyter.

Hirsch, Marianne, and Leo Spitzer. 2010. "Incongruous images: 'Before, during, and after' the Holocaust." In *Exposed Memories: Family Pictures in Private and Collective Memory*, edited by Zsófia Bán and Hedvig Turai, pp. 3–28. Budapest: CEU Press.

Hopkins, Pauline. (1902) 2004. *Of One Blood: Or, the Hidden Self*. New York City: Washington Square Press.

Horton, James O., and Lois E. Horton, eds. 2009. *Slavery and Public History: The Tough Stuff of American Memory*. Durham, NC: University of North Carolina Press.

Hughes, Langston. (1926) 2019. "I, too." Academy of American Poets, poets.org/poem/i-too. Accessed July 12, 2019.

Ickstadt, Heinz. 2010. "History, Narration, and the Frozen Moment of Photography in Richard Powers' *Three Farmers on Their Way to a Dance* and Theresa Hak Kyung Cha's *Dictée*." In *Exposed Memories: Family Pictures in Private and Collective Memory*, edited by Zsófia Bán and Hedvig Turai, pp. 55–66. Budapest: CEU Press.

Imber-Black, Evan. 1993. "Secrets in Families and Family Therapy: An Overview." In *Secrets in Families and Family Therapy*, edited by Evan Imber-Black, pp. 3–28. New York City: Norton.

Isaac, Rhys. 1999. "Monticello Stories Old and New." In *Sally Hemings and Thomas Jefferson: History, Memory and Civic Culture*, edited by Jan Ellen Taylor and Peter S. Onuf, pp. 114–26. Charlottesville, VA: University of Virginia Press.

Jolly, Margaretta. 2011. "Introduction: Life Writing as Intimate Publics." *Biography* 34, no. 1 (Winter): v–xi. MUSE. doi:10.1353/bio.2011.0007.

Jones, Edward P. 2003. *The Known World*. New York City: Amistad.

Jones, Gayl. (1975) 1987. *Corregidora*. Boston, MA: Beacon Press.

Junker, Carsten. 2010. *Frames of Friction: Black Genealogies, White Hegemony, and the Essay as Critical Intervention.* Frankfurt a. M.: Campus.

Karn, Alexander. 2012. "Toward a Philosophy of Holocaust Education: Teaching Values without imposing Agendas." *The History Teacher* 45, no. 2 (February): 221–40. JSTOR. https://www.jstor.org/stable/23265920.

Karpel, Mark. 1980. "Family Secrets." *Family Process* 19, no. 3 (September): 295–306. Wiley. doi:10.1111/j.1545-5300.1980.00295.x.

King, Martin Luther. 1998. "I have a Dream." In *The Heath Anthology of American Literature*, 3rd ed., edited by Paul Lauter et. al., pp. 2530–33. Boston, MA: Houghton Mifflin.

Langford, Martha. 2008. *Suspended Conversations: The Afterlife of Memory in Photographic Albums.* Montreal/Kingston: McGill-Queens University Press.

Leverette, Tru. 2006. "Traveling Identities: Mixed Race Quests and Fran Ross's 'Oreo'." *African American Review* 40, no. 1 (Spring): 79–91. JSTOR. https://www.jstor.org/stable/40027033.

Levy, Daniel, and Natan Sznaider. 2002. "Memory Unbound. The Holocaust and the Formation of Cosmopolitan Memory." *European Journal of Social Theory* 5 (February): 87–106. Sage. doi:10.1177/1368431002005001002.

Link, Jürgen. 1998. *Versuch über den Normalismus. Wie Normalität produziert wird.* Göttingen: Vandenhoeck & Ruprecht.

Link, Jürgen, and Mirko M. Hall. 2004. "On the Contribution of Normalism to Modernity and Postmodernity." *Cultural Critique* 57 (Spring): 33–46. JSTOR. https://www.jstor.org/stable/4140758.

Lukasik, Gail. 2017. *White Like Her: My Family's Story of Race and Racial Passing.* New York City: Skyhorse.

McBride, James. (1995) 1998. *The Color of Water: A Black Man's Tribute to his White Mother.* London: Bloomsbury.

McGlothlin, Erin H. 2006. *Second-Generation Holocaust Literature: Legacies of Survival and Perpetration.* Rochester, NY: Camden House.

McKay, Nelly Y. 1999. "Introduction." In *Toni Morrison's Beloved. A Casebook*, edited by William L. Andrews and Nelly Y. McKay, pp. 3–20. Oxford, UK: Oxford University Press.

Miller, Nancy K. 2010. "Beguiled by Loss: The Burden of third-generation Narrative." In *Exposed Memories: Family Pictures in Private and Collective Memory*, edited by Zsófia Bán and Hedvig Turai, pp. 29–41. Budapest: CEU Press.

Mitchell, Margret. (1936) 1964. *Gone with the Wind.* New York City: Warner Books.

Morrison, Toni. (1977) 1998. *Song of Solomon.* New York City: Vintage Books.

———. (1987) 2007. *Beloved.* New York City: Vintage Classic.

———. 1988. "Unspeakable Things Unspoken: The Afro-American Presence in American Literature." Tanner Lecture on Human Values, The University of Michigan, October 07, 1988. Accessed 29 April 2012. https://tannerlectures.utah.edu/_documents/a-to-z/m/morrison90.pdf.

———. 1989. "Melcher Book Award Acceptance Speech." *World Magazine of the Unitarian Universalist Association* 3, no. 1–2 (January/ February): 4–5.

Nash, Catherine. 2002. "Genealogical Identities." *Environment and Planning D: Society and Space* 20, no. 1 (February): 27–52. SAGE. doi:10.1068/d314.

———. 2003. "'They're Family!': Cultural Geographies of Relatedness in Popular Genealogy." In *Uprootings/Regroundings: Questions of Home and Migration*, edited by Sara Ahmed, pp. 179–206. New York: Berg Publishers.

———. 2004. "Genetic Kinship." *Cultural Studies* 18, no. 1 (June): 1–33. Taylor and Francis. doi:10.1080/0950238042000181593.

———. 2017. "Genealogical Relatedness. Geographies of Shared Descent and Difference." *Genealogy* 1, no. 7 (March). MDPI. doi:10.3390/genealogy1020007.

Nixon, Ron. 2007. "DNA Tests Find Branches but Few Roots." *The New York Times*, November 25, 2007. www.nytimes.com/2007/11/25/business/25dna.html.

O'Brien, Sharon. 1996. "Preface: Write now: American Literature in the 1980s and 1990s." *American Literature* 68, no.1 (March): 1–8. JSTOR. https://www.jstor.org/stable/2927536.

Obama, Barack H. (1995) 2004. *Dreams from my Father: A Story of Race and Inheritance*. New York City: Three Rivers Press.

Olney, James. 1984. "'I was born': Slave Narratives, Their Status as Autobiography and as Literature." *Calalloo* 20 (Winter): 46–73. JSTOR. doi:10.2307/2930678.

Pabst, Naomi. 2003. "Blackness/Mixedness: Contestations over Crossing Signs." *Cultural Critique* 54 (Spring): 178–212. JSTOR. https://www.jstor.org/stable/1354663.

Perreault, Donna. 1990. "What Makes Autobiography Interrogative?" *Biography* 13, no. 2 (Spring): 130–142. MUSE. doi:10.1353/bio.2010.0682.

Rhys, Jean. (1966) 2001. *Wide Sargasso Sea*. London: Penguin.

Root, Maria P. 1996. *The Multiracial Experience: Racial Borders as the New Frontier*. Thousand Oaks: Sage.

Rosner, Elizabeth. 2017. *Survivor Café: The Legacy of Trauma and the Labyrinth of Memory*. La Vergne, TN: Ingram.

Rushdy, Ashraf H. A. 1999. *Neo-Slave Narratives: Studies in the Social Logic of a Literary Form*. Oxford, UK: Oxford University Press.

———. 2001. *Remembering Generations: Race and Family in Contemporary African American Fiction*. Chapel Hill, NC: University of North Carolina Press.

Ryan, Tim A. 2008. *Calls and Responses: The American Novel of Slavery since Gone with the Wind*. Baton Rouge: Louisiana State University Press.

Salisbury, Stephan. 2010. "Slave's Escape commemorated at President's House." *The Philadelphia Inquirer*, May 22, 2010. https://www.inquirer.com/philly/news/breaking/20100521_Slaves_escape_commemorated_at_Presidents_House.html.

Sattler, Julia. 2018. "'I am the New America': Negotiating and Representing American Families in Mixed Race Memoirs." *Comparative Studies in Modernism* 12: 43–61.

Smith, Shawn Michelle. 2004. *Photography on the Color Line. W.E.B. Du Bois, Race, and Visual Culture*. Durham, NC: Duke University Press.

Smith, Sidonie, and Julia Watson. 1996. "Introduction." In *Getting a Life: Everyday uses of Autobiography*, edited by Sidonie Smith and Julia Watson, pp. 1–24. Minneapolis, MN: University of Minnesota Press.

Sollors, Werner. (1997) 1999. *Neither Black nor White yet Both: Thematic Explorations of Interracial Literature*. Cambridge, MA: Harvard University Press.
Spencer, Rainier. 2006. *Challenging Multiracial Identity*. Boulder, Co: L. Rienner Publishers.
Spickard, Paul. 2001. "The Subject is Mixed Race. The Boom in Biracial Biography." In *Rethinking Mixed Race*, edited by David Parker and Miri Song, pp. 76–98. London: Pluto Press.
Spielberg, Steven, dir. 1997. *Amistad*. DreamWorks Pictures. DVD, 155 min.
Squires, Catherine, Heather Harris and Kimberley Moffit. "Introduction." In *The Obama Effect: Multidisciplinary Renderings of the 2008 Campaign*, edited by Catherine Squires, Heather Harris and Kimberley Moffit, pp. xvii–xx. Albany, NY: State University of New York Press.
Stowe, Harriet B. (1852) 1981. *Uncle Tom's Cabin*. London: Bantam.
Thomas, Velma M. 1999. "Introduction." In *Finding a Place called Home: A Guide to African-American Genealogy and Historical Identity*, edited by Dee Woodtor, pp. ix–xi. New York City: Random House.
Thompson, Becky, and Sangeeta Tyagi. 1996. "Introduction. Storytelling as Social Conscience. The Power of Autobiography." In *Names We Call Home: Autobiography on Racial Identity*, edited by Becky Thompson and Sangeeta Tyagi, pp. ix–xvii. Abingdon: Routledge.
The Toni Morrison Society. n. d. "Bench By The Road Project." Accessed Dec. 28, 2019. https://www.tonimorrisonsociety.org/bench.html.
Twain, Mark. (1883) 2010. *Life on the Mississippi*. Memphis, TN: Books LLC.
Warren, Kenneth W. (2011) 2012. *What Was African American Literature?* Cambridge, MA: Harvard University Press.
Watson, Julia. 1996. "Ordering the Family: Genealogy as Autobiographical Pedigree." In *Getting a Life: Everyday uses of Autobiography*, edited by Sidonie Smith and Julia Watson, pp. 297–323. Minneapolis, MN: University of Minnesota Press.
Welzer, Harald, Sabine Moeller und Caroline Tschugnall. 2002. *"Opa war kein Nazi." Nationalsozialismus und Holocaust im Familiengedächtnis*. Frankfurt a.M.: Fischer Taschenbuch.
Whitman, Walt. (1855) 1983. *Leaves of Grass*. London: Bantam.
Wicomb, Zoë. (2000) 2002. *David's Story: A Novel*. New York City: The Feminist Press at CUNY.
Wiencek, Henry. 1999. *The Hairstons. An American Family in Black and White*. New York City: St. Martin's Griffin.
Williams, Kim M. 2006. *Mark One or More: Civil Rights in Multiracial America*. Ann Arbor, MI: University of Michigan Press.
Williams, Linda. (2001) 2002. *Playing the Race Card: Melodramas of Black and White from Uncle Tom to O.J. Simpson*. Princeton, NJ: Princeton University Press.
Winter, Jay M. 2008. "War, Memory, and Mourning in the Twentieth Century: Notes on the Memory Boom." In *The Merits of Memory: Concepts, Contexts, Debates*, edited by Hans-Jürgen Grabbe and Sabine Schindler, pp. 97–118. Heidelberg: Winter.
Zack, Naomi. 2010. "The Fluid Symbol of Mixed Race." *Hypatia* 25, no. 4 (Fall): 875–90. JSTOR. https://www.jstor.org/stable/40928661.

Zamora, Lois Parkinson. 2008. *The Usable Past: The Imagination of History in Recent Fiction of the Americas.* Cambridge, UK: Cambridge University Press.

Zinsser, William K. (1987) 1998. "Introduction." In *Inventing the Truth: The Art and Craft of Memoir*, edited by William K. Zinsser and Russell Baker, pp. 1–22. Boston, MA: Houghton Mifflin.

Index

Abel, Sarah, 87
Absalom Absalom (Faulkner), 171
Affirmative Action, 14, 21–22
African American literature, 16, 30–31
African American Lives (TV show), 14, 113
African ancestry, 8; immigration story and, 139–40, 145; national identity and citizenship relation to, 139–40; *One Drop* on, 115; *Pearl's Secret* on, 139–40; *Roots* approach to, 97; *Slaves in the Family* Africa travels in investigation of, 82–83, 140–41, 201; *The Sweeter the Juice* on, 138–40
Alabama, 178
American Dream: dominant narrative around, 119, 127, 144, 145, 150–51, 153, 155; *The Great Gatsby* and, 146–47, 149; identity construction around, 145, 150–51; immigration narrative and, 144–48, 150; metaphor, 145; multiracial identity and, 150–51; Obama victory and, 12; *One Drop* on, 146–47, 149–50; passing relation to, 47, 146, 150, 151; *Pearl's Secret* and, 149; privilege/middle-class dimensions of, 127, 144–46, 150; *Slaves in the Family* and, 147–50, 153; *The Sweeter the Juice* and, 145–46, 149, 150. *See also* national identity and citizenship
Americanization: conformity relation to story of, 151–55; dominant narrative around, 119, 144, 153–55; ethnic narrative tradition and, 27, 28; family album role in, 110, 118; genealogy and, 101; master narrative template for, 153–55; *One Drop* and story of, 146–47, 176–77; racial mixing story and, 101, 151–54; *Roots* narrative of, 138. *See also* national identity and citizenship
Amistad, 14
Assmann, Aleida, 89

Ball, Edward (memoir). *See Slaves in the Family*
Barthes, Roland, 107
Beaumont family. *See Pearl's Secret*
Beloved (Morrison), 33, 155, 174–75
Bergland, Betty Ann, 27
Berlant, Lauren, 17, 20, 123
Bildungsroman, 19
Birmingham, Alabama, 178
"Black and White" (Gardner), 96
Black Lives Matter, 188
blackness: Creoles notions of whiteness and, 60–64, 177, 180–82; DNA

213

testing debunking purity around, 89–90; genealogy role in representing, 97; loyalty issues around, 126, 128–29, 150; *memoir of the search* genre navigation of, 16–17, 19, 29, 37, 44; *One Drop* navigating identity around, 61–64, 177, 180–82; *The Sweeter the Juice* navigating notion of, 56, 61–64, 128–29
Boelhower, William, 27, 136
Bradley, David, 33
Brown, William Wells, 1
Broyard, Bliss (memoir). *See One Drop*
Bush, George W., 11
Butler, Octavia E., 1, 33

Camera Lucida (Barthes), 107
Carpentier, Alejo, 34
Celan, Paul, 67
census forms and data, 8, 21–22, 24, 75, 189
The Chaneysville Incident (Bradley), 33
Charleston, South Carolina. *See* South Carolina
Charleston Church Shooting (2015), 12
Charlottesville, Virginia, 12–14
citizenship. *See* national identity and citizenship
Civil Rights Act of 1964, 3
Civil Rights Era and Movement, 184; African American literature and narratives after, 16, 30–31; national identity and role in, 3, 130–33; *Pearl's Secret* on, 130–31, 165, 178; *Slaves in the Family* on, 65, 132–33; *The Sweeter the Juice* and legacy of, 3, 6, 164, 182; tamed memory of, 201
Civil Rights legislation: interracial relationships and, 44–45; multiracial identification impact on, 3, 8, 21–22
Civil War, 45, 146, 176; *One Drop* and, 177, 181; *Pearl's Secret* and, 149, 166, 171; slaves fighting in, 169; *Slaves in the Family* and, 65, 133, 148, 150, 161, 169–70, 174

Clotel, Or: The President's Daughter (Brown), 1
Code Noir, 143, 176
color line, 7; addressing, from present context, 29; dialogue initiation across, 81; Du Bois on, 18, 187; in family photographs, evidence of, 102, 106–11; family structure relation to, 54, 65; family trees and inclusion of, 92–93; in national identity and citizenship, 39, 124–25, 129; passing terminology and, 46; reader engagement around, 25; *The Sweeter the Juice* family impacted by, 56–57
The Color of Water (McBride), 6
coming out narrative: family secrets and, 54; *memoir of the search* narratives kinship to, 6, 25–27, 42, 47, 199; in *One Drop*, 22, 25–26, 54, 64, 76, 182; around passing, 47; privilege loss in, 26, 47
Confederate flags, 8, 13
confessional genre, 6, 18
Corregidora (Jones, G.), 33
Creole heritage and culture: blackness and whiteness notions in, 60–64, 177, 180–82; *One Drop* narrative on, 7, 60–61, 131–32, 142–43, 147, 159–60, 165, 175–77, 180–82
Critical Race Theory, 120
Cross, June, 6

DNA testing: ancestry beyond national context with, 89; emergence of and science behind, 111–12; family secrets unveiled with, 75, 112–14; identity construction and, 2, 8, 32, 88, 113–14, 126; *memoir of the search* use of, 32, 88, 113–15; national identity connections and, 89, 126; *One Drop* narrator on, 113, 115, 116; passing practices and, 113–15; purity notion debunked with, 89–90, 114; results, reliability of, 112–13,

115; *Roots* influencing practice of, 112; *The Sweeter the Juice* on, 113–14
Drake, Kimberly, 32
Dreams from My Father (Obama), 9, 152, 158
Du Bois, W. E. B., 18, 107, 128, 187–88, 192

Elam, Michelle, 4–5, 12, 27, 29–30, 122, 200
Explosion in a Cathedral (Carpentier), 34

family albums and photographs: absences unveiled in, 109–10; Americanization with, 110, 118; color line evidence in, 102, 106–11; diversity in style of, 104–5; expansion with family discovery, 89; family secrets and, 49, 50, 68; family trees relation to, 104; idealization of images in, 110, 111; interpretation factors with, 105–7; *memoir of the search* use of, 32, 88, 89, 101–2, 107, 109, 111; middle-class context in, 89, 107, 111, 116, 117; normalization role of, 111; passing practice and, 88, 103, 108–11; in *Pearl's Secret* research, 49, 50, 68, 103, 105–6; photography development history role in, 102; slave narratives use of, 32; *Slaves in the Family*, 50, 103–5, 109–10; speakability impacted by, 109; *The Sweeter the Juice*, 103, 104; trauma missing from, 110
family archive, 115–18
family scripts, 60, 196
family secrets: abandonment issues around, 46, 53, 56–60, 63, 67, 71–72, 77, 84, 117; absence and missing pieces theme with, 48–49, 55, 56, 65, 73, 76; bond around, 54; children impacted by internal, 51–52, 60; coming out narrative around, 54; dialogue initiation around, 77–84; dimensions of, 56–73; DNA testing unveiling, 75, 112–14; family albums and photographs relation to, 49, 50, 68; family structure and meaning relation to, 42–47; family trees in research of, 75, 78; forbidden fruit metaphor with, 69; frontier metaphor for investigation of, 45–46; genealogy conflict with, 92; identity construction and unveiling, 5, 42, 48–49, 56; intergenerational quality of, 35, 44–45, 71–72; introduction by narrators, 47–56; investigative approach to, 46, 48, 73–77; isolation and, 54–55; literary trend about, 17; *memoir of the search* approach to, 18, 28, 29, 32–33, 41–47; metaphor use around, 45–46, 69, 73–76; narrative suspense around, 43, 48; narrator personal life silence contrasted with unveiling, 23; national identity relation to, 56; *One Drop* approach with, 26, 42, 48–49, 53–54, 59–64, 74–76, 81; of passing, 42, 46–47, 59; *Pearl's Secret* approach to, 42, 49–53, 68–76, 78–81; privilege relation to, 28, 47, 51–53, 64, 69; quilt metaphor in unveiling, 73–74, 76; rape in, 70–71, 101; reader engagement around, 25; responsibility issues with, 46, 52–53, 72, 73; segregation and, 46–47; around sexual orientation, 59; of slavery, resolution around, 18, 184; *Slaves in the Family* approach to, 42, 49–53, 55–56, 64–70, 73, 74, 81–83, 147; Southern encounters aiding resolution of, 184; speakability and taboo around, 50–51, 53–54, 63, 66–67, 69, 84; *The Sweeter the Juice* approach with, 42, 49, 55–64, 73–74, 76–77, 79–81, 182; trauma around, 43–44, 52–53, 57, 112

family trees: color line inclusion in, 92–93; expansion with family discovery, 89; family secrets research and, 75, 78; function of, 90–91; immigration story and, 98–99; Indian Princess Grandmother Myth and, 70; *memoir of the search* approach to, 32, 88, 89, 92–95, 97–99, 103; middle-class context in, 89, 117; normalization and, 94; *Other* and, 97–98; *Pearl's Secret*, 98–101, 121; photographs relation to, 104; privilege justification with, 91–92; relatives absence from, 31, 88, 144; spatial and temporal connections in, 91; speakability/unspeakability around, 91, 94, 117; tree metaphor for structure of, 97

Faulkner, William, 34, 171, 201
Ferré, Rosario, 34
Finding a Place Called Home (Woodtor), 93
Fitzgerald, Francis S. K., 146–47, 149
forgiveness, 81–83, 201
Franklin, Stuart, 102

Gardner, Eric, 96, 136
Gates, Henry Louis, Jr., 13, 113, 115
genealogy: African Americans challenges with, 88, 95–96; Americanization and, 101; anxieties with, 89; autobiographical narrative relation to, 94–95; blackness and whiteness representations in, 97; family secrets conflict with, 92; identity construction role of, 2, 8, 32, 88, 113–14, 117–18, 126; *memoir of the search* genre approach to, 5, 31, 32, 87, 88, 92–97, 100–101, 113–15; metaphors, 34, 97; middle-class context in, 89, 117; normalization and, 89, 95–96; Old South connection made with, 100–101; *Pearl's Secret* use of, 98–101, 121; privilege relation to, 89, 91–92, 117, 118, 124; purity notion debunked with, 89–90, 101, 114; *Roots* influencing practice of, 29, 31, 93, 96–97, 112; self-help guides to, 29, 93; *Slaves in the Family* use of, 96; *The Sweeter the Juice* use of, 96, 113–14; trauma resolution role of, 89; trend of, 29, 31, 87–88, 93, 112. *See also* DNA testing: family albums and photographs: family trees

Getting a Life (Smith and Watson), 36, 152
Gone with the Wind (Mitchell), 29, 31, 128, 168
The Great Gatsby (Fitzgerald), 146–47, 149
Great Migration: displacement and separation with, 166, 182; long-term impacts and legacy of, 3, 157, 158, 182, 184; *One Drop* family impacted by, 182; in *Pearl's Secret* family history, 69, 171; *The Sweeter the Juice* on, 171

The Hairstons (Wiencek), 6, 35
Haizlip, Shirlee Taylor (memoir). *See The Sweeter the Juice*
Haley, Alex, 15
Handley, George, 34, 90, 100–101
Harlem Renaissance, 38, 187
Hemings, Sally, 8, 66, 94, 126
Henry, Neil (memoir). *See Pearl's Secret*
Herweg, Nikola, 17
Holiday, Billie, 69
Hollywood narratives, 128, 168, 182–83
Holocaust, 34–35, 67–68, 194–96, 203–4
hooks, bell, 97
Hopkins, Pauline, 1
Hughes, Langston, 3, 187

identity construction: active and passive nature of, 3–4; American Dream and, 145, 150–51; after desegregation, 30–31; DNA testing and, 2, 8, 32, 88, 113–14, 126; family secrets unveiling and, 5, 42, 48–49, 56; family structures and stories role in, 41–42; genealogy role in, 2, 8, 32, 88, 113–14, 117–18, 126; Great Migration impacts on, 3, 182; *memoir of the search* genre focus on, 30–33, 37; *One Drop*, 48–49, 61–64, 177, 180–82; *Pearl's Secret* on, 4, 21; in *Slaves in the Family*, 65, 68; spatial and temporal factors in, 3, 4, 9; *The Sweeter the Juice* struggles around, 2–4, 37, 56, 58, 80; tropes of mixed-race, 4–5. *See also* multiracial identity: national identity and citizenship

Immigrant Autobiography in the United States (Boelhower), 27

immigration/immigrants: African ancestry and story of, 139–40, 145; American Dream and story of, 144–48, 150; family trees and, 98–99; narrative paradigm of, 5–6, 27, 28, 37, 136, 145; national identity relation to story of, 119, 135–44, 151–52; *One Drop* narrative on, 140, 142–43, 146; *Pearl's Secret* narrative on, 136–37, 139–40, 142, 144; privilege/middle-class perspective in story of, 135, 137, 141–42; racial mixing narrative relation to white, 5–6, 136–38, 141, 151; *Roots* narrative of, 138, 140; slavery and European, 67–68, 143–44, 147–48; *Slaves in the Family* narrative on, 140–41, 143–44, 147–48; *The Sweeter the Juice* narrative on, 135–42, 144; white, national identity around, 119, 136

Indian Princess Grandmother Myth, 70

interracial intimate relationships: Civil Rights legislation on, 44–45; Jefferson–Hemings controversy and, 8, 66, 94, 126; Louisiana history on, 66, 143, 176; proof of, 94; taboo on slaveholder and slave, 66–67; Virginia history on, 44–45, 66

Jefferson, Thomas, 8, 66, 94, 126
Jim Crow, 29, 30, 120, 159, 171
Jones, Edward P., 14, 155
Jones, Gayl, 33
Judge, Oney, 125–26

Keating, AnnLouise, 97
Kindred (Butler), 1, 33
King, Martin Luther, Jr., 2, 163, 187
The Known World (Jones, E.), 14, 155
Ku Klux Klan, 69, 79

Langford, Martha, 111
Latin American slavery, 34
Levy, Daniel, 203
Life on the Mississippi (Twain), 126
life writing, 17, 18, 192
Link, Jürgen, 6
Locke, John, 173
Louisiana: interracial sexual relations in, 66, 143, 176; *One Drop* family history in, 7, 60–61, 131–32, 142–43, 147, 159–60, 165, 175–77, 180–82; segregation history in, 180, 181. *See also* Creole heritage and culture
Loving Legend, 45
Loving vs. Virginia (1967), 44–45
Lukasik, Gail, 6

Malcolm X, 140, 187
Mark-One-Or-More (MOOM), 8
master narrative, 39, 117, 153–55, 199–200
McBride, James, 6
McGlothlin, Erin, 35
media, research. *See* DNA testing: family albums and photographs: family trees: genealogy: research process and media
melodramatic form, 15–17, 31
melting pot, 39, 125, 142, 151–52
memoir of the search narratives: absence and missing pieces themes in, 31, 48–49, 55, 56, 65, 73, 87, 89, 91–92, 95, 100, 103, 109–10, 173–75, 188–89, 194; assumptions

reversal aspect of, 19–20; blackness and whiteness investigation role in, 16–17, 19, 29, 37, 44; coming out narratives relation to, 6, 25–27, 42, 47, 199; confessional nature of, 6, 18; conventional conformity in, 4, 32–33, 84, 85, 120, 151–55; defining, 5, 16–17; DNA testing role for, 32, 88, 113–15; educational identifications with, 25, 26, 117; family albums and photographs role for, 32, 88, 89, 101–2, 107, 109, 111; family secrets navigation in, 18, 28, 29, 32–33, 41–47; family tree approach in, 32, 88, 89, 92–95, 97–99, 103; genealogy practices role in, 5, 31, 32, 87, 88, 92–97, 100–101, 113–15; identity construction central to, 30–33, 37; intergenerational dimensions of, 22, 32, 35, 44–45, 71–72, 88–89, 94, 106–7, 109, 111, 116, 117, 161, 169, 189, 194, 195; intertextuality of, 15, 35–36; on language absence for race dialogue, 90; loyalty considerations and conflicts in, 52–53, 69, 73, 78, 80, 100, 126, 128–29, 136–37, 141, 150, 177, 197; mainstream entry of, 17, 36–39; master narrative relation to, 39, 154–55, 199–200; multiple perspectives in, 17; multiracial identity confronted in, 9, 116; on national identity and citizenship, 15, 19, 31, 33, 36, 39, 119–35, 144, 151–52; normalization and, 5–6, 17, 28, 36–39, 120, 151, 154, 199; Obama, 9, 152, 158; passing investigations in, 23, 31–32, 39, 42, 46–47; past investigated from present contexts in, 23–24, 29, 33–35, 43–44, 105–6, 201–3; personal matters silence in, 22–23; personal-political role in, 28–29; political climate giving rise to, 8–9; post-Holocaust literature relation to, 34–35, 194, 203–4; privilege/ middle-class context for, 17, 18, 22–23, 25, 28, 38–39, 46, 54, 72, 89, 92, 107, 111, 116–17, 124, 125, 127, 135, 137, 145, 153–54, 197, 200–201; questions over answers offered in, 20–21; reader empathy and bond in, 22, 25, 47–48, 102; reconciliation approach in, 18–19, 83–84, 121; research process and media in, 24–25, 87–90; responsibility for past in, 5, 19–20, 46, 72, 73, 123, 154, 203–4; silencing aspect of, 5, 15, 45, 53, 84, 92; slave narratives relation to, 32–34, 100; slavery approach in, 29; spatial and temporal factors in, 3, 4, 9; taboo and speakability role in, 5, 18, 33, 38–39, 50–52, 84, 91, 94, 117, 199; texts selected for investigation of, 6–7; themes and narrative strategies common in, 5, 27–29, 32–33, 37–39, 87; transnational reading of, 34, 184, 185, 191. *See also specific topics and memoirs*

memory boom, 192–93, 195–96

metaphors: American Dream, 145; for family secrets, 45–46, 69, 73–76; genealogy, 34, 97; multiracial experience, 45, 131; *One Drop* use of, 74–76; *Pearl's Secret* use of, 21, 69, 74; *Slaves in the Family* use of, 74, 179, 180; *The Sweeter the Juice* use of, 73–74, 131

middle-class context: American Dream from, 127, 144–46, 150; for family albums and photographs, 89, 107, 111, 116, 117; with genealogy/family tree practices, 89, 117; for *memoir of the search* narratives, 17, 18, 22–23, 25, 28, 38–39, 46, 54, 72, 89, 92, 107, 111, 116–17, 124, 125, 127, 135, 137, 145, 153–54, 197, 200–201

miscegenation, 1, 131

Mississippi, 137, 165, 174–75, 178

Mitchell, Margaret, 29, 31, 128, 168

MOOM. *See* Mark-One-Or-More
Morrison, Toni, 30, 36, 97; *Beloved*, 33, 155, 174–75; *Song of Solomon*, 157–58
multiracial identity: American Dream and, 150–51; as census option, 8, 21, 189; Civil Rights legislation and identification as, 3, 8, 21–22; Elam on problems with category of, 29–30; Indian Princess Grandmother Myth and, 70; *memoirs of the search* confrontation with, 9, 116; metaphors about, experience, 45, 131; movement around, 8, 9, 21–22, 45, 189–90; Obama on, 12; tropes around, 4–5

Nash, Catherine, 117–18
national identity and citizenship: African ancestry search relation to, 139–40; color line role in, 39, 124–25, 129; conformity relation to, 151–55; DNA testing role in, 89, 126; dominant narratives around, 119–20, 122, 142, 154–55; family secrets relation to, 56; family story relation to story of, 123–35; genealogy practices and, 121, 126; immigration story relation to story of, 119, 135–44, 151–52; *memoir of the search* narratives on, 15, 19, 31, 33, 36, 39, 119–35, 144, 151–52; mixed-race dimensions of, 120–23; Obama illegitimacy debate and issues of, 9, 12, 124; *One Drop* on family story relation to, 125, 131–32; *Pearl's Secret* on family story relation to, 120, 124–25, 129–31; perpetrator-victim relationship legacy in, 122; privilege/middle-class factors in, 124, 125, 127–30, 132, 137, 152–54; responsibility for past role in, 123; slavery and segregation role in, 16, 32, 120–23, 132–35; *Slaves in the Family* on family story relation to, 132–35; *The Sweeter the Juice* on family story relation to, 2, 3, 125–29, 131, 142; white immigrants story and, 119, 136
National Museum of African American History and Culture, 14
Native Americans, 2, 30, 68–69, 114, 141
Nazis, 35, 203. *See also* Holocaust
Negro Act of 1740, 172, 176
Neither Black Nor White Yet Both (Sollors), 46
neo-slave narratives, 2, 15, 33–34
Neo-Slave Narratives (Rushdy), 2
normalization: with family albums, 111; family trees role in, 94; genealogy and, 89, 95–96; *memoir of the search* genre and, 5–6, 17, 28, 36–39, 120, 151, 154, 199; of passing, 61; scholarship on, 6; of slavery and segregation, 135; storytelling role in, 6, 36, 154, 199; whiteness role in, 5–6, 61
North Carolina, 165, 182–83

Obama, Barack: American Dream and victory of, 12; illegitimacy debate around, 9, 12, 124; *memoir of the search* narrative of, 9, 152, 158; presidential victory, factors behind, 9, 11–13
O'Brien, Sharon, 17
Of One Blood (Hopkins), 1
Old South, 31, 101, 172, 178, 182–83
Olney, James, 32
One Drop (Broyard); abandonment issues in, 59–60, 63; African ancestry investigation in, 115; American Dream and, 146–47, 149–50; Americanization story in, 146–47, 176–77; blackness and whiteness navigated in, 61–64, 177, 180–82; childhood memories of South in, 159–60; Civil War and, 177, 181; coming out theme in, 22,

25–26, 54, 64, 76, 182; on Creole and Louisiana heritage and culture, 7, 60–61, 131–32, 142–43, 147, 159–60, 165, 175–77, 180–82; DNA testing used by narrator of, 113, 115, 116; education of narrator role in, 25; family secret approach in, 26, 42, 48–49, 53–54, 59–64, 74–76, 81; family secret dialogue initiation in, 81; Great Migration impacts in, 182; identity construction in, 48–49, 61–64, 177, 180–82; immigration story, 140, 142–43, 146; metaphor use in, 74–76; on national identity relation to family story, 125, 131–32; overview, 7, 48; passing in, 7, 26, 59–64, 132, 146, 160, 177; privilege role in, 54, 64, 125, 143, 180–81; on reconciliation, 131; research process and media for, 74, 75, 113, 115, 116, 167; segregation encounters for, 180, 181; Southern family/culture encounters and confrontations in, 177, 180–81; Southern history of slavery negotiation in, 175–77; speakability and taboo in, 53–54, 62–63; tragic mulatta motif and, 26

One Drop Rule, 1, 37, 123

Other/Otherness, 15, 67, 97–98, 191, 198

palimpsest narratives, 43–44, 154

passing, racial, 1; abandonment issues around, 46, 53, 56–60, 63, 67, 71–72, 77, 84, 85, 117; American Dream relation to, 47, 146, 150, 151; coming out narrative around, 47; defining terminology of, 46; DNA testing and, 113–15; in family albums and photographs, 88, 103, 108–11; family archive impact on, 118; family secrets and, 42, 46–47, 59; implications of, 7; *memoir of the search* reflections on, 23, 31–32, 39, 42, 46–47; miscegenation with, 131; as narrative trope, 5; normalization of, 61; *One Drop* on, 7, 26, 59–64, 132, 146, 160, 177; *Pearl's Secret* on impacts of, 53; segregation and secret of, 46–47; sexual orientation "passing" relation to, 25–26, 59; *The Sweeter the Juice* on, 53, 56–57, 61–62, 126, 129; taboo and speakability around, 47

Pearl's Secret (Henry): on African roots, 139–40; American Dream and, 149; childhood memories of South in, 162–63; Civil Rights Movement and, 130–31, 165, 178; Civil War and, 149, 166, 171; family albums and photographs use in, 49, 50, 68, 103, 105–6; family secret dialogue initiation in, 78–81; family secrets approach in, 42, 49–53, 68–76, 78–81; on family traditions challenges, 110; family trees and genealogy use in, 98–101, 121; forbidden fruit metaphor in secret unveiling in, 69; on Great Migration, 69, 171; guilt for narrator in, 69–70; on identity development, 4, 21; immigration story, 136–37, 139–40, 142, 144; intertextuality dimension of, 35, 36; *memoir of the search* terminology origins in, 16; metaphor use in, 21, 69, 74; Mississippi significance in, 165, 178; on national identity relation to family story, 120, 124–25, 129–31; overview, 7, 68; passing impacts in, 53; past investigated from present context in, 21, 23; privilege role in, 52, 69–71, 79, 124, 130, 163; rape in, 70–71, 101; research process and media in, 24–25, 49, 50, 68, 73–75, 98–99, 103, 105–6, 168, 178; *Roots* influence for, 35; segregation experience in, 162, 163; Southern family/culture encounters and confrontations in, 178–79; Southern history of slavery negotiation in,

166–69, 171; South impact evidence in, 159; speakability and taboo in, 51, 53, 69, 70; victim and perpetrator investigated in, 16, 23, 103
perpetrators: Holocaust, literature and education about, 35, 203–4; national identity and legacy of victims and, 122; *Pearl's Secret* on notions of victim and, 16, 23, 103; *Slaves in the Family* exploration of victims and, 68, 132–33; victims boundary blurring with, 72
Perreault, Donna, 21
photographs. *See* family albums and photographs
Playing the Race Card (Williams), 15–16
post-Holocaust literature, 34–35, 194–96, 203–4
post-racial era, 8, 14, 72, 116
postslavery narratives, 34, 100–101
privilege: American Dream from context of, 127, 144–46, 150; coming out and loss of, 26, 47; family secrets relation to, 28, 47, 51–53, 64, 69; family trees in justifications of, 91–92; genealogy relation to, 89, 91–92, 117, 118, 124; melodramatic form and, 17; *memoir of the search* narratives from context of, 17, 18, 22–23, 25, 28, 38–39, 46, 54, 72, 89, 92, 107, 111, 116–17, 124, 125, 127, 135, 137, 145, 153–54, 197, 200–201; national identity and citizenship relation to, 124, 125, 127–30, 132, 137, 152–54; *One Drop* on, 54, 64, 125, 143, 180–81; passing and, 47; responsibility with, 128; in *Slaves in the Family* family story, 51–53, 82, 160–61, 171–72; *The Sweeter the Juice* on, 22–23, 127–29, 142, 163–64; white, in American South, 49, 162. *See also* middle-class context

Quakers, 183

rape, 70–71, 101
reconciliation: Charleston Church Shooting and, 12; *memoir of the search* approach to, 18–19, 83–84, 121; *One Drop* on, 131; *Slaves in the Family* on, 24, 29, 67–68, 81–83, 162, 201
Remembering Generations (Rushdy), 43–44
reparations (for slavery), 8, 14, 191
Requiem for a Nun (Faulkner), 201
research process and media: family archive creation from, 115–18; *memoir of the search* narratives, 24–25, 87–90; *One Drop*, 74, 75, 113, 115, 116, 167; *Pearl's Secret*, 24–25, 49, 50, 68, 73–75, 98–99, 103, 105–6, 168, 178; slavery documentation use in, 94, 134–35; *Slaves in the Family*, 50, 73, 88–89, 96, 103–5, 109–10, 134, 135, 167–68, 179–80; *The Sweeter the Juice*, 73–74, 76–77, 96, 103, 104, 113–14. *See also* DNA testing: family albums: family tree: genealogy
responsibility: collective, for past, 13–14, 19–20, 83, 123, 129, 154, 201; complexity with notion of, 14; with family secrets, 46, 52–53, 72, 73; *memoir of the search* narratives and, 5, 19–20, 46, 72, 73, 123, 154, 203–4; with privilege, 128
Revolutionary War, 134, 147–48, 161, 173
Rhys, Jean, 34
Roots (Haley); genealogy practice influenced by, 29, 31, 93, 96–97, 112; immigration narrative in, 138, 140; influence of, 15, 16, 29, 31, 35, 37–38; mainstream conventions and, 16, 37–38
Rushdy, Ashraf A. H., 41; on family secret narratives, 43–44; on intertextuality, 36; on national responsibility for past, 19–20, 123;

on neo-slave narratives, 2; on past reconsideration trend in 1990s, 13; on reparations, 14
Ryan, Tim, 38

Sankofa, 14
Scott, Walter, 126
Second-Generation Holocaust Literature (McGlothlin), 35
Secret Daughter (Cross), 6
segregation, 178; African American literature output relation to, 30; Church, 180; documentation, 94; family archive and, 116; identity construction after end of, 30–31; Jim Crow, 29, 30, 120, 159, 171; long-term consequences of, 4; Louisiana history of, 180, 181; memories of South and, 159–65; national identity relation to legacy of, 16, 32, 120–23, 132–35; normalization of, 135; *One Drop* encounters with, 180, 181; passing secret prior to, 46–47; *Pearl's Secret* experience of, 162, 163; *Slaves in the Family* ancestors views on, 161; *The Sweeter the Juice* experience of, 164, 165
sexual orientation, 25–26, 56, 59, 182
Silko, Leslie Marmon, 30
slaveholders: *Slaves in the Family* on ancestors as, 7, 24, 50–51, 55–56, 64–67, 73, 103–5, 132–34, 140–41, 148, 158, 160–62, 165, 167–76, 179–80; slaves sexual relations with, 66–67
slave narratives, 2, 15, 32–34, 100
slavery: *Beloved* on recognition of, 33, 155, 174–75; Civil War soldiers from, 169; collective responsibility for, 13–14, 20, 83; European immigration story and, 67–68, 143–44, 147–48; forgiveness for family participation in, 81–83, 201; history of Southern, negotiating, 5, 8, 165–77; Holocaust relation to, 67–68; Latin American, 34; long-term impacts, investigation of, 4, 34, 68; media and publications around, 13–14; *memoir of the search* approach to, 29; Morrison on memory of, 174–75; music and cultural appropriation with, 175; national identity relation to legacy of, 16, 32, 120–23, 132–35; Negro Act of 1740 and, 172, 176; 1990s discourse about, 8–9, 13; normalization of, 135; present context in investigation of, 33–34; reparations for, 8, 14, 191; resolution around family secrets of, 18, 184; *The Sweeter the Juice* on, 169–71, 173; Three-Fifths Compromise with abolition of, 148, 173–74; transnational nature of, 82; trauma, public commemoration of, 14–15
Slavery and Public History, 13–14
Slaves in the Family (Ball); Africa travels and investigations in, 82–83, 140–41, 201; American Dream and, 147–50, 153; on Boston King slave in family history, 134; childhood memories of South in, 160–62; Civil Rights Movement and, 65, 132–33; Civil War and, 65, 133, 148, 150, 161, 169–70, 174; conventional narrative conformity in, 4, 153; family albums and photographs use in, 50, 103–5, 109–10; family secret dialogue initiation and approach in, 81–82; family secrets in, 42, 49–53, 55–56, 64–70, 73, 74, 81–83, 147; forgiveness for family past in, 81–83, 201; genealogy practices in, 96; guilt and reconciliation with past in, 24, 29, 67–68, 81–83, 162, 201; identity construction in, 65, 68; immigration story, 140–41, 143–44, 147–48; metaphor use in, 74, 179, 180; on national identity relation to family story, 132–35; overview, 7; privilege role in, 51–53, 82, 160–61, 171–72;

research process and media for, 50, 73, 88–89, 96, 103–5, 109–10, 134, 135, 167–68, 179–80; segregation views in, 161; slave treatment by ancestors in, 65–66, 133; on South Carolina slaveholder family history, 7, 24, 50–51, 55–56, 64–67, 73, 103–5, 132–34, 140–41, 148, 158, 160–62, 165, 167–76, 179–80; Southern family/culture encounters and confrontations in, 177–80; Southern history of slavery negotiation in, 167–76; South impact evidence in, 159; taboo/speakability issues in, 49–51, 53, 66–67, 147; texts influencing, 35; Three-Fifths Compromise and, 148, 173–74; victim and perpetrator relation investigated in, 68, 132–33

Smith, Sidonie, 36, 152

Sollors, Werner, 31–32, 46

Song of Solomon (Morrison), 157–58

The Souls of Black Folk (Du Bois), 18, 187–88, 192

The Souls of Mixed Folk (Elam), 4–5, 12, 200

South: childhood memories of, 159–65, 182–84; encounters and confrontations in, 177–85; history, making peace with, 179, 180, 182–85; history of slavery, negotiating, 5, 8, 165–77; Hollywood depictions of, 128, 168, 182–83; Morrison depictions of, 157–58; Old South culture of, 31, 101, 172, 178, 182–83; racist violence in contemporary, 12–13; *A Streetcar Named Desire* iconic of Old, 182–83; taboo with heritage from, 49–50, 162; trauma around heritage and memories in, 158, 162, 170, 183–84; white privilege and comfort in, 49, 162

South Carolina: Charleston Church Shooting in, 12; Negro Act of 1740, 172, 176; *Slaves in the Family* slaveholder history in, 7, 24, 50–51, 55–56, 64–67, 73, 103–5, 132–34, 140–41, 148, 158, 160–62, 165, 167–76, 179–80; Sullivan's Island and slavery in, 174–75

speakability. *See* taboo and speakability

Spencer, Rainier, 22

Spickard, Paul, 9

Stowe, Harriet Beecher, 31

A Streetcar Named Desire, 182–83

"The Subject Is Mixed Race" (Spickard), 9

Sweet Diamond Dust (Ferré), 34

The Sweeter the Juice (Haizlip); on African roots, 138–40; American Dream and, 145–46, 149, 150; blackness and whiteness notions navigated in, 56, 61–64, 128–29; childhood memories of South in, 163–65, 182; Civil Rights Movement legacy and, 3, 6, 164, 182; color line impacts in, 56–57; on DNA testing, 113–14; familial abandonment in, 56–58, 63, 77; family secret dialogue initiation and approach in, 79–81; family secrets and, 42, 49, 55–64, 73–74, 76–77, 79–81, 182; genealogy in, 96, 113–14; Great Migration addressed in, 171; identity struggles in, 2–4, 37, 56, 58, 80; immigration story, 135–42, 144; metaphor use in, 73–74, 131; on national identity relation to family history, 2, 3, 125–29, 131, 142; overview, 6–7; passing role in, 53, 56–57, 61–62, 126, 129; photographs use in, 103, 104; privilege role in, 22–23, 127–29, 142, 163–64; research process and media for, 73–74, 76–77, 96, 103, 104, 113–14; segregation experience in, 164, 165; sexual orientation secret in, 56, 59; Southern family/culture encounters and confrontations in, 182–83; Southern history of slavery negotiation in, 169–71, 173;

speakability and taboo in, 53, 59, 63; trauma in, 57, 58; Virginia family history in, 6–7, 165
Sznaider, Natan, 203

taboo and speakability: family albums and photographs, 109; family secrets, 50–51, 53–54, 63, 66–67, 69, 84; family trees and, 91, 94, 117; *memoir of the search* genre addressing, 5, 18, 33, 38–39, 50–52, 84, 91, 94, 117, 199; *One Drop* on, 53–54, 62–63; around passing, 47; *Pearl's Secret* on, 51, 53, 69, 70; slaveholder and slave sexual relations, 66–67; *Slaves in the Family* on, 49–51, 53, 66–67, 147; Southern heritage, 49–50, 162; *The Sweeter the Juice* on, 53, 59, 63
Thomas, Velma Maia, 93
Three-Fifths Compromise, 148, 173–74
Till, Emmett, 164–65
"Todesfuge" (Celan), 67
tragic mulatta motif, 4, 26, 39, 61
trauma: family albums and, 110; family secrets and, 43–44, 52–53, 57, 112; genealogy role in resolution of, 89; public commemoration of slavery and racism, 14–15; scientific detachment in addressing, 201; Southern encounters aiding recovery from, 183–84; with Southern heritage and memories, 158, 162, 170, 183–84; transmission of unresolved, 72
Trump, Donald, 13
Twain, Mark, 126
Types of American Negroes (Du Bois), 107

Uncle Tom's Cabin (Stowe), 31
Unite the Right rally, 12–14
University of Virginia, 12, 25, 62, 181
unspeakability. *See* taboo and speakability

victims: Holocaust, 35, 204; national identity and legacy of perpetrators and, 122; *Pearl's Secret* on notions of perpetrators and, 16, 23, 103; perpetrator boundary blurring with, 72; *Slaves in the Family* exploration of perpetrators and, 68, 132–33
Virginia: interracial relationships in, 44–45, 66; *Song of Solomon* set in, 157; *The Sweeter the Juice* family history in, 6–7, 165; Unite the Right rally and violence in, 12–14; University of, 12, 25, 62, 181
Voting Rights Act of 1965, 3

Wallace, George, 178
Warren, Kenneth W., 30
Washington, Martha, 125–26
Watson, Julia, 36, 152
What Was African American literature? (Warren), 30
White Like Her (Lukasik), 6
whiteness: Creoles notions of blackness and, 60–64, 177, 180–82; DNA testing debunking purity around, 89–90; genealogy role in representing, 97; *memoir of the search* genre navigation of, 16–17, 19, 29, 37, 44; normalization relation to, 5–6, 61; *One Drop* navigating notion of, 61–64, 177, 180–82; *The Sweeter the Juice* navigating notions of blackness and, 56, 61–64, 128–29
white supremacy, 12–13, 26, 69, 79, 168
Whitman, Walt, 3
Wide Sargasso Sea (Rhys), 34
Wiencek, Henry, 6, 35
Williams, Linda, 15–16, 18, 31
Winter, Jay M., 195
Woodtor, Dee Parmer, 93

Zinsser, William, 18

About the Author

Julia Sattler is based at TU Dortmund University in Germany. In her research and teaching, she investigates the intersection of activism and writing from a variety of angles—from questions of citizenship and social justice to twentieth-century female poetry. She is currently working on a second book project relating the narration of urban transformation processes in the German and American Rust Belts from an interdisciplinary angle.

www.ingramcontent.com/pod-product-compliance
Lightning Source LLC
Chambersburg PA
CBHW020743020526
44115CB00030B/863